ADULT EDUCATION:
INTERNATIONAL PERSPECTIVES FROM CHINA

CROOM HELM SERIES IN INTERNATIONAL ADULT EDUCATION

Edited by Peter Jarvis, University of Surrey, in association with the ICAE.
Consultant Editors: Chris Duke and Ettore Gelpi

ADULT EDUCATION IN CHINA
Edited by Carman St John Hunter and Martha McKee Keehn

COMBATTING POVERTY THROUGH ADULT EDUCATION
Chris Duke

LIFELONG EDUCATION AND INTERNATIONAL RELATIONS
Ettore Gelpi

NEW PERSPECTIVES ON THE EDUCATION OF ADULTS IN THE UNITED STATES
Huey Long

ADULT EDUCATION:
International Perspectives From China

Edited by
CHRIS DUKE

CROOM HELM
London • Sydney • Wolfeboro, New Hampshire

Croom Helm Ltd, Provident House, Burrell Row,
Beckenham, Kent, BR3 1AT

Croom Helm Australia Pty Ltd, Suite 4, 6th Floor,
64-76 Kippax Street, Surry Hills, NSW 2010, Australia

British Library Cataloguing in Publication Data

Adult education: international perspectives
from China.
1. Adult education
I. Duke, Christopher
374 LC5215

ISBN 0-7099-4509-4

Croom Helm, 27 South Main Street,
Wolfeboro, New Hampshire 03894-2069, USA

Library of Congress Cataloging-in-Publication Data

Adult education.

1. Adult education — China. 2. Comparative education.
I. Duke, C. (Christopher)
LC5257.C6A35 1987 374'.951 86-16817
ISBN 0-7099-4509-4

Printed and bound in Great Britain by
Biddles Ltd, Guildford and King's Lynn

EDITOR'S NOTE

The Croom Helm Series in International Adult Education brings to an English-speaking readership a wide overview of developments in the education of adults throughout the world. Books are planned in this series of four different types:

a) about adult and continuing education in a single country
b) having a comparative perspective of two or more countries
c) studies having an international perspective
d) symposia of different countries having a single theme.

This book is of the second type, but in this case it presents a perspective from the Conference organised by the International Council for Adult Education and adult educators in the People's Republic of China. This book contains the Conference papers and a brief summary of the discussion that ensued. Both the papers and the discussions are valuable and it is hoped that this book will provide another perspective upon the world of adult education.

Chris Duke, editor of this volume, was recently associate secretary general of the International Council for Adult Education and is Professor of Continuing and Adult Education at the University of Warwick, U.K. He was formerly at the Australian National University in Canberra, so that he is ideally equipped to edit a volume such as this. In addition, Yvonne Heslop, at the Australian National University, must be thanked for producing the excellent camera ready copy for this volume.

Peter Jarvis

THE INTERNATIONAL COUNCIL FOR ADULT EDUCATION

This book is published by Croom Helm in conjunction with the International Council for Adult Education. This Council is a non-governmental, voluntary partnership of people and organisations working together to promote the education and learning of adults in order to help create a human-centred, responsible and social world.

The Council was formed in 1973 and now comprises national and regional organisations and associations from eighty countries and there is also liaison with other groups and organisations.

The Council has a secretariat at its headquarters in Toronto, Canada.

This is the only organisation of its kind in adult education. It is based upon the contention that people have the capacity to learn how to accomplish many things that can change the conditions of their own lives and also improve the conditions within which they live and work. Thus adult education is seen as a power towards both learning and action, so that people can play an informed part in all economic, social, individual and political development.

The work of the ICAE centres around the following:

- Strengthening of the capacity for service and action of national and regional organisations.
- Leadership training at all levels.
- Research, that is both participatory and applied.
- Information exchange.
- Contributing towards the development of adult education as a field of study.
- Advancing the knowledge, skills and competencies of individuals and groups.

Thus all ICAE programmes and activities are co-operative in nature and emphasise:

- self-reliance
- indigenous solutions
- local level experience
- participatory approaches.

If you wish to know more about the ICAE please write to:

The International Council for Adult Education,
29, Prince Arthur Avenue,
Toronto,
CANADA M5R 1B2

CONTENTS

Foreword

It was my first visit to China, but I felt quite at home while I was there, because both the Chinese and the Japanese are very similar in their appearance and use the same Chinese characters, and so I could easily understand the meanings of signboards and writings. Although there was unhappy history between us in the past, I could feel that the situation has been changing for the better.

The first four-day observation tour gave us fruitful experiences with the real situation of Chinese adult and youth education. I was much impressed with the zeal that the Chinese people showed for their studying at spare-time universities, at workshops, at communes, etc., and also for establishing cooperative relations with other countries.

Kazufusa Moro'oka Japan

It was so good for me to share that time with people who have such a good background and rich experience. Dialogue and confrontation were good too. But above all it was good to see that dreams can come true. That unemployment, hunger, violence, competition, noise, may be overcome. That all are entitled to education, a good one too. That local autonomy and local power are not just words preached in the desert. That workers know - better than we do - their needs and interests. That they **do** assume life and fate in their own hands. That poverty is not a mortal sickness but something to be shared in order to ensure human rights. Be sure I learned a lot...Maybe, some day, I will have the opportunity of putting some of these learnings into practice.

Marcela Gajardo Chile

Preface

"We are unifying the contradictions", Wang Wenlin observed during one of the working group sessions of the Shanghai Symposium on Theories, Applications and Systems of Adult Education. No undertaking was entered into to publish the Symposium Proceedings, because the difficult and ambitious nature of the meeting cast doubt upon the possibilities for integration of understandings and perspectives. Not only was this the first international adult education meeting to take place in China. Apart from the great diversity within that large, fast-changing country, foreign participants also represented a huge diversity of experience and approaches, drawn as they were from all continents, all major cultural and political systems, and from countries in vastly different stages of 'development'.

In the event the contradictions were well canvassed, but the quality of deliberation, the capacity on the part of most who took part to listen and to respond across barriers of language and experience, suggested to all those at the meetings that there would be merit in drawing together the major papers, comments and themes emerging from plenary and group dialogue, as one set of proceedings. The proceedings follow in the main the structure of the Symposium which, at the suggestion of the Chinese members of the planning group a year earlier, analysed in turn: aspects of the **theories** underpinning adult education practice around the world; the **applications** of these theories in relation to literacy, industrial and rural production and development; and the **systems** adopted to make the necessary provision and to prepare adult educators for their work.

The lead papers were generally made available to participants, in Chinese, French or English, prior to the Symposium. They were briefly introduced or amplified by the authors, after which a small panel commented on selected issues or threw comparative light upon what had been said. An opportunity for comment and question from the full Symposium was followed by more extended periods of discussion in mixed working groups - Chinese and English or Chinese and French. The results of these further deliberations were reported back to the full Symposium during later sessions. Each of these elements of discussion is reflected in the summaries which accompany the papers in this book.

The group discussions were also an invaluable opportunity for those taking part to reflect upon, clarify and compare notes on the intensive four days of visits and studies at adult education sites of many kinds in urban and rural Shanghai with which the twelve day Symposium commenced. This shared experience, scarcely less interesting to participants from other parts of China, provided an anvil on which participants could together hammer out a common understanding and test the generalisations and illustrations from the formal plenary sessions against a shared reality. This, together with the willingness to listen and learn which more than anything characterised this distinguished international gathering, was the key to the success of the meetings.

The International Council for Adult Education is deeply appreciative of the substantial assistance provided by the Canadian International Development Agency (CIDA) towards the costs of the Symposium, and for the assistance of IDRC especially to assist with dissemination. China provided very considerable overt and hidden support as well as cordial and generous hospitality through the Adult Education Association of China and the host Shanghai Adult Education Research Society; its members combined to make the Symposium an unforgettable experience for foreign adult educators, many of whom were visiting China for the first time. Special thanks are owed to Charles Wong of the Chinese University of Hong Hong, who was indispensable and unflagging in resolving communication, logistical and other problems, and tirelessly self-sacrificing prior to and during the Symposium. These proceedings are dedicated to him and Yvonne Heslop, whose meticulous and unstinting efforts and professionalism made both the Symposium and these Proceedings possible.

I THEORIES

Chapter 1

Major Issues and Directions.

Professor Gordon Selman attempted the formidable task of providing a general historical overview of the development of adult education. This was followed by Yao Zhongda's analysis of adult education for the development of productive forces in China, which aroused much interest among foreign participants and provoked critical exchange among the Chinese. Selman brought out the connectedness of things past and present - the continuities through change. He identified underlying social purposes and valuing of human dignity in the adult education tradition, presenting it as both a movement and a profession. Liberal and instrumental, individual and social purposes, are indicated in the paper, as is the place of both governmental and private effort. The needs of disadvantaged groups and for democratisation attract mention, the concept of lifelong learning being seen as highly influential. There is now much more exchange and mutual influence between adult educators in different countries than formerly. Overall the paper conveys a sense of the shift from periphery to central public policy stage, an impression strongly reinforced by Yao so far as China is concerned. Both papers find schooling alone inadequate and illiteracy still a major challenge. Yao suggests the presence of laws dictating the growth of adult education which go beyond matters of culture and ideology, while stressing the importance of correct political leadership.

A. Adult Education: An Awakening Force

Gordon Selman

Rudyard Kipling pointed out that "there are nine and sixty ways of constructing tribal lays, and every single one of them is right". The same sort of situation is faced by anyone attempting a general historical overview of the development of adult education. The number of choices open to the author is exceeded only by the number of possible pitfalls. One is reminded of the response of a Canadian Prime Minister, admittedly a man noted for his caution in such matters, who responded to an awkward inquiry by saying, "To that question I must answer yes and no, and qualify both - but don't quote me." Similar caution is perhaps appropriate in the face of the formidable subject entrusted to me on this occasion.

The nature of adult education is such that to describe its state at any given time, in any one country, is a daunting enough task. To describe it adequately over the span of its historical development, and in the many nations, is well nigh impossible. One of the most striking characteristics of adult education as a field is its diversity and the fact that it is so widely dispersed throughout society, much of it in the private sector and virtually invisible to the casual observer. It is far from a tidy enterprise, which is at once a problem and a source of strength. Indeed it might be argued that a tidy mind is a distinct disability in dealing with the subject.

The story of adult education over the past two centuries is intimately linked with the struggle of humanity for freedom and dignity, for progress and development - for the good life. It has gained significance, even majesty, not so much as a particular or specialised aspect of human activity, not for itself, but because of the goals it has served and continues to serve. Learning, and its handmaiden education, are vital dimensions of the continuing struggle of mankind towards what Moses Coady of the Antigonish Movement in Canada termed "the good and abundant life".

Adults have throughout the history of mankind been helped by their society to learn the things it was thought important and appropriate for them to know. The task before us, however, is to examine particularly the modern adult education movement as it has existed in the last two centuries or so, during which time new and specialised forms of provision have been made to assist adults to learn what they, and their society, wished them to know.

Research and reflection on the history of adult education in various parts of the world indicate a number of themes or perspectives which are relevant to the story everywhere.

The Individual and the Society

One of the most important dichotomies in the field, and to some extent a point of creative tension, has been represented by the concepts of education for individual development and education for citizenship. The concepts are of course, inseparable. Only individuals can learn. But the use to which they put their knowledge, skills or attitudes may be either largely personal in emphasis or directed towards community life. Much of the earliest British adult education activity described by Kelly (1970), such as study groups on science and efforts to teach people to read the scriptures, were clearly undertaken for the purpose of individual growth and development. In the case of the Danish Folk School, the struggle for national ethnic revival in several Central European countries in the nineteenth century, or the Canadian National Farm Radio Forum - and the number of possible examples is legion - the purpose was clearly education for the individual as citizen.

Liberal and Instrumental Learning

There has throughout the history of adult education been emphasis upon that education which develops the powers of the person as ends in themselves (here termed liberal education) and education which is undertaken to strengthen the person's capacity to carry out other tasks (instrumental). The line between the two is a mysterious one. It was said of the Danish Folk School, for instance, that without ever mentioning the word butter, they trained generations of farmers to make the best butter in Europe. And the Workers' Educational Association of Britain, through a liberal education curriculum, helped to produce a corps of leaders for organisational and public life. The same can be said of the Swedish Study Circle movement. In all of our countries, we have examples of the instrumental approach, such as the agricultural extension movement in the United States, the public health education effort in the People's Republic of China, the Yugoslav Worker's Universities and other Third World programmes designed to produce the skills required for the process of development.

The Movement and the Profession

In perhaps most, if not all, countries, adult education in its many forms began as a people's movement and frequently was seen as an instrument for improving society. Many of those providing leadership for adult education saw it as a way of improving the quality of life, promoting citizen participation, social justice and equity. The names of Mao, Mansbridge, Grundtvig, Freire and Nyerere come to mind, as do many others. In recent decades we have in many countries promoted the professionalisation of adult education. Specialised training has been provided in order to create a corps of leaders, researchers, administrators and other specialists for the field. Particularly notable efforts to this end have been made, for instance, in the socialist countries and the United States, for instance. In many societies, there has developed a type of professional approach which tends to be committed more to the standards and problems of practice (and often to institutional and self-interest) than to the more traditional goals of the adult education movement. The result is sometimes a tension in the field, a competition of aims and priorities.

Private and Public Sponsorship

The differing political and social arrangements in our countries have produced strikingly different organisational approaches. For many nations, however, this has been historically - and is - an important perspective on adult education. In my own country, and many others I am familiar with, adult education, in the early decades of its development, was sponsored predominantly by the private, voluntary, non-governmental sector. With the emergence of what has been termed "the strong remedial state", the public authority has accepted this as well as other instruments of intervention and to an increasing degree, adult education has been provided by the public sector. In many more revolutionary situations this shift has come about dramatically. Many of us have actively sought an enlarged role for the public authority, believing that some needs can be met adequately only by government action. At the same time, many believe that there is a power, a dynamic, in the private and voluntary sector which can facilitate learning and outreach in ways and to an extent not possible for the public authority. The channeling of public funds through non-governmental organisations for the support of adult education is a prominent feature in the Scandinavian countries, an approach which seeks to combine the advantages of public and voluntary contributions. But in all countries there has been concern for strengthening the public role in the interests of broadening provision, setting standards and promoting equity in the system.

Response and Initiative

Generally adult education has developed as a response to individual and societal needs. It would be strange if this were not the case. Many examples spring to mind, such as the mechanics' institutes of nineteenth century Britain, the part time post-secondary programme in the U.S.S.R., vocational education as a response to the needs for development in the Third World, the large-scale literacy campaigns in many countries, and the paid educational leave policies in several European countries. Indeed it is possible to write the history of adult education in my own country, and I suspect in others, in terms of the major advances which came as a response to the crises and dramatic changes in our lives as a people. What has followed upon many of the revolutions of the present century provides notable examples, including, of course, that of China. It has long been debated by educational philosophers and historians whether educational provision can or should bring about intentional social change. Opinion is divided and the record at best unclear. Current voices in the field (Botkin, 1979) are calling upon adult education to be more pro-active rather than reactive in its outlook, and for a shift from what is termed 'maintenance/shock' learning to 'innovative' learning. We have long had a tradition in adult education for the promotion and facilitation of social change as one of adult education's major tasks. In many countries, the efforts of adult education leaders to promote and advance towards a system of lifelong learning may be among the most important initiatives ever taken by the field.

These perspectives - in some cases, contrasting tendencies - account for many of the forces and points of view which have shaped adult education through its modern history to the present day. The second part of this paper will be devoted to certain developments which have been of particular importance in the most recent decades, especially the last twenty-five years, during which time the nature of the international community has changed so profoundly.

Education and Development

Significant evolution in thinking has taken place over the past few decades with respect to the concept of development and the role of education in the development process. There has been increasing realisation that development must be seen in many dimensions as well as the economic. Much literature has focused on "the educational core of development" and latterly on the crucial role to be played by nonformal as well as formal education, if development programmes are to live up to their potential. There is widespread discussion of the shortcomings of much development effort over the past generation and concern about cynicism in some quarters. Many issues for discussion on the role of adult education in development are contained in the "Design for Action" developed by the 1976 conference of the International Council for Adult Education held in Dar es Salaam (Hall & Kidd, 1978, 284-5):

the **educative dimension** of all strategies for economic, social, cultural and political development;

participation of the people in decisions;

policies responsive to **basic human needs;**

implementation of the **Unesco Recommendation** on the Development of Adult Education;

regional and national **organisations** to develop adult education capacity; action to **assist countries** least developed in adult education;

training for adult education through regional centers;

accent on particularly **deprived groups** in society: women, illiterates, peasants, migrants;

research that emphasises participatory methods of investigation and evaluation;

integrated rural development;

workers' education for those in the rural sector;

promotion of and respect for **indigenous cultures**:

adult education **content** concerned with development issues of food, health, environment.

Recognition of the essential role of adult education in the development process has surely been the most important single fact in the history of the field in our generation. President Nyerere has put it well:

> First, we must educate adults. Our children will not have an impact on our economic development for five, ten or even twenty years. The attitudes of adults, on the other hand, have an impact now. (Institute of Adult Education, 1973:4)

Of particular significance in the relationship between adult education and development has been the field of literacy education. The functional literacy projects sponsored by Unesco from 1967 to 1973 for its Experimental World Literacy Programme, the recommendations of the first World Conference of Ministers of Education on the Eradication of Illiteracy, in Tehran in 1965 and which proposed and created the mechanisms for the EWLP, the Persepolis Declaration of the 1975 International Symposium for Literacy, and the large-scale literacy campaigns in many countries, are some of the significant features and achievements of an enterprise devoted to the world's most compelling educational task. That in spite of much successful effort, the absolute number of illiterate persons in the world is increasing, is recognised by all educational authorities as an urgent call to further effort. That there will be, according to optimistic predictions, at least 900 million adult illiterates by the year 2000 (Lowe, 1982, 62) is a fact which will continue to place literacy education at the head of the international community's educational agenda.

The Impact of Technology

One of the most obvious features of the development of the field in recent decades has been the influence of increasingly rapid technological change on both the educational needs of our people and the methodologies of the field. The situation varies widely from one country and region to another. To take only one example, but perhaps it is one of the most dramatic: the impact of technology on what used to be called correspondence instruction and now is usually termed distance education. A method which was highly developed in many countries in the inter-war period of the 1920s and 1930s but began to languish in many regions after the Second World War has been augmented and transformed as a result of the application of recent technological developments. A methodology which was seen by many as out of date and very restricted in its use has now returned to centre stage of adult education.

Meeting the Needs of Special Groups

It was a remarkable feature of the Tokyo Conference in 1972 that there was such a broad base of agreement among the nations represented - no matter what their stage of development or political orientation - that increased priority must be attached to meeting the educational needs of certain groups which our systems of adult education had not served adequately. Foremost among these were the most educationally disadvantaged in our populations. Great emphasis was placed on what was termed the democratisation of the field, and since that time great efforts in many countries have been devoted to serving such disadvantaged groups more effectively. The education of women was also identified by virtually every participating nation as a priority and important progress has been made in some areas. The list of special needs is long, and one can but mention several others: the urban and rural poor, migrant workers, ethnic minorities and handicapped persons. Judging by international surveys and reports, many countries have made concerted efforts in these and other areas of special need.

Provision in Public Policy

One of the most striking changes in the period between the second (1960) and third (1972) Unesco World Conferences on Adult Education was the development of public policy in this area. That trend has continued apace. Just as adult education as a field of practice is decentralised in our societies, so public policy with respect to it has appeared in various sectors, such as labour, welfare, economic planning and development, agriculture, health and of course education. Education and training have come to be seen increasingly as indispensable means of intervention to cope with a complex of problems such as chronic high levels of unemployment, including youth unemployment, the need to upgrade or alter the skills of the workforce and the increasing burden of welfare costs. As a result, adult education has been transformed from what in many cases was a marginal state of genteel poverty and obscurity to a major role in public policy and practice. Adult educators accustomed to seeing their area neglected even in plans for the broad field of education have now seen it come to the fore in national social and economic policy. For many, the process began or was accelerated with **Learning to Be**, the report of the Unesco International Commission on the Development of Education, in 1972. The rest of the decade has brought many important policy recommendations and actions, including international consensus on the Recommendation on the Development of Adult Education, adopted by the Unesco General Assembly in 1976.

Lifelong Education and the Learning Society

Although the concept and reality of lifelong learning are in some respects as old as recorded history (and we are aware of The 1919 Report in Britain and the declaration of the Montreal Conference in 1960) the active promotion of the concept as a basis for policy development perhaps dates from the Unesco Faure Report (**Learning to Be**) and subsequent elaborations by Unesco, the Organisation for Economic Cooperation and Development (OECD) and other inter-governmental organisations. Adult education does not 'own' the idea of lifelong learning - far from it - but adult educators have played a major role in the development of the idea and represent what must be a major element in its implementation. Many adult educators are particularly accepting of one of the central ideas inherent in lifelong learning, the focus on learning, as distinct from education. There is a realisation and reliance on the fact that seen in a lifelong and lifewide perspective, the growth and development of the individual is influenced by all the elements of society, not just those formally designated as educational. Indeed some proponents of lifelong education see the diversity of sources of assistance for learning, including self-directed learning of all kinds, as important protection for the individual against some of the forces seeking to influence him or her (Gelpi, 1979). The intellectual and philosophical thrust behind the concept of lifelong education and the related ideas of **education permanente** and recurrent education has had profound impact both on our field and on broader circles of national policy, and will continue to do so.

A World Community of Ideas

One of the most beneficial and profound changes in the field of adult education in recent decades has been the creation of an international community of ideas. If it was ever the case that the flow of influence, advice and assistance was overwhelmingly a one way flow - from the more to the less developed nations - this has now ceased to be the case. The experience and ideas of the Third World are having profound impact on the First and Second. Concern for development and the struggle to improve our approaches to adult education are things which we share. The international conferences on the field and on specialised aspects of it are of great importance. They are but the tip of the iceberg of international sharing and mutual benefit. Montreal, Tokyo, Tehran, Persepolis, Dar es Salaam and Paris remind us of important efforts to share experience and launch new lines of development. An increasing number of instruments has been developed to promote communication at the international level. To the traditional avenues available to the scholarly world have been added the work of Unesco (of central importance to our field) and that of other intergovernmental organisations, the regional adult education bodies, and since its formation in 1973, the International Council for Adult Education. Through these and many other international instruments, we have created the means to support and learn from each other.

The history of adult education to the present day is wonderfully complex. It is interwoven with the story of the struggle of the human family to achieve its individual and social goals. The record of the past reveals impressive and inspiring achievement. As the poet John Milton reminded the leaders of his day, "peace hath her victories no less renowned than war". The past also contained its problems, frustrations and disappointments. It is both the lessons of the past and a vision of a possible future which arm us for our further efforts.

REFERENCES

The following includes the sources referred to in the text and a few other works which were the most useful among the many consulted.

Anderson, L. & Windham, D.M. (Ed.), 1982, **Education and Development**, Lexington, Lexington Books.

Botkin, J., Elmandjra, M. & Malitza, M., 1979, **No Limits to Learning**, Oxford, Pergamon.

Coombs, P.H., 1968, **The World Educational Crisis: A Systems Analysis**, New York, Oxford Univ. Press.

Gelpi, E.,1979, **A Future for Lifelong Education**, Manchester, Manchester Univ., Manchester Monographs, vol 1 and 2.

Hall, B & Kidd, J.R. (Ed.), 1978, **Adult Learning: A Design for Action**, Oxford, Pergamon.

Institute of Adult Education (Tanzania),1973, **Adult Education Handbook**, Dar es Salaam, Tanzania Publishing.

Kelly, T., 1970, **A History of Adult Education In Great Britain**, Liverpool, Liverpool Univ. Press, (Second edition).

Kidd, J.R., 1974, **Whilst Time is Burning**, Ottawa, International Development Research Council.

Learning to Be, 1972, Report of the Unesco International Commission on the Development of Education, Paris, Unesco.

Lowe, J.,1982, **The Education of Adults: A World Perspective**, Paris, Unesco, Toronto, OISE Press, (Second edition).

Simmons, J. (Ed.), 1980, **The Education Dilemma**, New York, Pergamon.

Titmus, C., 1981, **Strategies for Adult Education**, Chicago, Follett.

World Bank, 1980, **Education Sector Working Paper,** Washington, World Bank.

B. Adult Education Theory and Development in China

Yao Zhongda

In the world of today, adult education, as an important integral part of the nation's education and as a new domain, is being paid great attention and held in high esteem by more and more national governments and non-governmental organisations. Looking far and wide at the world situation, the reason why educational undertakings in the developed countries are flourishing has, without exception, something to do with the relevant development of adult education; even some developing countries that are advancing more rapidly have realised the truth that to develop adult education vigorously is the only way to make the national economy develop successfully and to develop education suited to that economy. For this reason, adult education is gradually being given its rightful place in many countries. This is an objective law independent of the wills and acts of people with lofty ideas, but shaped following the development of productive forces and the course of human growth. In a sense, it is not subject to political views or social systems; it has a foothold throughout the world and in the whole of human society.

Theoretical Basis

There was once a revered professor, Lu Shiying, in China. In **Education in the Countryside**, written more than half a century ago, he expounded: "school education is one stage of life, short in time and simple in content", but the knowledge acquired after growing up is "more complicated and extensive than that acquired at school". This shows his understanding of the objective fact of the importance of adult education, though it does not touch the essence of its inexorable development.

Why has it happened that adult education is increasingly flourishing as a worldwide trend? As early as one hundred and twenty years ago, Karl Marx pointed out emphatically in **Capital** that "the degree of skills of the existing population is always the pre-condition of production as a whole; it is therefore the principal accumulation of wealth and the most important result of antecedent labour; its form of existence, however, is living labour itself". To put it in clearer terms, the ground for the development of adult education is that the uninterrupted development of productive forces demands the continuous raising of the educational level and technical skill of the labour force. This is the theoretical basis for the certain development of adult education.

It is beyond question that adult education is developing and will go on doing so. But in different countries, owing to many different circumstances, there are inevitably disparities in the way adult education starts, its course of development, forms of organisation, content requirements, forms of management, etc. For instance, in the Federal Republic of Germany, adult education has a history of over one hundred years. It developed following the industrial revolution, but as a national policy, it was formally included in the constitution only in 1919: all the federal states must promote the popular education system which includes adult education centres.

It is said that adult education in the United States began when attention was drawn to the need for remedial education for young people after World War I. But it was only after upsurges in 1953 and 1957 that adult education was spurred to faster development. The reasons were on the one hand the need for vocational training for ex-servicemen prior to employment, and the pressure of rapid development of modern science and technology on the other. However it was not until 1962 that adult education appeared in the laws in the United States. In that year, the Training and Education Bill for the labour force was passed by Congress and in 1963, as part of the Law of Economic Opportunity, the Adult Basic Education Act was adopted, also. Afterwards, additional acts were formulated respectively in 1965, 1966 and 1968, expanding the scale of adult education. At present, adult education is developing extensively in the United States as well as in the Federal Republic of Germany.

In the past few years, the development of adult education in China has aroused great interest among organisations and individuals in adult education in quite a few countries, and is understood by more and more friends through mutual exchanges in various ways.

Course of Adult Education Development in China

China is a developing country. There are now different opinions as to when adult education emerged. Some hold that it came into being side by side with human society, which can be traced back to earliest times. Others say that it began during the period of the Old Democratic Revolution (1911 - 1919). Still others maintain that it sprang up in the wake of the New Democratic Revolution. What is the correct view on this remains to be further investigated. However, one thing is certain: as a democratic right or as a part of welfare services, adult education, initiated by the pioneers of the Democratic Revolution and established by pioneer educators, started quite early in China. But on a regional or national level, it was only during the period of the Second Revolutionary Civil War (1927 - 1937) that the development of adult education came to be connected directly with the development of productive forces and the advancement of social progress, becoming a policy and an integral part of, or at times even the most important part of, the whole education effort of the country. Moreover, it began to develop with clear objectives, with planning and leadership. At the time the education policy of the Chinese Soviet Government in the Central Soviet Area was "to raise by every means the education level of the workers and peasants. For this purpose, every possible political and material support must be given to the masses." Under the guidance of this policy, adult education was carried out extensively in the Soviet areas. According to the records, in the 2,932 towns registered in 1933, 6,462 night schools and 2,388 literacy classes were set up, and nearly 250,000 workers and peasants took part in study.

The most outstanding time in the development of adult education was the later period of the War of Resistance against Japan and of the Third Revolutionary Civil War (1942-1949). What took place in the Anti-Japanese Democratic Base Areas and Liberated Areas was the result of a belief that cadres were the vanguard of the masses, who needed more than anyone else to be trained and improved: the adult in the countryside is the main force in war and production; one step advanced by them will bring forth one step in war and production. The Democratic Governments of all the Base Areas therefore formulated their national education policy: "cadre education is first and mass education second. As for the former, the improving of the present is more important than the training of future cadres, and for the latter, adult education is superior to children's education." The implementation of this policy played a major role in promoting the development of the Large Scale Production Movement in the Base Areas, and in training large numbers of cadres to greet the victories of the War of Resistance Against Japan and the Revolutionary Civil War.

Nation-wide large scale development of adult education in China began after the founding of New China. It was, on the one hand, a continuation and development of the fine tradition of the Revolutionary Base Areas during the war years, and on the other hand, which was a more important factor, impelled by the objective contradiction between the backwardness left behind by old China (more than 80 per cent of the adult population were illiterate) and the demands made for culture [i.e. education (Ed)] by the rapid development of productive forces in New China. This understanding was reached not after but before the founding of New China. In May 1949, at the Second Plenary Session of the Seventh Congress of the Chinese Communist Party, Chairman Mao Zedong pointed out sharply to the whole Party, cadres at various levels and the broad masses in the Base Areas: "our cadres must do their utmost to learn the techniques of production and the method of managing production as well as other closely related work such as commerce and banking". He added at the same time: "if we know nothing about production and do not master it quickly, if we cannot restore and develop production as speedily as possible and achieve solid success so that the livelihood of the workers, first of all, and that of the people in general, is improved, we shall be unable to maintain our political power, we shall be unable to stand on our feet, we shall fail". That same year he emphasised again in his well-known work **On the People's Democratic Dictatorship** "we shall soon put aside some of the things we know well and be compelled to do things we don't know well". "We must learn what we do not know." "If we dig into a subject for several months, for a year or two, for three or five years, we shall **eventually** master it."

Correct ideological guidance is based on objective understanding of reality and rational analysis of the conditions required to open up the way to a bright future, which is very precious. However, the more important thing is practice, and the testing and developing of a theory in practice.

In the second year after the founding of New China, 1950, the first National Conference on Worker-Peasant Education was convened by the Ministry of Education under the Central People's Government. The Conference pointed out that "the central task at present for the nation is to restore and develop rapidly the country's production and construction, which depends mainly on the two forces of workers and peasants on the production front. If educational work does not cooperate to heighten the ideological consciousness and raise the level of culture and techniques of the two main forces, the new attitude towards labour and creative spirit required by the production and construction will not arise, which will do harm to the central task; and our educational work will lose contact with reality." This conference laid a solid foundation for the development of various aspects of adult education then and for the future, such as ideological mobilisation, organisation of teaching, leadership, management, guaranteed resources, etc.

The 1950s saw the flowering of the first phase of adult education following the founding of New China. The main manifestations were:

(1) It developed in all walks of life, including cadres and staff members of central and local government institutions at various levels, workers and staff members of factories, mines and other industrial enterprises, members of rural cooperative teams, craftsmen of cities and towns and urban residents, etc. Most of them went to night schools and literacy classes.

(2) Besides laying emphasis on wiping out illiteracy, spare-time middle schools or colleges were set up according to the different demands of various kinds of people. As well as the majority who took part in spare-time study, worker-peasant accelerated middle schools and classes for advanced studies were established for cadres, advanced staff members and model workers, allowing them to be released from work for study with the same salary. Thus, the demands for continuous learning of knowledge and techniques by people with different educational levels were basically satisfied.

(3) It lasted quite a long time and yielded remarkable results. In the mid- fifties, although the development of adult education was influenced to varying degrees by political movements and had its ups and downs, generally speaking there was no long pause, especially in worker education and rural literacy work. "Ten months of pregnancy ends in one day's birth." Up to 1959, the number of illiterates in the adult population dropped from over 80 per cent at the beginning of the founding of New China to 43 per cent. But during the long period of 15 to 16 years from the late fifties to the mid-seventies the country was in the grip of political movements coming one after another, and economic development suffered severe setbacks. As a result, adult education both general and technical was regarded as heresy and it virtually came to a complete halt. It was only in 1976 when the ten-year nation-wide internal disorder was finally terminated, and especially after the Third Plenary Session of the Eleventh Congress of the Communist Party of China which decided to shift the stress of the whole Party to economic construction, that adult education could be restored and developed systematically again.

Trends in the Future

China is a socialist country and a rapidly developing one. The development of socialism is guided by the science of historical materialism, the basic viewpoint of which is that of production, i.e. all social activities must be subordinated to and serve the development of production. This includes educational undertakings, especially adult education.

China has entered a new historical period. The general task put forward by the Government is to unite people of all nationalities in working hard and self-reliantly to achieve, step by step, the modernisation of industry, agriculture, national defence and science and technology, and to make China a culturally advanced and highly democratic socialist country. At the same time, the general objective for the two decades between 1981 and the end of this century is to quadruple the value of gross national industrial and agricultural production. For this purpose, in accordance with the State's requirements of "working vigorously to popularise primary education, strengthen secondary vocational education and higher education and develop educational undertakings of all types and at all levels in both urban and rural areas, including training classes for cadres, workers, staff members and peasants, and literacy classes, in order to train all kinds of specialists and raise the scientific and education level of the whole nation", all walks of life are developing programmes of adult education to meet the requirements of the development of production and to raise the level of knowledge of personnel of all types. From this we can foresee that the second period of full bloom of adult education will certainly occur following the upsurge of economic construction. It differs from the first upsurge in this respect: to eliminate illiteracy is still an important task, but in the national perspective it is not the focal point of the work and is now replaced by balanced and continued development of adult education of all types and at all levels, with stress on continuously raising the cultural level.

In short, adult education in China has developed under the circumstances that its culture was backward and it had to suit the needs of rapid development of productive forces. It has been carried out for a long time, taking as primary the work of popularising basic knowledge of culture. Now, with the requirements of technology for raising the educational level of cadres, workers and peasants, new changes are taking place in adult education in the targets of enrolment, forms of organisation, content, teaching methods, and in other ways. Problems in adult education in China that need to be explored are daily more closely approximating those in technically advanced and culturally developed countries.

C. Panel Commentary and Discussion

Professor Moro'oka explored ways of classifying and so clarifying the nature and diversity of adult education - social education as it is known in Japan. Five characteristics were identified: self-directed independent learning; environment-based learning; human relations training; voluntaryism; and community-oriented activities. Secondly, he recalled a five-way categorisation of adult education areas as a kind of 'basement for comparative studies': physical health; social and human relationships or communication; economic development; cultural self-fulfilment; and political decision-making. These are alternatively described as: health, welfare and family living; fundamental and literacy education - remedial; vocational technical or professional competence; self-fulfilment; and education for civic, political and community competence. Moro'oka was able to identify each of these from the previous study visits around Shanghai and considered them a sound framework for analysing the adequacy of adult education systems.

Mulusa concurred with Selman in finding adult education broad and confused, without precise boundaries. Although Selman's historical and thematic treatment was helpful it did not uncover the reasons for the confusion: Western country adult educators had spent too long in sterile definitional matters; even in Kenya now there was debate as to whether adult education was a 'discipline'. Inherent contradictions should instead be examined such as whether adult education was to assist the transmission of knowledge, technology and culture between generations or, rather, to transform society, thus disrupting the existing order. Mulusa sought a sharper distinction between different concepts, and between such different practitioners as Cuba's politicised functionaries in the literacy campaign, Kenya's less committed literacy campaign salaried teachers, and those at higher levels for whom specialised tertiary qualifications are essential. He called for expression of different views about the expanded role of government in adult education - 'intervention' as he expressed it, a term that Chinese speakers later observed had no meaning for their own context where government 'leadership' was expected. Mulusa referred specifically to some Western criticism of Political Education in Tanzanian adult education as being indoctrination. Selman's paper "steered clear of such troubled waters, but this is an issue that needs to be discussed openly at such a gathering". This is tied up with the call for more pro-active adult education, echoing Nyerere's 1976 challenge that adult education could not be neutral.

Mulusa went on to applaud the stress upon education for the full development of people rather than merely for economic growth; goals like participation in decision-making should be included. He added a sceptical note on the potential of new technologies and distance education; for example "the Kenyan Correspondence Course Unit has only survived on captive audiences handed down by the Government". He concluded by reiterating the need to concentrate on productive research and development rather than wasting energy eg. on arguing what adult education is. "Because of this wastage of energy, adult education is not yet a strong awakening force. It looks to me like a force which is in the process of waking up, and asking very basic questions like who are we, where are we and where are we going."

Dr Cunningham echoed Mulusa's concern with the political. She found Selman's "a very soft view" , painting "a very rosy picture of adult education - as if we are workers clad in shining armour". "It does not seem to me that the paper stresses the political aspects of adult education - it is not neutral." One needs to go beyond the 'individual versus society' dichotomy, beyond saying that adult education is liberal in intent. 'Society' usually means the values of the dominant culture, which may not be in the best interests of the poor, women, or minority groups. Those lacking power seldom contribute to defining societal values. 'Liberal education' likewise lends itself to different definitions as to how to 'develop the powers of the person as an end in itself'. "Mr Yao is more explicit on this point. He suggests that 'correct ideological guidance' is needed to open up a bright future for adult educators." While thus welcoming this putting of cards on the table, Dr Cunningham questioned Yao's apparently exclusive stress on productive forces, asking if this went far enough. With such a restriction "how will people gain an appreciation of the power of cultural values within the society? In my experience empowerment of people also comes from their ability to understand and critique social control as it is expressed through the power of culture." In the United States individualism and equality are such strong cultural norms that those not experiencing equality get blamed for this as a personal failure, leading to 'deficit mentality' adult education, where structural explanations might better be sought.

Subsequent discussion elucidated several of these points, sometimes only after intensive group clarification of meanings and assumptions. Yao's 'development of productive skills in the labour force' attracted much interest; it was suggested that it should be understood widely to refer to all skills of human development with direct or indirect implications for production. The Chinese programmes themselves, it was argued, bore out this wider meaning of development of productive skills. Dialogue among Chinese participants suggested other angles. One looked to enrichment and diversification of adult education with increasing prosperity. Another stressed the 'spiritual' as well as the material as a form of production. Some felt that Yao's paper was too narrow, that adult education has a richer, spiritual meaning beyond raising productivity: there was a role in 'the two civilisations, material and spiritual'. Also adult education could be indirectly related to future production; not every part could be seen as directly related, although the system was still too narrow. Against this another Chinese participant argued in support of Yao's apparent preoccupation with production (which indeed reflected his particular responsibility for workers' education rather than the whole gamut of adult education in China), that societal evolution **is** based on productive activities: adult education did and **should** in this view serve only production. The balance of opinion among Chinese and non-Chinese alike was however that it served different purposes, and could be claimed to relate across the board to production only in a broad and indirect sense - in China as elsewhere.

Group reports summarised this. Thus: "several foreign delegates felt that the statement 'education is always subordinate to production' was in conflict with what they had observed on the visits (especially the Workers' Palace). This point was clarified by several Chinese delegates, pointing out that education for productivity involves not only jobs skills, but also the development of ideological and personal knowledge and skills. This 'well-rounded' concept of worker education is important if people are to be both productive in their work as well as serving the goals of their country." And in another group, divergent views coalesced as Chinese members tried to explain:

> The tremendous demand for technical skills and the mobilisation of adult education for the modernisation effort, and the widespread application of knowledge to scientific and technological advancement, were seen as immediate and imperative concerns. But at the same time the current needs and the future perspective of adult education in terms of individual/personal advancement, and spiritual/moral/cultural/ideological advancement, were considered as of equal significance. In this context it was felt that 'productive skills', or rather the 'productive force' should not be interpreted only in terms of material advancement, but should also include non-material aspects...in terms of both society/state and the individual. Adult education should help the country to develop, to get ahead, in all areas, and help the individuals to be well qualified, competent, and able to understand the world situation.

Another group report took this matter up with reference to the popular will and the role of government:

> It was agreed that a common definition [of adult education] was not possible, since differing social and political situations call for different forms of adult education. This is related to the difficulty of defining development. In nations where the government reflects the wishes of the people, then development is easier to define and it is easy to see how ideology and production can go together in adult education, as in China. But, as in many developing countries, if governments do not reflect popular will, then ideological factors come first and adult education can be seen as a force for liberation. A Chinese participant noted that the Chinese focus of study is productivity through the two civilisations - material and ideological - and that development that concentrated solely on material development would be bad...

The role of adult education in politics and production perhaps dominated the first round of clarification and analysis, though expressed in various ways. One speaker questioned Selman's set of dichotomies on the ground that they could and did interweave and co-exist rather than necessarily contrast. Another on the other hand challenged his apparently neutral stance, asking whether adult education could be allowed to be an instrument of power elites. (It was in fact often thus misused, in Selman's view.) To another question Yao reiterated that the key in China was the Government's 'current policy' - what others tend to call the political will.

The same issues spilled over into discussions about the role of legislation in supporting adult education. It was recognised that styles vary between countries so that to generalise was hard; also that badly managed legislation could be counterproductive. The law worked well in China, it was argued, and the rapid development of adult education without the law in that country was held unthinkable by some Chinese participants. Here the interests of people and Government coincided: hence the inappropriateness of using the term 'intervention' in this context. In some, particularly Scandinavian, countries, Rubenson pointed out, there were important 'collectives', middle groups mediating between the individual and society and playing a moderating part for certain interests, with government funds given to the collective for adult education purposes. Trade unions and free churches, for example, used such adult education to promote their own goals. While this helped in some societies, the group report of this discussion noted that "China and Iraq saw no conflict between government interest and public benefit in the current practice of Government intervention in adult education". Some of these questions touching politics, government, and the role of adult education for liberation, were taken up in the papers and discussions summarised in the next chapter.

D. Trends and Issues for the Future

Professor Rubenson, commenting on academic addresses by Dr Hunter and Wang Wenlin to an open session of the Symposium, observed that adult education had been a major policy issue and area for a mere twenty years. He identified several relevant factors.

Economic changes, and the ascendancy of human capital theory: up to three times the return was claimed by some for investment in people compared with other forms of capital investment. Such investment was also seen as a means of reducing inter- and intra-generational inequalities.

Recognition of the persistence of inequality, despite comprehensive education for example, led to radicalisation, very marked among adult educators in Scandinavia, which was linked there to unions' demands for industrial democracy which included a demand for adult education.

The absence of a visible structure for adult education was a near-universal phenomenon. More diverse higher education led to diversification of non-traditional modes of entry, including especially recognition of non-academic expertise. Discussion about how to change the regular formal education system was now very general.

Education and training related to employment was now the single most important facet of adult education in industrialised countries: training to meet new labour market requirements. This trend was led by governments and employers, and equity counted for little in it. General education as distinct from specific training was very rare in this work. For manual workers it was largely restricted to on-the-job training; wider educational opportunities tended to be restricted to the senior levels. A Swedish study had revealed that only 25 per cent of unskilled workers were given any opportunity to learn on the job, compared with 80 per cent of senior salaried personnel. Adult education was thus tending to contribute to polarisation within society.

Dr Hunter summarised issues and directions having priority for the future, and elaborated in her paper:

greater clarity regarding the social, economic, and political intention of programes of literacy/basic education;

responsiveness to the desire of the bypassed adults for formal education, of equal quality with the education provided for the already educated elite of the society;

development of high quality educational software that will enable more effective use of new technologies within the educational enterprise;

serious consideration of the relation between training and productivity: does such a relationship exist?

greater availability of educational counselling services that have the needs of the potential learners as the central focus;

public and private support for all forms of adult education, not disproportionately for worker training;

constant vigilance to avoid increasing the distance between an educated few and the masses;

concern for the rights, educational access, and training of workers employed by the transnational corporations;

greater emphasis in worker education on intellectual development, creativity, and skills needed for social analysis;

creation of educational forms and processes to address global issues in the context of concrete local reality;

provision of discrete training for educators working in different forms of adult education, with all sharing a common focus on appropriate connections between local and global issues.

E. Adult Education and the Future: Major Issues and Directions

Carman St. J. Hunter

The Task

The variety of issues facing adult educators and the complexity of arrangements for the provision of adult education within any one country have generally defied even the best efforts at comprehensive description. An overview of the world scene is even more elusive. This symposium is an invitation to each of us to enter as fully as possible into the range of challenges and responses to the needs of adults that characterise the diverse forms of adult education throughout the world so that both our vision and our practice may be enhanced.

Definitions and Distinctions

First, to provide some parameters to aid our discussions, a few simple definitions and distinctions. We define adult education as any planned educational experience for adults that takes place outside the regular, accredited school, college, and university system of the country. Such education may constitute either a first or second chance for adults who have not been able to benefit from the regular system for whatever reason. In some cases, adult education may lead to accreditation - and may even be on a par with the regular system as is the case in China. In other cases, no accreditation is sought or offered; study is undertaken for the sake of acquiring specific knowledge or skills or for the pleasure of learning.

The definition of who is an **adult** differs from one society to another. Here adults are defined as all those who are so considered within their own society.

It is further necessary to be able to distinguish among different forms of adult education as a basis for international understanding and discussion. Three categories suggest themselves as helpful for this purpose:

fundamental or basic education (literacy)
work-related or updating education
discretionary education.

These forms can be differentiated by goals and assumptions, primary focus, participants, funding sources, administration or sponsorship, and approach or methodology. In most nations, all three forms exist simultaneously, the degree of priority depending upon social and economic factors among others.

New Questions and New Issues

International adult education conferences were once relatively calm, deliberative assemblies. Participants, whether policy-makers or practitioners, came largely from already industralised countries. The most commonly discussed issues caused little furore:

relations between adult education and the regular system;
increasing the status and resources of adult education;
participant motivation;
establishing effective administrative structures;
improving methods and materials;
establishing the concept of education as a lifelong process.

In recent years the climate and concerns of adult education gatherings have changed. While the same issues continue to emerge and receive attention, others arouse more passion. This has largely come about as a result of the increasing number of participants from pre-industrial and industralising nations. Their search for ways to redress inequalities and injustice in access to education, especially in societies where the majority of the population has been excluded from the regular system, has stimulated a different way of looking at the existing systems and examination of new issues long considered beyond the scope of purely educational concerns. They ask:

Who benefits and who is left out of educational programmes for adults?
Are illiteracy and low levels of education the cause of poverty or its results?
In what ways do adult education structures reinforce social and economic distance?
Should adult education serve primarily individual or national goals?

Strong feelings are raised on both sides of each question. Industralised nations have, as a result of these debates, become more conscious of the disadvantaged minorities within their own borders. Whatever differences exist with respect to other issues, there is agreement that a major priority for all nations is to provide effective education for those who have been most excluded in the past. The difficulty is in knowing **how** to achieve this goal.

Basic Education Including Literacy: Issues and Directions

In many countries, the only unit within the ministry of education that deals with adults is mandated to develop policy and programmes that deliver literacy training, primary school equivalency, or, in industralised nations, secondary level equivalency for the most excluded portion of the population. Whether those who have been left out are a minority, as in highly industralised countries, or a majority, as in pre-industrial nations and in those seeking rapid modernisation, they are the nation's poor, living on the fringes of or outside the dominant social and economic structures. They include both rural and urban poor.

While there are innumerable issues that must be faced by those responsible for adult education in any country, including funding strategies, locus of planning and curriculum development, staff training, research needs and effective evaluation, there is one that is central and determines the direction taken with respect to all of the others. This central issue is the **intent or purposes** of literacy and basic education. Without clarity on that one issue, confusion ensues at every level and the lack of consistency between methodology and purpose causes considerable pain for programme providers, adult education practitioners, and, most seriously, for participants.

What purpose has priority for literacy/basic education provision within adult education? That is the determinative question within any society. Three quite distinct policy intentions can be discerned by analysing literacy/basic education programmes even when the policy-makers may not themselves have been clear at the start. Any one of the three may include some emphases from another policy intention but one always has priority:

> to provide a first step in the process that will enable adults to achieve academic equivalence with the regular system of schooling;
>
> to provide terminal education for certain groups within the population that will increase their productivity as workers, enhance qualities that contribute to good citizenship, and improve the quality of family life;
>
> to provide skills and basic knowledge necessary for social analysis, creative problem-solving, and active participation in reshaping the structures of social and economic life in the community and beyond.

The majority of literacy/basic education programmes seek to achieve the first of the three purposes. Providers have worked with varying degrees of success to adapt both their content and methodology to the particular needs and experience of adults as contrasted with those of children. Many have been highly successful in stimulating adult learners to make spectacular gains in short periods of time. However, there are several obstacles to full achievement of the goal of delivering equivalent education to large numbers of adults. Countries in the early stages of modernisation encounter difficulties financing adult education programmes and working to universalise primary education for children at the same time. Another impediment to providing adult education equivalent to the academic courses of the regular system is that modernisation requires placing a priority on scientific and technological training and a consequent narrowing of the focus of adult programmes compared with those of the regular system. In addition, the need to train the brightest and best minds as rapidly as possible requires high levels of selectivity. In the end, those who benefit from this effort could become another elite.

The second purpose has been particularly important in the provision of literacy/basic education for rural populations. Sometimes the planners and teachers have concentrated their efforts on transmitting the content they have determined to be essential for the participants to learn. Consequently their methodology has been rigid. Others with the same basic purpose have managed to develop curricula and materials more closely related to the experience and needs of particular learners. Their methods have been more participatory. Critics of this second purpose, however, are quick to point out that the end result is a dual system of education. They claim, further, that it constitutes an attempt to socialise the poor, making them into docile workers and citizens, lacking both knowledge and skills to initiate any change in their basic situation. They point out that both national and foreign capital have an interest in making the peasants dependent on the market, both as producers and consumers.

The third purpose is both more difficult to achieve and more controversial because it envisages education for full participation in social and economic change. Advocates of both the second and third purposes frequently refer to the use of participatory methods and approaches; however the former are generally referring to educational processes that take place within the learning group itself with implications for the personal and family life of the learners in such areas as health, nutrition, family planning, self-help economic enterprises and the like. Those seeking to realise the third purpose employ the same methodology within the learning situation but also seek to enable social, political, and economic analysis that results in action in these areas. The learning agenda is generally broader than in the case of the second purpose, and may seek the underlying causes for problems in family and community life. It may stress the structures of society rather than the failure of knowledge, information, or skills among people locally.

Two illustrations of the confusion caused by lack of clarity about which purpose a given programme seeks to achieve may be of some help as we seek to understand why the issue of intention is so important with reference to basic education and literacy programmes.

(1) Literacy campaigns in countries that have recently undergone dramatic social change have generally been based on the third purpose. Literacy training was placed in the context of mobilising the energies, interests, and commitment of the masses for participation in the change process. Literacy was presented as essential to this larger purpose. Educators from other parts of the world have often declared their desire to learn from the successes of China, Tanzania, Cuba or Nicaragua in promoting literacy. They have assumed that the educational methodology could be replicated apart from the basic purpose of the campaign which was fundamentally political. Experience seems to indicate that this is impossible.

(2) Adult education field workers are more likely than policy-level personnel to espouse the third purpose. Perhaps this is because they do not carry national-level responsibility or because they live closer to the poor whom they serve. Whatever the reason, they often dedicate themselves with considerable fervour to carrying out basic education with the objective of enabling people to transform their social reality. The result may be that when the people identify and begin to act on the real obstacles to their development, the entrenched interests of dominant groups resist and the people are the losers. Responsible adult educators cannot ignore the inevitable results of espousing purposes that are not also supported by those ultimately responsible for the programme. Adult educators need not necessarily give up on the third purpose but they should, at least, be fully aware of what they are doing.

What is the Future?

One thing is clear. The demand for adult basic education will increase. Those originally deprived of access to education are asking for formal education or its equivalent. They want what has apparently worked for others. Even programmes that intend only minimal change for participants will continue to be the means for awakening a greater thirst to know and understand the world. Governments will be pressed to provide access, not to second-class education, but to something more substantive. This demand will be in conflict in many nations with the desire of landowners, factory owners and managers, and government employees to use education as a means of preserving things as they are. It will also be in conflict with international interests that presently seek out under-educated adults for the cheap labour they require to maintain profits.

In addition to the important role of adult educators who have consciously placed themselves on the side of the poor, application of the potential represented by technology can provide access for the formerly isolated, even those in rural villages, to fields of knowledge long hidden in books they never saw. At present technology is far ahead of the software created for educational use. This need not always be the case.

Modernisation itself will create more jobs in the market economy that require higher levels of education, thus contributing to the spiral of demand. Perhaps nations undergoing modernisation can avoid the mistakes of many already industrialised nations by being more aware of the dangers of focusing on products to the exclusion of human concerns. Many problems in the western world today result from the absence of the study of languages, history, literature, and the social sciences from functional skill training programmes. Mass education need not exclude concern for individual development in the context of social and economic development.

Work-Related Education: Issues and Directions

A young man, apprenticed to a master glass-blower, becomes skilled in creating the beautiful objects for which his village is famous. A woman observes an assembly-line worker, then takes her place on the line, and within a week may be up to full production capability. In an antiseptically clean laboratory at a small factory, young women are taught by older workers to bond hair-thin gold wires to silicon chips that will end up in hand calculators in some distant part of the globe. These scenes represent three different industrial eras, simultaneously present in the same country or in different parts of the world. They all utilise the same method of worker education: training by a more experienced worker. This informal training still represents the most common form of worker education. In recent times, however, formal training has come to play a more significant role.

In capitalist economies, worker training is almost entirely privately sponsored. While governments may provide vocational programmes, once the worker is employed, that form of provision is generally no longer available. In socialist economies, worker education is more commonly provided by government agencies. Yet the difference of sponsorship alters very little the diversity of types of provision. China has perhaps the most comprehensive system of government-sponsored worker education in the world. It is a rational and well coordinated system that responds to worker educational needs at every level. In the United States, for example, a combination of private industry, labour unions, and cooperating institutions provide roughly equivalent services but they are not centrally planned or coordinated. Both provide in-service training, short and long-term courses leading to promotions, economic advantages for the worker, and, in some cases, to advanced degrees. In China these degrees are awarded through the adult education system that parallels the regular system. In the U.S., industry may reach agreement with local institutions to accept industry training for credit and the conferring of engineering or other degrees. What counts for the worker is that study opportunities are available and that the training is recognised. In capitalist countries, the stress may be placed on advantages for the individual while in socialist economies, greater emphasis is placed on contributions made to the country's progress. However, in reality, the major incentive behind both government and employer-sponsored training is increased productivity. Raising the GNP and gaining a larger share of competitive world markets are behind the upgrading and retraining of both industrial and agricultural workers everywhere.

In all economies, labour organisations play a central role in worker education. In some cases, they sponsor training themselves through a wide variety of courses and also by establishing educational institutions which they finance and run for the benefit of workers and their families. In industrialised nations, trade unions have been in the forefront of negotiating educational benefits for workers as part of their contracts. Private employers, governments, trade unions and workers all see the need for more extensive training for the work force. The need to upgrade skills to keep up with the changing demands of increased technology, to facilitate the shift of workers to new jobs as industries move to new locations, and the underlying objective to increase social equality by making training accessible to all workers, appear to guarantee greater emphasis on this form of adult education throughout the world. A number of serious issues cannot however be ignored by responsible planners of this form of adult education.

Hard data are urgently needed to establish some tangible indication of the relation between education and productivity. At present, planners have practically nothing to go on when they are faced with the question of how much to invest in training. A positive connection is assumed but no reliable research has established exactly what that is.

Another important issue is the need for some form of educational brokering services. Even where significant opportunities are available for worker education, the workers themselves are often unaware of how to take advantage of the plans and of the specific opportunities that best match their experience and objectives. This is, of course, a particular problem of nations that do not have centrally planned economies.

As national governments and industry become more heavily committed to financing work-related education, there is considerable fear that, having made heavy investments in this particular form of adult education, they may tend to neglect other important forms. Literacy and basic education needs may not be fully met and discretionary education may be accessible only to those who can afford the necessary costs themselves.

The recent tendency in industry to divide and redivide the labour process in order to increase productivity, to reduce 'inefficiency' and to control the cost of labour has resulted in what is now called 'deskilling'. Workers need only master very small tasks, thus allowing less well-trained and less costly personnel to do most of the work with the better trained managerial class able to supervise productivity. As this trend continues, along with the decreasing need for traditional manufacturing jobs, fewer workers will be needed, with those who are at the managerial level requiring more costly and more intensive training. This demand for the brightest and the best may lead to greater educational inequalities within worker education.

There is an anomaly in the expressed dedication of major industries to the increased education of the workforce while, at the same time, they are transferring so many operations overseas. There they employ vast numbers of undereducated workers, especially women, to make designer jeans, electronic parts, and children's toys. The cycle may be beginning all over again with the exploitative conditions of 19th century England and North America being repeated throughout the world. The struggle for worker rights, including access to education, is an issue that should preoccupy adult educators both in the home countries of the transnational corporations as well as in the host countries.

A further economic factor that raises the most serious challenges of all for adult education is apparent in the post-industrial nations. Its implications cannot be ignored by those embarking on the path to modernisation. Both basic education and the increased access of workers to advanced levels of education are creating a mismatch between expectations and opportunities. This is not a new phenomenon. What is new is the lack of assurance that there will be continuous economic expansion with ever greater material rewards for everyone. Paul Barton who has long studied the field of work-related education sees the role of adult education in the future in a new way:

> There may be another transition underway, one that will transform our definition of productive roles in the society and economy. Have we defined our identities and measured our own worth too much according to the status of paid employment in the industrial economy? As important as traditional modes of success are, are there no other outlets for the desire to contribute? If society values the continued development of the mind, the enhancing of skills, and the transfer to all citizens of the knowledge hidden in

> books and in the minds of a few, then the pursuit of learning itself will become a "productive" role and offer greater opportunity for employment in the learning industry at the same time. Expanded learning opportunity may in this way further our transition from uninhibited GNP growth to a new kind of growth.(1)

Paul Barton goes on to speak of the continued development of the mind as the frontier of the future, a frontier in the mainstream of human evolution. He declares that it is through the well-educated and developed mind that we will discover new human purpose and meaning for the future. The worker, to participate in making a new future, requires an education far broader than skills for a specific job. Workers' education must provide the tools for analysing what is happening in the society and in the economy if workers are to direct and shape the changes that will affect their lives.

Discretionary Education: Issues and Directions

The first two forms of adult education discussed, literacy/basic education and work-related education, differ from the third form, discretionary education, in that both are seen as essential prerequisites to the modern state. Without a literate citizenry and a workforce trained for production, it is claimed that a nation will always remain at a disadvantage; therefore the provision of basic education and work-related education have become priorities for nations beginning the modernisation process. Discretionary education has grown up quite apart from any public policy. It includes a wide array of options for learning, assumed by the groups and institutions that offer them to be responsive to the affluent. Discretionary education first flourished in already industrialised societies where those who already had higher levels of formal schooling were most ready to take advantage of the alternatives for further study. In recent years, however, the social and economic background of participants, as well as the accessibility of this form of education, have substantially broadened.

In China the Workers' Palaces provide discretionary education. Many who follow TV and radio courses at home are also involved in this form of education, as are the many persons who are engaged in self-study. As more and more people complete various levels of education provided by the Adult Education Division of the Ministry of Education, one imagines that opportunities for discretionary education will increase in China. In North America and Europe the trend toward the provision of endless numbers of options for individual choice has grown so rapidly that there is every indication it will continue in the same direction. Adult education in this form appears to be another consumer commodity for individual consumption, entirely dependent upon the market and, therefore, unplanned and uncoordinated. Highly motivated adult learners are able to satisfy their desire to learn. One feels compelled to ask, however, where this proliferation is going and how it contributes to the dream of lifelong education in the learning society. Is it enough to provide an infinity of choices to be taken up by the members of a society who already have the most schooling, the highest incomes, and the self-confidence to pursue further learning?

The first two forms of adult education each serve a definite social purpose: one to provide educational opportunities to those who have been left out or left behind; the other to strengthen the nation's productive capacity. For these reasons they are incorporated in public policy and, to a degree, in public funding, but it is difficult to imagine public or private agencies investing heavily in an enterprise without a clear social value. Individual pursuit of learning does not appear sufficiently compelling a purpose to win wide support when resources for all forms of education are shrinking.

Meanwhile, the overwhelming issues that threaten the future are increasing in both urgency and complexity. In what way do they impinge upon the educational enterprise? We have been able to affirm the need to educate workers, from the machine operator to the inventor of new machines, because they contribute to the nations's future. Building on the thought of Paul Barton, is it not possible that we now need to marshall the resources of the human mind and spirit, not to create and run our machines but to resolve some of the unanswered questions that our immense technological capability poses for the world? Perhaps the new frontier for adult educators is to discover how to translate these global questions into concrete concepts and new educational processes that will enable adults to address these issues in the context of their local and personal experience and in the light of their reflection on the human wisdom of the past.

Some of these issues include:

peace and disarmament;
justice, including the relations between rich and poor within and between nations;
ethical issues and questions concerning the uses of science and technology;
the environment;
human rights;
international aid and trade policies.

Each of these global issues has its repercussions in the lives of people, even those in remote villages. The task of the adult educator would be to help make the concrete connections and to assist in determining the resources necessary to turn discussion into learning and action.

John Lowe, reflecting on the recommendations of the 1972 Tokyo conference on adult education, sponsored by Unesco, suggests that more imaginative use of mass media, coupled with nonformal education approaches, might enable local communities to identify their own problems and set about solving them through their own efforts, aided by essential public resources and assistance. He goes on to observe that these activities need not bear the label 'education' or even 'learning'(2). The problem with discretionary adult education as it has evolved has been its excessive emphasis on individual development. Can individual potential develop in isolation from development of the potential of the social structures within which individuals live? The approach we are imagining here is one that envisages the widest possible opportunities for individual learning, with the fruits of that learning being applied to the search for solutions to the real issues that threaten nations and humanity as a whole.

In this connection, it is interesting to recall the model provided by the Chinese in the early days after the 1949 revolution, when every Chinese belonged to a small learning group at work, at school, in the neighbourhood, all dedicated to discovering the implications of the vast changes taking place for individuals and for the society as a whole. Our Chinese hosts would probably be the first to point to deficiencies in that particular model, but it has at least symbolic appeal as an indication that a whole society can be mobilised and a structure put in place that allows all citizens to learn from and with one another.

Many of the same concerns were reflected in the European Conference on Motivation for Adult Education sponsored by the German Commission for Unesco in February 1984. Many delegates there spoke of the need to include within adult education the means to address international and global issues locally (3). No particular level of skills or credentials is required for people to address these issues. While those who have benefitted from more extensive educational opportunities may bring the resource of greater understanding of the past, participants in a village literacy circle will bring their own resources to the examination of the threats to survival or the implications of justice for living together in an interdependent world. What is suggested here is a particular vision of a learning society in which individual pursuit of learning gains in meaning and purpose as it is applied within learning groups - by whatever name they are called - to the quest for new ways to live together in one world.

Adult education is not one unified discipline. Practitioners in the field are usually working in only one of the three forms distinguished here. Perhaps in the future we will need to make clearer distinctions among the kinds of training appropriate for each form of adult education.

While all who work directly with adults will need to become more skilful in making the connection between global issues, local issues, learner resources and other available resources, each form makes its own demands on the educator. If there is a choice between costly academic training of a few professional leaders and supervised in-service training of fieldworkers, the decision will need to be reached in the context of how best to improve the quality and extension of services in each of the three forms. Most of the knowledge regarding the common preoccupation with 'how adults learn' has been based on work in industrialised countries with already educationally advantaged adults. Wherever the priority is on literacy/basic education, field workers can probably benefit more from on-the-job training with sufficient provision for reflection on what they are learning from the learners than from academic study. All adult educators will need both more study and practice themselves in understanding and applying social theory to their work. How else can they help workers, for example, to understand the social relations of production in their own society and begin to act strategically in ways that will improve their lives in the future? In the same way, the challenge of discovering the best ways to grapple with global questions in a concrete local context can only be addressed by doing it. Different strategies will be called for in each society, and will vary from one group to another within that society.

One future trend seems to stand out above all others: adult education can no longer be viewed as the transmission of knowledge, information, or skills to those who lack them. Rather, the focus is on utilising knowledge, information and skills from every possible source in the interest of human development within a social context.

REFERENCES

(1) Barton Paul E., 1982, **World Transitions**, New York, Mcgraw-Hill, pp. 185-186.

(2) Lowe John, 1982, **The Education of Adults, a World Perspective**, Paris, Unesco, OISE Press, 2nd edition, p. 217.

(3) Boshier Roger, 1983, "A European Perspective on the Unesco 1984 Conference", **Convergence**, XVI, 4, p. 44.

THREE FORMS OF ADULT EDUCATION*

Categories	Literacy/Basic Education	Work-Related Education	Discretionary Education
Goals/ Assumptions	To provide academic equivalency with the regular system;	To increase worker productivity, especially for advanced scientific and technological jobs;	To meet the demands, needs, interests of adults for continued learning opportunities;
	To provide terminal education for certain population groups;	To make the nation more competitive in international markets;	To enable adults previously outside the job market to seek employment;
	To provide skills and knowledge for social analysis, problem-solving and participation in reshaping structures.	To raise the GNP and, in this way to improve the quality of life for the people.	To assist adults outside the workforce and older adults to make more enjoyable or productive use of their available time.
Primary Focus or Content Area	Basic Literacy and numeracy skills	Specific job-related skills and processes;	Courses, workshops, seminars, learning circles in most diverse fields corresponding to the interests, curiosity, ambition of the adult population;
	Information and practical skills for functioning in modern society, sometimes called basic competency or functional literacy eg. training in health, nutrition, agriculture, self-help economic activities, community development etc.	Advanced mathematics; science, and technology;	Study may be related to work or leisure, to vocations or avocations: eg. health, family, consumer interests; civic, political and commun-
		Engineering skills, computer science;	
		Labour studies;	
		Retraining for new jobs;	

Categories	Literacy/Basic Education	Work-Related Education	Discretionary Education
Primary Focus or Content Area contd.	Social analysis, consciousness raising; Courses leading to primary and/or secondary school certification; Cultural activities, traditional music, dance drama, and crafts; Planning and leading actions for a better community.	Secondary school equivalency certification (in some countries); Agricultural science; Management and leadership.	ity competence; public and international affairs, peace environment; group dynamics; self-fulfilment; music, arts dance, theatre, crafts; home repairs, carpentry; learning how to do anything. Skill development in every imaginable field for employment options, volunteer activities, leisure pursuits or sports.
Participants	Those with little or no prior schooling; school leavers; Poor and by-passed adults minorities, women, older people (in industrialised nations this population may constitute a minority; in industrialising nations it may be a majority);	Workers who have reached or surpassed the basic level of education expected in their society; More management level personnel than low level workers in most societies; Workers chosen because it is thought that additional training will equip them for increased contribut-	Persons seeking vocational change or a new job. Unemployed workers without employer backing for additional training. Generally those sufficiently affluent to assume the cost of their further education; Persons with already high

Participants contd.	Age level depends on definition of an adult in any given society.	ions in their field and/or greater responsibilities; Farmworkers who have shown special skill, interest or aptitude.	levels of education. Self-directed and highly motivated learners;
Major Funding Sources	Government: national state or provincial, county or municipal; International/inter-governmental agencies; Private foundations and corporations; Volunteer services.	Industries or other employers - either through direct funding of training courses or through negotiated benefits; Labour unions; Government-supported training programmes.	Fees paid by individuals; Bursaries, scholarships paid by the sponsoring agency; Government or foundation grants.
Administration	National government campaigns with considerable local administrative freedom; State/provincial, county or municipal educational agencies; Unions or mass organisations;	Directly by employers in work-site training programmes; Indirectly by employers administering tuition aid benefits, time off, etc; Various levels of government; Labour unions;	Any institution or agency offering learning opportunities: eg. libraries, museums cultural or professional associations external degree granting institutions, recreational organisations, mass organisations, political groups private voluntary and community agencies, institutions of

Categories	Literacy/Basic Education	Work-Related Education	Discretionary Education
Administration contd.	Private, voluntary organisations; Universities.	Institutions of the regular system where workers use tution aid or paid study benefits.	the regular school or university
Approach/ Methods	Complete spectrum from academic to open learning groups: Academic approach characterised by: - Centrally prepared materials; - teacher domiance of the classroom; - emphasis on academic skills and performance testing; - fixed schedules; - grade level orientation; Open approach characterised by: - locally prepared materials; - learner-oriented curriculum; - community and individual	On-the-job training and apprenticeships; Part-time work, part-time study arrangements that relate study to work; Formally taught academic courses; Workshops and seminars, especially for management training; Short-term hands-on training courses; TV, radio and correspondence courses followed by related class work at the job site; Formal university and	Traditional academic courses; Nonformal community learning groups using similar methods to those described under literacy/basic education; Experience-based training; Radio, TV, cassettes and computer-based methods; Adult learning centre groups and individual study; Self-study based on individual learning plans.

Approach/ Methods contd.	problem-solving; - schedules and sites determined by learner preference/availability; - use of drama, music, dance, games, pictures, stories to nurture creativity; Individual tutoring; Radio and TV.	graduate level courses at the work site or at outside institutions.

*__Note__: The form of adult education that predominates in any society is generally assumed to **be** adult education. At present the predominant form in pre-industrial societies is literacy/basic education. In China, work-related education is considered synonymous with adult education. In North America and Europe, discretionary education is the form usually taken to be adult education. In fact all three forms exist simultaneously in most countries.

Chapter 2.

Liberal and Popular Adult Education

Jennings sketches the history of liberal adult education in Britain, noting the different meanings and contexts of 'liberal' and its affinity to 'liberty'. His sketch of purposes as well as practices through the century from the 1860s indicates a belief in the abilities of the masses as in no way inferior to the elite. The diversification of provision and the emergence of new subjects in more recent times echoes Chinese predictions, referred to in the previous chapter, of a shift from studies of a narrowly functional kind, with increasing affluence. Noting trade union demands for distinctly functional studies, Jennings concludes with the irony that in present circumstances of rapid economic and social change it is the more liberal kind of adult education which proves the most 'relevant' and functional.

Cadena, writing from the very different circumstances of Latin America today, also incidentally conveys the importance of understanding the socio-economic context of adult education, especially where it is intended to bring about purposeful social change. The historical perspective brought to issues of adult education for social change was stressed also by Gajardo, whose tabled paper is published in part below. Gajardo, responding to Cadena's paper, pointed out that popular adult education approaches in Latin America date back to the 1890s, though they gained 'theoretical and methodological status' only in the 1960s. She emphasises the reformist inclinations of several modernising Latin American governments which sought to incorporate 'marginal groups' into the norms and values of modern consumer society. The theory of dependency developed in that continent explains why this approach failed to overcome social inequalities, even before the change to the much harsher repressive circumstances which were general by the mid-seventies: "political parties and people's organisations were strongly repressed and democratic experiences came to an end...In this context we may say that popular education, as part of people's movement approaches to adult education, emerges in a context where spaces for social responses are highly restricted. Traditional political behaviour has been abandoned if not definitely suppressed." It is in this context that one needs to read Cadena's analysis of the popular adult education and peasant movements to bring about change.

A. The Evolution of the Liberal Tradition

Bernard Jennings

Liberal adult education may be defined in three ways:

by the **content**: social, economic and political studies; the arts and humanities; and scientific studies accessible to the non-specialist;
by the **purpose**: education for intellectual development and effective social action;
or by the **process**: the pursuit of thoroughness and objectivity through the critical analysis of freely expressed arguments.

A comprehensive definition would include all these.

The progenitor of the liberal tradition in British adult education was James Stuart (1843-1913), who planned the system of university extension teaching which was launched by the University of Cambridge in 1873. The idea of liberal adult education is much older, but 'tradition' implies continuity and cohesion, which makes it plausible as well as convenient to begin with Stuart rather than Socrates.

When James Stuart moved from his native Scotland to Cambridge, he was shocked by "the grievous class distinctions" which he regarded as "one of the great dangers and difficulties in this country of England" and which contrasted with the more open society and wider educational opportunities of Scotland. He realised also that middle-class women had few opportunities for serious academic study. Women were barred from the ancient universities of Oxford and Cambridge.

In 1867 Stuart, who now had degrees in classics and mathematical sciences, began a series of experimental lecture courses in the industrial towns of the north of England, in association with middle-class women's educational organisations and working-class groups such as the Rochdale Co-operative Society (the model on which the modern consumer co-operative movement was based). He was asked to talk about education. He offered instead a course on Astronomy, through which he could demonstrate the principles of scientific enquiry. "I am anxious to do that which is true education, to assist them in forming an opinion for themselves ... For I believe that education generally consists far too much in the learning of simple unsuggestive facts."(1)

The argument put forward by Stuart, that in liberal education - learning pursued for its own sake to develop the intellectual powers of the individual - the process is much more important than the content, can be overstated. As Stuart was beginning his pioneering work, the Liberal politician, W. E. Gladstone, on the eve of becoming Prime Minister for the first time, wrote a study of poems of Homer entitled **Juventus Mundi** (youth of the world), with the purpose of bringing out the Homeric ideas which were relevant to his time.

> ... the power of opinion and persuasion as opposed to force ... the hatred, not only of tyranny, but of all unlimited power ... the reconciliation and harmony between the spirit of freedom on the one hand, the spirit of order and reverence on the other.

Classical Greece was seen as the birthplace of liberty, which Lord Acton described as "the delicate fruit of a mature civilisation ... not a means to a higher political end. It is itself the highest political end." The words 'liberty' and 'liberal' (whether applied to learning or to politics) have the same Latin root - 'liber', meaning 'free'.

When Gladstone was an Oxford undergraduate about 1830, he had attended a class on Aristotle's **Rhetoric** which included two future governors-general and one viceroy of India; a future governor-general of Canada; two political dukes and two other men who became cabinet ministers; and eight who became heads of Oxford colleges or professors (2). Liberal education was, therefore, a form of vocational training for the governing classes. Because they would have to deal with broad problems, they needed a general education which both developed their mental powers and nurtured values appropriate to the responsible discharge of their public duties. There are parallels with the education of the governing classes in Imperial China, although an Oxford education in the nineteenth century was a much less exacting experience. At a more modest level of public service, the same liberal education was seen as an appropriate preparation for entry to professions such as the church, the law and the civil service - indeed, these were known as the 'liberal professions'.

The two main arguments used against a broad education for the common people, whether as children or as adults, were that a liberal education would frustrate people who had no chance of entry to the liberal professions; and that the ideas appropriate for governors would be dangerous in the possession of the governed. Educating the labouring classes, an M.P. told the House of Commons in 1807,

> would teach them to despise their lot in life, instead of making them good servants in agriculture and other laborious employments to which their rank in society had destined them ... It would enable them to read seditious pamphlets, vicious books and publications against Christianity ... instead of teaching them subordination ... it would render them insolent to their superiors (3).

The contrary view had been put by Adam Smith in **The Wealth of Nations**

(1776)

> An instructed and intelligent people ... are always more orderly than an ignorant and stupid one ... they are less apt to be misled into any wanton or unnecessary opposition to the measure of government (4).

By 1867 the extension of the right to vote in parliamentary elections to a substantial number of working men had made it imperative for the government to "prevail on our future masters to learn their letters". The author of that remark, Robert Lowe, a Liberal M.P. with an anti-democratic outlook, argued that 'gentlemen' should transfer their attention from the classics to economic and political issues

> to assert the superiority over [workmen] which greater intelligence and leisure is sure to give, and to conquer back by means of wider and more enlightened cultivation some of the influence which they have lost by political change ... The lower classes ought to be educated to discharge the duties cast upon them ... [and to] defer to a higher cultivation when they meet it (5).

From the viewpoint of a progressive Liberal such as James Stuart (he was later an M.P. on the radical wing of the party, supporter of votes for women) there was no threat to social harmony in the aspiration of working-class activists, with their co-operative societies, savings banks and mutual improvement societies. The threat came from the barriers between social classes, which Stuart sought to lower through a system of academic adult education in which "rich and poor, men and women" studied together.

His contacts with the intelligent workmen of Rochdale (at whose prompting he added a discussion class to his original scheme of formal lectures) convinced James Stuart that "the highest class of education, if properly adapted, was capable of being appreciated by, and of real use to, the general mass of the people". He argued also that only a scholar who was a master of his subject could make it accessible to lively but untutored minds. If the universities allowed this work to pass into other hands, their influence on national life would decline. He went so far as to assert that "it is not only our duty to ... encourage demand for education ... but to endeavour to call it up where it does not exist or has not had the energy to express itself" (6).

Cambridge University began a regular programme of extension courses, mainly in large towns, in 1873. Oxford and the few other universities then in existence followed suit a few years later. They did not, however, provide any funds beyond the cost of a modest central administration. It was therefore necessary for the local committees to attract a fee-paying lecture audience of 100 or more, at the same time catering for the smaller numbers of earnest students by means of a discussion class and written work, leading to an optional examination. Even so the fee for a 12-lecture course, unless subsidised by some local organisation, was the equivalent of a week's wage for a labourer, or about half of the weekly earnings of a skilled worker.

Between 50,000 and 60,000 people were attending extension courses in the early 1890s, with Oxford and Cambridge serving about 170 centres all over the country. History and literature were the leading Oxford subjects but science was popular in the Cambridge programme and in London. Nearly two-thirds of the audiences were middle-class women and girls, but the working-class response - about 10-15 per cent of the total - disappointed the university men whose aims included "the breaking down of intellectual caste and the university extension of the intellectual franchise". Workers were kept away not only by financial difficulties but also by fear of manipulation and by a general sense of alienation from middle-class activities. The only lasting successes with working-class groups were achieved in partnership with a strong local workers' organisation, usually a co-operative society (7).

This tenuous link was developed into a strong partnership by a young co-operator, Albert Mansbridge, who founded the Workers' Educational Association in 1903. The W.E.A. had two main aims - to unite working-class organisations (co-operatives, trade unions, church and chapel societies, political clubs etc.) for educational purposes, and to build a more effective bridge to the universities. The latter was achieved through a complex agreement worked out with Oxford in 1907-08, which the other universities adopted during the next few years. The W.E.A. - a decentralised, voluntary, workers' organisation - achieved the following: long, sustained courses, usually 72 meetings, spread over three years, for groups small enough to make effective dialogue possible; an equal share in class administration at the university; and for the local W.E.A. branch freedom to choose the subject and 'a controlling voice' in the selection of the tutor. Mansbridge and the W.E.A. wanted high-quality tuition, in subjects of concern to the workers, taught by university scholars who would both sympathise with the aspirations of their students and recognise their experience as valid evidence for academic study. Furthermore the W.E.A. needed, and secured, government grants, because the workers could afford to pay only nominal course fees.

Mansbridge could not have achieved this remarkable victory without the help of powerful allies - Oxford scholars who wanted to raise the academic standards of their university and at the same time democratise its entry; churchmen whose consciences were troubled by contrasts between wealth and poverty; and political leaders who were both impressed and reassured by Mansbridge's policy line. He argued that the education of working-class leaders would promote the peaceful solution of social problems, such as low wages, bad housing and unemployment. He was the master of creative ambiguity, saying at the same time "education is necessary for working-class emancipation" and "education **is** emancipation". Mansbridge had a great respect for the liberal values of the universities, and his doctrine that profound learning inevitably leads to sensible action was one with which university men felt bound to agree.

The smooth voice of Oxford proclaimed the view that, as the University of Oxford had always educated the ruling classes, the Labour M.P. or the trade union leader would need

> an Oxford education as much, and will use it to as good ends, as the civil servant or the barrister. It seems to us that it would involve a grave loss both to Oxford and to English political life were the close association which has existed between the University and the world of affairs to be broken or impaired on the accession of new classes to power.

The W.E.A.-university alliance was attacked from both sides: from the political right by those who regarded the higher education of workers as a social danger, or objected specifically to 'workers' control' of the curriculum and the selection of tutors; and from the left by some Marxists who refused to have any contact with 'capitalist' universities, and formed the Labour College educational movement in opposition. The W.E.A. declared itself to be impartial **as an organisation** on political issues - with the exception of education for which it had very radical policies - leaving political **activity** to its members working through other bodies such as trade unions or the Labour Party (8).

The partnership between 'labour and learning' raised some important questions about the nature of liberal education. Could the concepts of education for social purpose, and education for its own sake, be reconciled? Would the political commitment of the students (usually to the moderate left) interfere with the pursuit of knowledge? The first and greatest tutorial class tutor, R.H. Tawney, gave the traditional W.E.A. answer to the second question in a fiftieth anniversary lecture (1953)

> ... the way for a ... movement to achieve impartiality is not to attempt to chase all the partialities out, for being human we can none of us be other than partial. It is to draw as many as possible

of the partialities in ...(9)

An earlier (1910) statement had associated objectivity with the thoroughness of a good university education

> it is scientific, detached and impartial in character ... it aims not so much at filling the mind of the student with facts or theories as at calling forth his own individuality, and stimulating him to mental effort ... it implants in his mind a standard of thoroughness, and gives him a sense of the difficulty as well as the value of truth (10).

A report on adult education written at the end of the first world war, and usually known as the 1919 Report, was greatly influenced by the success of the W.E.A. and the university tutorial classes. Liberal adult education was declared to be a 'universal need', in contrast to technical education which had only an instrumental value. "Adult education is a permanent national necessity, and inseparable aspect of citizenship and therefore should be both universal and lifelong" (11). This was not a new doctrine. It had been preached to co-operative societies in the 1880s, and can be traced back much earlier.

The 1919 Report stressed the virtues of voluntarism, not merely voluntary attendance at classes, which was taken for granted, but the organisation of classes by a democratic voluntary movement such as the W.E.A. Voluntarism was never an essential part of the liberal tradition, but could be described as an important enrichment of it. The same report recommended the establishment by each university of a department of adult education with an academic head. This idea was gradually adopted, but only a few university departments embarked upon an independent role. Most were content to identify liberal adult education with the W.E.A. - university partnership.

Sidney Raybould, who became Director of Extramural Studies at Leeds University in 1946 and was for the next twenty years one of the main upholders of the liberal tradition, wrote in 1949 that

> the most remarkable achievement of the W.E.A. has been in persuading working-class students to undertake serious and thorough courses of study, which have permanently altered, and improved, their tastes, their standards of judgment, their capacity to think independently and responsibly, and their ability to further the causes in which they are interested (12).

By 1933 fifteen W.E.A. students had become M.P.s, all Labour (the Liberal Party had been replaced by Labour as the main rival to the Conservatives), 1,800 were local councillors and 250 magistrates. The attitudes of Conservatives to this phenomenon ranged from toleration, on the grounds that the Labour movement was being educated to be 'responsible'; through disquiet at the training of 'socialist shock troops'; to the rejection of the whole idea of teaching political subjects to workmen. The W.E.A. argued that, unlike the Labour College movement, it taught people not **what** to think but **how** to think. One Conservative critic retorted that W.E.A. students came "determined to learn how to think what they were already thinking" (13).

The first majority Labour government was elected in 1945. Seventy Labour M.P.s, and fourteen members of the government, had been W.E.A. students or tutors. In most large towns the local council was Labour-controlled, and some W.E.A. activists stepped into key roles such as chairman of the education committee. In a mood of optimism the W.E.A. took up its post-war task, defined in a policy statement of 1947 as "the education of our citizens for the work of national and international reconstruction". Yet within a few years the idea of liberal education for social purpose was being seriously questioned. The achievement of the Labour government in maintaining full employment and improving welfare services weakened the drives against social injustice. The continuing intractability of problems in Britain (recurrent economic crises and low industrial productivity) and abroad (the Cold War and regional conflicts such as Palestine) undermined a fundamental belief of the liberal tradition - that the road of learning leads to a land of wisdom, that knowledge is power, that the education of citizens brings the solution of social problems. These propositions seemed to be at best only partly true. The counting of small gains may console reformers in retrospect; it does not inspire them in prospect.

The relative decline in the demand for subjects such as economics and international relations did not mean that liberal adult education as a whole was losing support. Far from it. Provision has expanded considerably, restrained only by the level of government financial support. The liberal tradition has continued to evolve. One of the pressures has been the rapid growth of academic knowledge, and of the degree of specialisation, within universities, which themselves underwent a major expansion, especially in the 1960s. The old-style generalist, who would teach a large segment of an undergraduate degree course single-handed, or cover two or three subject areas in adult education, has been replaced by academics in both fields whose scholarly reputation depends upon their publications, usually in a relatively narrow area. The development of new subjects on the extramural frontier has continued - several subjects now taught within universities such as industrial relations were pioneered in adult education - but the latest, local history, has produced groups of devoted adult students doing serious local research over several years and bringing out substantial books and papers.

In this age of specialisation, the adult education providers have found themselves increasingly catering for the already well educated, rather than the educationally deprived, by means of relatively short courses. Some university adult educators have erected this practice into a principle, declaring that their mission is the further education of university graduates, which would allow them to occupy a lofty 'quaternary' pinnacle, on top of the primary-secondary-tertiary stages of education. Most of the academics and voluntary workers in adult education have, however, clung to James Stuart's view that the university teacher should have the skills needed to make his subject **accessible** to adults willing to make the necessary effort, and to the traditional W.E.A. idea that the **experience** of mature adults is both relevant and valuable in the study of humane subjects.

One feature of the nineteenth century liberal tradition which has been greatly weakened, is the assumption that a broad liberal education is a suitable preparation for a range of professions. Professional training has become much more specific. The emphasis on functional rather than general studies has invaded the adult education field from, perhaps, an unexpected direction. The education department of the Trades Union Congress, which is concerned mainly with the training of shop stewards (voluntary workplace representatives), has insisted on a curriculum specific to the function - industrial relations law and practice, communication skills etc. - instead of a broader study of economic and political issues. The W.E.A. and university adult education departments have tried to widen the curriculum, mainly by providing extended courses, but the T.U.C. line has been dominant. By a tragic irony the growth of mass unemployment has exposed the limitations of a system which produces shop stewards who are the best minute-takers in the world, and can work out redundancy payments in seconds with the aid of their electronic calculators, but have little understanding of the economic and political forces which have overwhelmed them.

Liberal adult education can count, at best, on only half-hearted support from the present British government, which is obsessed with the need for industrial training. The same attitude has emerged in several other countries. The main defence of the liberal tradition currently put forward is based upon the need for the fruitful use of increased leisure, but the **social** case for liberal adult education is even stronger. Britain's political institutions, electoral system and local government (the independence of which is rapidly being eroded) are in urgent need of re-appraisal. The potentialities of collective voluntary action when the working week and the working life have been shortened offer another item for the agenda. It may even be found - as some people believe - that Britain's economic problems are rooted in social institutions and attitudes. If so, adult education of the liberal kind becomes even more 'relevant'.

This paper has dealt with liberal adult education in the British context. An analysis of the liberal idea on an international scale would be a much lengthier and immeasurably more complex task.

However, the liberal tradition derives much of its strength from the universality of one fundamental principle, the needs of man as a social being, the idea that we achieve our fullest development only as willingly active citizens. The first President of the W.E.A., William Temple, defined liberal adult education as "the disciplining of the judgement, the enlivening of the imagination and the widening of the sympathy" - in other words the cultivation of the powers which make us more truly human.(14)

REFERENCES

(1) E. Welch, 1973, **The Peripatetic University**, Cambridge, pp. 25-29.

(2) G. Watson, 1973, **The English Ideology** pp. 19-20, 32-3.

(3) M.E. Sadler, 1980, "National Ideals in Education", in P. Gordon (ed.), **The Study of Education**, Vol. I p. 58.

(4) A. Smith, 1776, **The Wealth of Nations**, Everyman edition 1910, Vol. II. p. 269.

(5) **Hansard**, CLXXXVII, 15 June 1867; R. Lowe, "Primary and Classical Education", in D.A. Reeder (ed.), 1980, **Educating our Masters**, Leicester, pp. 125-6.

(6) Welch, pp. 21-2, 30, 35-7; N.A. Jepson, 1973, **The Beginnings of English University Adult Education** p. 66.

(7) B. Jennings, 1975, **New Lamps for Old? University Adult Education in Retrospect and Prospect**, Hull, pp. 4-8.

(8) B. Jennings, 1973, **Albert Mansbridge** Leeds, and 1979, **Knowledge is Power: A Short History of the W.E.A. 1903-78** Hull, Ch. I.

(9) R.H. Tawney, 1964, **The Radical Tradition** (Penguin edition 1966), p. 94.

(10) A. Mansbridge, 1913, **University Tutorial Classes** p. 145.

(11) Adult Education Committee of the Ministry of Reconstruction, **Final Report** (Cmd. 321 of 1919), p. 5.

(12) S.G. Raybould, 1949, **The W.E.A., the Next Phase** p. 77.

(13) Jennings, **Knowledge is Power**, pp. 47-50.

(14) Jennings, **New Lamps for Old**, pp. 25-6.

B. Popular Adult Education and Peasant Movements for Social Change

Felix Cadena

The Context

As Latin America approaches the 21st century, a century and a half after gaining independence from the Spanish and Portuguese empires, the overall situation is critical, but there is hope.

In this century, we have seen technological advances enabling space flight, but have also seen a rebirth of interest in the knowledge which ancient indigenous cultures applied to the preservation of health and the ecological equilibrium.

The victims of atrocities and genocide, who have seen, for generations, the blood of those who struggled for social change spilled freely - especially in Central America, the Southern Cone, and Brazil - have now seen several of their tormentors vanquished. Sometimes the aggressors themselves, faced with evidence of their defeat and the scorn of the world, have had to leave and take their place in the garbage can of history.

Latin Americans have aspired to the 'American way of life', and the 'affluent society' - in the name of which their resources have been despoiled, and the peasants have been reduced to paupers by the exploitation of the international division of labour. Now, with the contraction of the economy, social injustices are aggravated; national debts grow; and every sort of aggression is justified by the doctrine of 'defence of America's vital interests'.

The 'Conservative revolution' which fuels Reagan's megalomania seeks to crush any attempts at people's liberation, by force of arms and with the help of those who would sell their own country. They are no longer trying to coopt social movements, but physically to eliminate them, on the pretext that to strive for liberation is merely to align oneself in the struggle between the USA and the USSR. If America cannot 'save' a country, as it did Grenada, it thinks it can at least mortally wound it and make it lose prestige.

'Yet despite everything, there is change'

In the face of such aggression, and such a vision, the Latin American people - especially the peasants - have continued their strategy for survival, in a resistance struggle which has been going on now in some cases for over five centuries.

Not counting simply migrating, there are two prongs of this strategy, which may or may not both occur at the same time.

One is open conflict in self-defence, or to regain property and rights.

The other is the continuing struggle of resistance.

The first comes about when people see that aggressions against their interest leave them no choice but direct confrontation. This leads to the seizing of land, occupation of government buildings, and sometimes even to armed struggle.

Such actions, requiring great commitment, sacrifice and heroism, are neither spontaneous nor the result of some transport of emotion.

Although the misery and oppression in which the peasants have lived would give grounds for thousands of confrontations, the peasants have learned to beware of being tricked, not only by their exploiters, but by irresponsible people who incite them to absurd actions. These struggles arise out of a growing process of organisation, analysis and action carried out by peasant movements.

They leave behind important experiences which become part of the historic memory of the organisations, and contribute to a collective history which will one day help greatly to transform the unjust structures of our countries.

Nevertheless, such actions rarely involve the majority of the peasants. Over 90 per cent of them are simply caught up in the constant day-to-day struggle for resistance - a calmer struggle, less violent on the surface, but hardly less cruel and bloody. Thousands have fallen victim to disease, famine, and sometimes even bullets.

The Triumph of Survival

The strength of this resistance comes from the knowledge and skills that people have had to develop over the years just to keep going. They endured the Aztec and Inca empires, outlasted the empires of Charles V and Philip II, and are now defending themselves from the empire of Reagan and his allies.

Nevertheless, this resistance takes a terrible toll on the peasants. Nor do current political dynamics in many countries allow them to contribute effectively to a widespread popular movement which would transform each nation and ultimately put an end to world-wide imperialism. It is only slowly and with difficulty that this spontaneous, unorganised resistance develops towards a conscious, strongly organised movement with clear political focus.

Particularly in the countryside, there is a real lack of tools for class organisation. The traditional types of association, while effective in regulating the internal relations of an agrarian community, are unable to form larger organisations which could confront the system. Unions and cooperatives often fail to connect with the situations and with the thinking of the rural people; and political parties in many countries are no longer trustworthy. Only the 'agricultural unions', the 'coordinators', or the 'fronts for popular unity' form a fairly reliable base. But the tendency of these groups to see economic and political aspects in isolation drives unnecessary wedges between them.

Popular adult education can play a very important role in developing spontaneous resistance into class-conscious social movements, and in consolidating the organisations thus formed.

To understand this role, we must first distinguish between several types of educational activity.

Peasant Education

In any rural society there is a series of processes, mechanisms and relations of production, socialisation, accumulation and the reproduction of knowledge.

These are based on social structures, such as the family, productive organisations, religious and political groups, etc. These imply a set of educational practices which reproduce and transmit knowledge about reality, or about historical facts reflected in reality. Setting aside externally-stimulated programmes, there is a constant flow of educational activities within a community, generally of a non-formal type. These can have a far greater impact than more direct formal educational processes.

Education 'for' peasants

Such education is determined and created outside the rural community. It encompasses a broad range of perspectives, falling between two extremes:

> On the one hand, there are programmes quite consciously conducted in opposition to the peasants' interests: like demagogic manipulation to prevent political organisation; servile instruction for modernisation; or proselytising for religious sects which defend individualism and encourage excessive consumption.
>
> At the other end of the scale are programmes claiming to proffer knowledge to the peasants in a paternalistic manner, without taking into account the viewpoint of the inhabitants. This describes most formal education programmes, and many 'community development' projects as well.

All these programmes share:

a disregard for the expectations, needs and processes of the peasant community;

the assumption that social change can be reduced to pushing the assimilation of the knowledge and values of industrial urban culture, which is considered superior to the culture developed by peasants.

Education 'with' peasants, 'for' their class interests

This type of education is often initiated from outside the rural community, and requires an external agent, such as an animateur, popular educator, social mediator, etc. What distinguishes it from the former type is its interest in strengthening the processes of peasant society, drawing on educational work, and pinpointing the political dimension of social practices.

Such programmes begin with an attempt to identify the problems, expectations and concrete daily needs of rural inhabitants, and involve a commitment to help solve them.

What distinguishes them is that they bring to this analysis a set of criteria and strategies the fundamental goal of which is to fight the unjust situation in which the people live. In other words, to struggle against the hegemony attained by a minority class, which has imposed a model of development keeping most of the inhabitants of our countries dominated, dependent and exploited.

Finally, the main goal of the popular educator should be to help the people reclaim their collective history, so that they can bring about structural changes necessary to ensure that their needs and wishes - both in their daily lives and on a broader cultural level - are fulfilled according to their own interests: in other words, the building up of popular power.

Building Popular Power

What do we mean by popular power? I do not mean representatives of the people taking over formal state power structures through a military coup or mobilisation. First, such a revolution seems unlikely to succeed, because of the growing cynicism with which the modern empire simply invades countries where revolutionary processes occur. Secondly, if such a governmental change is not accompanied by popular education work, the representatives of the people, with the best of intentions, run the risk of merely becoming the new overlords - all in the name of the people.

Popular Participation

Popular education can be distinguished from other types of education for social change not only by its goal but by several concrete aspects:

> The new society is not only a goal for the future. Popular education seeks in its daily work to implement the new social relationships suggested by the principles of an alternative society.
>
> Another aim is to expand the number of organisations and of people committed to such a society. A key point in this concept of social change is the development of a 'critical mass' great enough to prevail over the privileged minorities which now hold power in oppressed societies.

To avoid falling into vague and useless generalisations, we should specify that 'participation' means more than carrying out educational work 'horizontally', without imposing solutions from above. It should contribute effectively to all the factors leading to popular power:

> the growth of critical consciousness;
> the development of the capacity effectively to transform reality;
> the strengthening of class organisations.

In each of these areas, participation should be viewed as both a process and a result.

Let me give some illustrations:

> **Critical consciousness as a process,**
> critical consciousness includes the ability:
> to identify obstacles to development;
> to describe and analyse the causes and consequences of such obstacles; understanding the relationships between local and national levels, and between economic, political, social and cultural actions;
> to distinguish between the surface appearance and the essential nature of phenomena;
> to evaluate resources and to choose the best alternatives, keeping in mind that social reality is a constant struggle of class interests.

As a result, real participation means first and foremost helping people consciously to appropriate their own reality.

Effective action to transform reality

As a process, this means improving people's capacity to:
locate and integrate the necessary resources to respond effectively to problems;
acquire technical, administrative, accounting, legal skills, etc., and to make them their own;
plan specific activities in a way that will lead to the desired goals.

As a result, it means gaining greater influence over processes in which the organisation becomes involved, with the goal of controlling some of these processes. It also means equalising the distribution of goods and services and conditions.

Strengthening class organisation

As a process, this implies:
Strengthening real internal democracy and self-management;
greater consciousness of real class interests, and increasing group membership;
making the principles of organisation real in people's own lives as well as in external relations.

As a result, this synthesises all the above factors. They can be grouped in two categories:

On the one hand, the capacity to defend one's class interests, and to define the type of society which would serve them.

On the other hand, coordination among various groups, which will allow them to grow as a social force, enabling people to change society structurally to make it less hegemonic and more responsive to people.

I hope that I have made clear the ways in which Popular Adult Education differs from other educational practices within movements for social change, which have all too often limited themselves to proselytising, economic improvement, or training their own leaders.

C. On Social Change and People's Movement Approaches to Adult Education in Latin America

Marcela Gajardo

People's movement approaches to adult education are not new in Latin America. To a certain extent they arise with the emergence of political movements and popular organisations which, for decades, have been struggling for social transformation or for the improvement of life and working conditions of those groups which have been systematically excluded from social, economic and political life in this continent.

An overall view shows that people's efforts for education and other social needs began as early as the twenties. This may be exemplified with cases such as the Mexican Revolution which, led by the peasant movements, altered the land tenure system as well as peasant and rural communities' educational organisational processes. Experiences in Peru involving intellectuals (such as J. Carlos Mariategui, one of the most thoughtful and incisive social and political analysts of his age) and popular organisations raised issues which even nowadays seem to be influencing popular education movements. Bolivia and Ecuador provide us with interesting indigenous experiences and, in a more formalised way, there are the activities carried out by the worker and peasant unions in Chile and Argentina during the thirties.

However, it was not until the sixties that adult education, and more recently popular education, acquired a certain theoretical and methodological status. This coincided with a series of changes at societal level in most Latin American contries. First Cuba, in the late fifties, initiated a revolutionary process which implied a radical change of all processes and prevailing institutions. Further, it altered existing relations with the U.S. and established a socialist state diametrically opposed to existing capitalist structures and relationships, both internal and external.

Most of the Latin American societies at the time, with the exception of some countries in Central America such as Nicaragua and Haiti, were subjected to a general process of modernisation and expansion of the industrial base. Changes were introduced in the agrarian structure, too. The agrarian reforms in Chile, Peru and Columbia are a good example of this. Governmental programmes of integrated rural development were experienced in other countries. Community development programmes were introduced at local and grass-root levels. In the educational sphere some countries implemented educational reforms and most carried out adult education programmes in different areas and at different levels: literacy campaigns and basic education were mandatory. Plans for technical and social training were developed in a good number of countries. Education linked to community development and education for self-management in people's enterprises acquired progressive importance at a time when countries such as Brazil under J. Goulart, Peru under the government of Velasco Alvarado, Chile under the administration of Frei and later Salvador Allende, Bolivia under the government of J. J. Torres, among others, were implementing reform-oriented social transformations.

Although initiated from above, people's movements were not alien to these transformations. Social and economic transformations gave new force to the emergence of popular organisations and consolidation of existing ones, particularly within the workers' and peasant movements. But, development-oriented policies were not formulated to meet popular interests and needs. They were basically formulated with the purpose of integrating the so-called 'marginal groups' into the norms, values and consuming patterns of a modern society. Nevertheless, this scheme soon showed its deficiencies for overcoming social inequalities which were a consequence of structural limitations imposed by a system now widely known as dependent capitalism. The theory of dependence, which accounts for this phenomenon, emerged as a native Latin American scheme of interpretation of social and economic processes. As a radical approach to reality it soon began to influence other areas of social and cultural concern, among them adult education.

Latin Americans are highly indebted to Paulo Freire for the formulation of an approach to literacy and adult education processes which demands the educator's commitment to the reality, needs and interests of people's movements. Freire's originated as a methodological proposal, a literacy method for and with the people, and culminated with the explication of an overall problem: the political significance of education, and particularly adult education, for the people's movement and its organisations.

> The thought of Paulo Freire is essentially a situated thought and any attempt to promote it to an abstract universality, on the grounds of the acknowledged efficiency of his literacy method, at once misrepresents and disfigures it. The situation which occasioned the Freire approach, as he himself takes pain to explain, is the emergence of the popular masses into the national political scene in the so-called 'underdeveloped' countries, more precisely in Latin America. This is a situation pregnant with the most exciting as well as the most dismal possibilities ... It is a situation, therefore, which calls for reappraisal of the meaning and methods of education.(1)

Experiences in adult education and popular organisation during the sixties and mid-seventies were highly influenced by Freire's thought in Latin America. Moreover, even in the context of our present panorama where reformist political experiences have given place to the imposition of authoritarian political styles and a liberal type of economic policies (except for a few countries, among them Nicaragua), Freire's thought continues to influence people's movement approaches to adult education and to what is at present known as popular education.

> Paulo Freire's approach played a significant role in the development of adult education with popular organisations. He showed the way in which these activities could contribute to structural social transformation-oriented processes and the contribution education can make to the development of a critical consciousness of social reality and social-economic relationships. Such a standpoint has definitely marked those adult education experiences which aim at supporting conscientisation and liberation processes.(2)

These experiences have both a quantitative and qualitative importance in Latin America. Quantitatively, they have multiplied themselves in various societies. Where social changes are taking place they are developed as governmental programmes or led by non-governmental organisations. In authoritarian contexts they are generally assumed by non-governmental and popular organisations which support people's movements strategies. As an example we can find the offical popular education programmes in Cuba and Nicaragua which include both the modification of educational structures for enabling universal access to basic education and literacy campaigns and training programmes for workers and peasants. The use of institutional spaces to support people's education programmes is well exemplified by the case of Brazil where various experiences are being promoted through official channels. But it is undoubtedly in the area of non-governmental organisations that popular education and people's movements approaches to adult education seem to have flourished.

Qualitatively these experiences show that, in Latin America, existing approaches to adult education have progressively moved towards a more radical approach which sees the adult learner as one who belongs to a social class which shares conditions of poverty and oppression, as social groups which have been deprived of their right to participate in economic, social and political life. The adult learner is no longer defined in terms of age and school attainment but on the basis of identification with people's movements. In this way adult education coexists with trends which emphasise class connotations and political orientations:

> In Latin America we can recognise the coexistence of different adult education approaches as well as different, and sometimes opposed, adult education trends. Two settled trends and an emerging one may be distinguished from existing experiences. The first one based on developmentist and modernising theories which aims at the incorporation of popular masses into existing structures and socio-political processes. The second one based on the premises set forward by the capital dependency theory which sees in adult education the possibility of promoting higher degrees of organisation and, further, collaborating with liberation processes either supported from above or conducted by the people's movements. Last, but not least, the popular education trend which aims at instating a new social order, a new hegemony ... (3).

Popular education has an explicit political connotation. This may be attributed to the fact that such a concept is used in traditional democratic societies but mostly under authoritarian regimes in most of the countries in the continent.

Spaces for social response are highly restricted at present. New social actors have appeared on the scene sometimes in a spontaneous and violent way, sometimes in a more organised way, concerned with a wide range of issues such as work, human rights, improvements in living and working conditions, health, means of transportation, education. These are the so-called basic needs, and many experiences in popular education deal with them. Others are oriented towards the recuperation of a cultural identity which is being denied or threatens to disappear. Movements dealing with popular culture and historical memory aim at this. Within the people's movements new groups are emerging as organised and mobilised forces: ethnic groups, women's movements, youngsters, workers and landless peasants, artists and intellectuals, among others. These groups are the constituency of non-govenmental organisations. Confronting institutional and political forces they are part of the civil society willing to address existing conditions by means of creative and original strategies for survival, based upon collective organisation and social mobilisation.

Cadena's statements on Popular Adult Education and Peasant Movements for Social Change sit within this context. Popular and people's movement approaches to adult education today emphasise the capacity of specific social groups to bring about change. For such approaches change occurs essentially through groups or movements able to take initiatives and successfully to carry out new experiences. This does not mean that past experience has been forgotten or set aside. On the contrary aspects related to "the growth of critical consciousness", "development of the capacity effectively to transform reality", "the strengthening of class organisations", were all present in the approaches which saw adult education as part of a wider approach to social transformation. What is new is the explicit commitment of popular education to people's movement projects for social transformation. This raises new issues for discussion. Many questions have yet to be asked concerning the way in which popular education and people's movement approaches to adult education visualise the overall educational processes of the working classes and people's movements. What is the role of the State and of the civil organisations? Do people's movement approaches to adult education have to do only with adult education practices which in turn have to do with their social struggles (for land, education, dwellings, work) and specific matters related to social interests and needs? Or do they have to do, too, with all educational practices both formal and non-formal? Should educational systems (and other educational institutions) play a part in educational processes which aim at providing knowledge and skills both for adults and children? Or must they be considered simply a means for social and economic reproduction?

These issues are today in the minds of those researchers and practitioners who deal with people's movement approaches to adult education. Although the trends seem to emphasise a major preoccupation with popular education, understood as that which tries to meet popular needs and interests and which often occurs outside existing institutions, there is also a progressive interest in understanding the way in which people's movements and the working classes may make efficient use of existing opportunities.

This is the present challenge for people's movement approaches to adult education. To a certain extent we have to explore new alternatives within existing conditions, having in mind that long-term goals for people's movements and popular organisations have to do with the construction of a new social order based upon democratic principles of social and political understanding.

REFERENCES

(1) Coutinho, J., Preface to Freire, P. 1971, **Cultural Action for Freedom**, Harvard Educational Review, Monograph Series No. 1.

(2) Garcia Huidoro, J.E., "La relacion educativa en proyectos de educacion popular", Gajardo, M. (Org.) 1983, **Teoria y Practica de la Educacion Popular**, IDRC-MR81s,

(3) Gajardo, M., 1983, **Educacion de Adultos en America Latina. Problemas y tendencias,** Unesco/OREALC, Chile.

D. Panel Commentary and Discussion

Dr Wijetunga posed several challenging questions both about the liberal tradition and about Latin American popular adult education:

'Education' in itself, whatever its orientation, can be considered a process of social transformation. In that context both the liberal tradition in adult education and popular adult education should contribute to social change. But does the equation end there?

'Social change' itself means vastly different things under different circumstances. 'Social change' in one context could mean adaptation, integration, and harmonisation of even conflicting and contradictory elements, all of which in the long run would lead to the maintenance and stablisation of the status quo or, in other words, the preservation of the basic foundations of society, with all its diverse stratification.

In another context, 'social change' necessarily means those processes which usher in structural changes, in terms of political, economic and social relationships, people's organisation and mobilisation, and even the transfer of power to a new class of people, so that the oppressed masses can overcome the prevailing unjust situation. As a precondition for this, there is the need to understand the all-pervading reality, and the process of achieving it in popular adult education.

What should be our approach to the understanding of these two processes? Should we look at them subjectively, or only objectively? The only common factor between the liberal tradition and popular adult education would seem to be 'social change', and even in that, is there more divergence than convergence?

Is the liberal tradition essentially a by-product of industrialisation and the emergence of organised urban labour, especially in the European countries? Or is it something familiar only to Britain? If so, is it only a minor tradition, with many limitations, both for universal application and in terms of effective and far-reaching social change? Does the British tradition, as described here, reflect a subtle move to keep the enclaves of tradition and class interest intact, and immune from contamination by labouring classes, by offering them some crumbs? In doing this, are the agents of organised labour, as purveyors of adult liberal education, collaborators in this process?

As an adult educational process, what relevance has this tradition outside Britain especially for Third World countries, in terms of numbers which could be reached, and in terms of the total effect on their lives? My own country, Sri Lanka, has imbibed this tradition, though very grudgingly conceded by the authorities, but even after a decade or so it remains a very marginal activity. How has the liberal tradition thrived in those places where it has been practised for some considerable time, and what are its future prospects?

Popular adult education, as Cadena describes it, should necessarily lead to class confrontation, if not now then at some future date. Dr. Ambedkar, the leader of the Indian harijans, had as his motto, "Educate, organise, and agitate". So therefore adult education should lead to mobilisation of people for winning their rights and changing their situation. Here my dilemma is, will the established order allow it? Will it not nip in the bud the people's movements? It is here that 'survival' has relevance and meaning. How well have these movements survived, and thrived? Can Cadena be more specific, with a few concrete examples?

Guy Saez compared the French approach to popular education with the British liberal tradition in the late nineteenth century; the first popular universities were started by unions and intellectuals early this century. The focus was on why we had to know, what and for whom. One practical application was the modernisation of agriculture before and after World War Two. Peuple et Culture started in 1945. Its popular education was not only a method of adult education but in itself a project for social transformation. Through collective action it addressed the individual in the social context, seeking transformation through participation in all sectors. Saez reflected a concern to avoid the subversion of popular education to become merely an instrument of economic purposes, reiterating the need to fight for a democratic, participative society, and to insist upon the cultural element in development. Despite differences between the French and English experience his comments resembled Jennings' in the contrast with the Chinese preoccupation with production reflected in chapter one above.

Lea Cousineau drew on another French tradition of popular education, that of Quebec, to take up a question also raised by Gajardo about using and changing the formal system in the interests of equity and social change. In Quebec adult education is referred to in a global context covering all forms of adult education, formal or nonformal, vocational, popular, general or literacy education. "In our society men and women are constantly fighting to preserve their right to learn and to get their part of the knowledge resources. We claim a general access for everybody to the formal system at the secondary school, college and university." This goes hand in hand with efforts to reinforce popular and workers' organisations, women's groups, unions and popular groups all of which "have developed educational practices largely inspired by the Latino-american experiences for some of us or by European experience for others".

Cousineau posed the following questions:

> Can we, and how can we, develop real links between unions, women's groups and the formal education systems?
>
> How can we obtain services from the university without losing our own identity and our own objectives?
>
> How can we collectively use university and college resources without losing control over our own information and learning activities?
>
> How can we significantly change the traditional practices of the formal education system?

In Quebec these questions have given birth to new practices:

> a written protocol between universities and unions, popular and women's groups about adult education. Within such an agreement biologists and chemists have been able to work on workers' health and give specific education with the union's animateur, putting together their own scientific expertise and the important knowledge workers have acquired day by day in their work.

There was also the question of access to the regular education system. Adults returning to study "are not in any way ignorant people. Even if they do not have diplomas they possess a large amount of knowledge from their own life and experience and from their activities in unions and popular groups." Formal accreditation of this kind of knowledge was being actively promoted - for the "formal recognition of non-formal knowledge". Difficult though this was for universities it was a matter of justice and equity, especially for women.

In plenary discussion questions were raised about workers' organisation, which, it was suggested, was crucial both to precede education and as a basis for action. Another question concerned the strength of popular adult education in Latin America today: could it generate a 'critical mass' and bring about social change, and if it was sufficiently organised for this, would any resulting change be allowed? Would it be only very slow and limited? Jennings, responding to questions about workers' organisation, referred to W.E.A. links with the trade unions, and the strength that derived from members being members of different organisations, some of which - such as churches and cooperatives - were quicker and more active than unions at that time. He also addressed the question of how far popular movements can gain power through knowledge, and not trigger off conflict and further oppression. He saw a major problem in Britain as workers' apathy and reluctance: how to persuade the powerless to take action to acquire knowledge leading to power.

Reports from the groups added further dimensions to the discussion. One group was sceptical about the extent to which adult education could bring about any kind of radical social change. It was felt that no real change could occur unless there was government support and direction. Pre-revolution Chinese experience was cited to suggest the limits within which adult education without government support could effect real change.

Another group asked, similarly, whether adult education could change the political structure of the country and create more justice if it is controlled by government. While this was held to be the case, it was pointed out that there were also non-governmental organisations effectively involved in adult education, and that in some capitalist systems individual government agents may subvert the system from within.

Another group concentrated especially on the Chinese experience regarding links between adult education and social change. A "short but graphic and informative history of Chinese adult education from around the time of the founding of the Communist Party in China", especially for the pre-liberation period, "showed a number of points of similarity with the recent and current situations in many developing countries":

> From its beginning, the Communist Party of China was involved in adult education, often carried out under very difficult and dangerous circumstances. Prior to liberation, it carried out educational activities sometimes openly, sometimes clandestinely or semi-clandestinely, and also supported educational efforts made by other progressive forces. The main task at this time was to gain power, and this involved armed struggle, production and education. In their efforts to educate, motivate and raise the consciousness of the people before liberation, the political component of education was stressed more than the cultural.
>
> After liberation, there was of course greater emphasis placed on cultural education. Adult education continued to maintain prominence ... There was at the same time a movement from a non-formal to a more formal system of adult education. But the two principles underlying Chinese education continue to be its collectivism and social consciousness, such that the Chinese people are encouraged to supervise the bureaucracy eg. by criticising the abuse of privilege by high-ranking officials.

The fourth group report nicely captured the links between the apparently diverse experiences confronting delegates: the immediate Chinese experience alongside British liberal traditions and Latin America's contemporary struggle:

> Discussion began with Chinese delegates feeling they were somewhat remote from the topics. However, further discussion revealed a number of commonalities between China's experience and that of other countries. For example, popular education in China began at the beginning of the 20th century as an 'awakening force' in political terms. Its early activities were hampered by the lack of power of the educators. Later on it became more systematic through night schools for peasants at which they learned not only for the purpose of 'awakening' in preparation for liberation but also agricultural production skills. In some ways this process is similar to the concept of popular adult education.
>
> It was noted however that there are also similarities between this process of popular education and the concept of liberal adult education. The difference is that liberal adult education has beeen based on achieving change through an **evolutionary** process - while popular adult education has frequently been to prepare for change through a **revolutionary** process.

The group went on to give other examples of liberal education: the Danish Folkschules and the Swedish Study Circles. "These examples show that not all liberal education began from educational institutions like universities. Some commonalities were noted between the Folkschules and Study Circle-activities and those which are carried out in [Chinese] Workers' Cultural Palaces."

Summing up the session, the Chairman highlighted the following:

- what was the relevance of the two presented studies to other societies?

- how effective were popular adult education movements to bring about change, especially in the context of very repressive regimes?

- should not adult education movements directed to bringing about social change also take on board such humanitarian considerations as food, health and survival?

- what happens, in terms of possible bureaucratisation and loss of flexibility, when popular adult education movements are 'adopted' by government?

what alliances can and should adult education enter into with 'non-educational' reform groups and movements - unions, women, and so on?

how can the reform of the formal education system be addressed, and what is the desirable relationship between nonformal and formal sectors?

Chapter 3

Adult Education Research

A. Research in Adult Education: Major Areas of Theory and Inquiry

Ana Kranjc

Preface

It would be a massive task to present the fundamental theory of adult education, ongoing research in this field and outstanding issues, with or without solutions. It is more realistic to embark on such an undertaking for pedagogy, where the education systems studied are more uniform and exhibit more similarity than can be traced or even anticipated in adult education. The variety of phenomena, the diversity of forms and ways in which adults acquire knowledge, by their very nature defy scientific generalisation and the formation of a more unified theory.

Because of the variety, dissimilarity and lack of interrelatedness, due to the social, cultural, economic, political, technical and scientific conditions in which research in adult education is carried on, this paper seeks simply to identify various ways in which scientific solutions might be developed and offered, focusing on description rather than on a hierarchical classification of research findings. What follows is but a rough categorisation of developments so far; it cannot aspire to the level of exhaustive analysis or precise evaluation. Cross-cultural comparisons and rough estimates of the heterogeneous phenomena of adult education in various parts of the world reveal specific features of different environments, but fail to do justice to each individual system of adult education or to the different experts.

Scientific Foundations

Work on the scientific foundations of adult education varies around the world; the place science concerned with adult education occupies in different areas vis-a-vis other scientific disciplines varies greatly. What differs in particular is the complex of relationships between scientific knowledge about adult education and the most closely related disciplines: sociology, psychology, anthropology and a few others. Roughly speaking, there are three typical situations, and three basic ways of forming a scientific theory of adult education.

Research on and theory of adult education remaining within the boundaries of pedagogy

(Countries in which pedagogy has the status of a separate scientific discipline.)

Pedagogy developed primarily as inquiry into the laws underlying teaching and learning, and as a search for more generalised understanding of these laws. Initially the child's school-period was very short (between ages 6 and 10), but when compulsory education was extended to 6, 8, 10 or even 12 consecutive years of the child's life, reaching into the adolescent years, the research tasks of pedagogy as a science expanded. The subject has been extended to an increasingly longer period of chronological age.

Pedagogy has also been expanding horizontally. From one decade to another there was a growing number of school subjects; there emerged new types of vocational and technical schools. The network of schools spread in all directions. Instruction at school became increasingly determined by general social development, social circumstances and cultural development, presenting new research areas and new problems.

Along with the expansion of pedagogy as a science goes the development of research in adult education. Attempts are made to discover the basic regularities and to elucidate phenomena occurring in adult education, especially in countries where the main emphasis is on the education of adults, or on the second level of education, with formal accreditation. Such countries pay less attention to informal education, liberal education and continuing education, since the practice of adult education follows the lines established for regular school education.

This kind of situation is found mostly in societies where education is undergoing rapid change, where compulsory education is being extended, and where new kinds of schools are being rapidly opened to meet the economic, socio-political, technical and cultural needs of the society. In such circumstances adult education is but an additional instrument of the education system, performing what the regular school has failed to do. It is understandable that in theoretical and practical respects also the science of adult education cannot simply free itself from pedagogy and start up independently.

It is characteristic of societies where the government exercises official pressure on and strong control of education that research in adult education is kept within strict limits. While such control is possible in traditional forms of education, with etatism penetrating into all details of the functioning of regular schools, it is not feasible in the broader forms of independent, informal adult education. These are intended to offer adults learning ways to knowledge, personal development, and a wealth of diverse pursuits. In the abovementioned systems such forms may even decline. Other, broader phenomena of adult education are touched neither in practice nor in science. This type of research in adult education remains within the province of pedagogy and reflects the typical phenomena of the 'too-school-like' educated society.

It is not political influence alone which keeps research in adult education confined to the narrow framework of pedagogy. A similar picture can be found in certain developing countries where - in view of the lower level of economic and social development - the regular school system remains the only realistic basis for adult education. Here adult education tends to be realised only in this way; alternative ways (distance education, multi-media education, educational influences of communications in compact urban settlements) remain as yet unexplored. In such cases theory of and inquiry into adult education are restricted to formal schooling and pedagogy.

Research into adult education as a meeting-point of related disciplines

Elsewhere, adult education is studied on an interdisciplinary basis, from the perspectives of sociology, psychology, biology, economics, medicine and other sciences, as necessary. Such foundations also provide the basis for research in and the theory of adult education. This is the approach characteristic of the English-speaking countries. Each of the sciences mentioned above has its own interpretation of phenomena emerging in adult education. Sociology treats, above all, social phenomena and interprets the underlying regularities in terms of social groups in the educational process. Psychology preserves for its scientific domain the typically individual approach; it observes the individual's learning in all its specificity. Other disciplines involved in the study of adult education likewise remain, each for itself, inside the province of its own subject and research methods. However, the problems studied by these disciplines with specific reference to adult education are multifarious, practically defying attempts to arrange them in a well-composed whole.

Disagreements among the various disciplines treating adult education can give no more than a mosaic of individual details, a mosaic composed of sociological or psychological or biological research problems. Comprehensiveness in the study of adult education cannot be achieved in an inter-disciplinary way.

A critical assessment of this second typical situation does not negate the possible value of the inter-disciplinary approach. But inter-disciplinary studies must also be based on the foundations of their own identification of phenomena. This is not possible unless adult education is the subject of a special science, focusing exclusively on it and developing specifically appropriate research methods not borrowed from other disciplines.

This second typical approach provides only partial insights into and partial answers to issues involved in adult education. Therefore its cognitive potential is limited. Partial insights do not remain in isolation. They appear in horizontal sets and widen the horizons of what is known about adult education. Predominantly suitable for direct application, they can be applied also in situations similar to those in which they were obtained. Multi-disciplinary treatment of adult education precludes a deepening of understanding. It precludes the forming of a unified theory, because the generalising value of partial insights, partial understanding, is too low.

Such investigations tend to exclude the study of phenomena making up adult education through time and across space. Research results revealing sociological, psychological or economic laws governing adult education are a reflection of the current moment; they provide a description rather than a causal pattern. They omit the longitudinal axis within adult education; what is sought is relations with **external** phenomena. Thus adult education becomes related to the society, social groups, personality characteristics, economic phenomena, and the like.

There is no denying the significance of the inter-disciplinary approach for the explication of phenomena, for the study of laws operating in a given field. But if this is the only approach, if a particular science and theory of the field is not being developed, then the essence escapes us. We keep ourselves on the fringe of the phenomena; we look at them mostly from the outside and fail to consider their internal regularities. The results of multi-disciplinary approaches are not commensurable; the question of how far investigations cover and exhaustively represent the field of adult education remains unattended. This usually causes little concern, since high value is placed on the applicability of findings. It is the pragmatic aspects which predominate. Research work follows up immediate practical activities in adult education. The influence upon efficiency is obvious.

Formation of a distinct science - andragogy

When discussing the various types of research activity and the formation of theory, one cannot ignore the experimental work stemming predominantly from Central Europe. Here the endeavours of specialists have been concentrated above all on the formation of a separate scientific discipline concerning education of adults, called andragogy (and by some andragology). Efforts dating back 40 or 50 years have by now borne the first fruits.

In the process of developing andragogy as a science of adult education, special attention has been paid to clarifying distinctions between pedagogy and andragogy, since both disciplines are concerned with education. By and large scientists agree that the two disciplines are only relatively independent of each other, since both of them centre around education. They come under the province of 'educology' which brings together general insights having high generalising value, which are satisfactory and valid both in pedagogy (education of children and young people) and in andragogy (education of adults). The question of more or less independence of andragogy as a science is advocated in different ways and extreme points of view can be found on both sides. In support of a wholly independent science are those who term it andragology. They follow not so much pedagogy as other social sciences, and seek to form the science of adult education, with no particular regard for pedagogy.

Discussion of the relation between pedagogy and andragogy has found echo in other continents, even if the theory is not being built on the same foundations. Some try to contrast andragogy with pedagogy, emphasising its freshness and specifics. Others plead for it as a superordinate discipline which has a broader concept and is more socially determined, in contrast to pedagogy which is restricted mostly to school education. The extremes either deny andragogy any scientific status whatsoever or see in it the only way towards a more comprehensive concept of adult education. Those directly engaged in developing andragogy at first emphasised above all the difference from pedagogy: specificity of the subject of education (adult persons), and of the psycho-social conditions under which adult education is carried on.

Gradually the initial efforts began to take a different course. During the last decade we notice (in countries in which andragogy has expanded) even opposite tendencies. Specialists have now started to discover points commonly shared by pedagogy and andragogy, since they have come to believe that andragogy has become established to a degree where it is no longer of questionable status. Still, instances of the influence of pedagogy on andragogy are commoner than in the other direction.

At the beginning of the development of andragogy scientists were concerned mostly with formulating fundamental categories and laws underlying adult education. Gradually out of **general andragogy** there evolved other andragogic subdisciplines, which deal with specific spheres of adult education. Only the most characteristic are mentioned here:

Andragogic didactics studies the methods and forms through which adult education will be efficient: eg. mass forms of education, learning in small groups, and individual ways of learning.

Industrial andragogy including education in the specific conditions of work in a factory setting; training for current demands on the job; work for the revision of knowledge needed because of technical innovations, scientific developments, and restructuring of the economy.

Rural andragogy promotes the transfer of knowledge for such purposes as the production of food and the development of social relations in the countryside. It serves as the basis for cultural development in the rural environment.

There are daily more unresolved questions about education for leisure time, mostly as a consequence of diminished working hours as well as unemployment. Thus a person trained for work in industry may turn out to be one-sided and too narrow when he or she loses a job. At school he or she received a more or less one-sided vocational training and now may be unable to get employment. **Leisure-time andragogy** inter-relates insights and findings that can hopefully contribute to man's activity in a wider area, and in a more creative way.

Family andragogy concerns the training of people for family roles (partners, parents), a kind of training not offered in school; what can be gained from everyday experience is not enough for happy and successful family life.

Penologic andragogy is devoted to the education, re-education and vocational training of prisoners. Similarly, **army andragogy** and **andragogy of handicapped persons** deal with the educational activity appropriate to these specific situations.

The decades through which andragogy has been developing have also seen certain mistakes and shortcomings. Research workers' direction of interest primarily towards their own subject has caused neglect of linkage with other subjects. The inter-disciplinary approach is almost unknown in countries which have set out to develop andragogy. The deficit of sociology, psychology and economics in adult education is more than obvious. Solution to theoretical issues will be possible only when the development of our own unified science is possible and when linkage with related disciplines can also be established.

Major Areas of Inquiry - Problems for Research in the Future

The principal trends reveal only the chief guide-lines of development. There appear unsolved problems which obstruct the further development of adult education. The concept of life-long education gives rise to new phenomena that have to be coped with if learning is to be successful. Transition into a society utilising computer science is not possible with the old ways of education. The educational process is gradually ridding itself of unnecessary formalism and is increasingly oriented towards actual learning. Adult education, seeking extra-mural forms of education, must provide for: unity in the education system; integration of adult education with the work and life of people; functional evaluation of knowledge; motivation for education; international relations in accumulation and use of knowledge.

Unified educational system - internal integration

Adult education has its roots in the pre-school and school periods. Although conceived in a different way, it is heavily dependent on previous education. Attempts to achieve a unified system through legislation have brought out points of contact and regularities which interrelate various learning methods, develop motivation for education and preserve learnability from early childhood until old age. This could provide objective foundations of linkage. Attempts at formal linkage have in practice shown that "the stronger overpower the weaker", that traditional schooling prevails over adult education and thus deprives it of its essential character. Therefore the precondition for successfully putting together adult education and regular schooling is first the recognition of equivalent status, to be followed by mutual influence in both directions. Also the school must take into account what is to follow after students have completed their regular schooling; conversely, adult education must take into account the earlier educational basis.

The unity of the education system, in accordance with the concept of life-long education, is dependent on the complementary functions of different educational fields, and on a rational internal division of labour in the realisation of educational goals and objectives.

Adult education in life and work - external integration

How to develop efficient ways for acquiring knowledge outside formal school institutions, in relation to the vocational, working, and cultural activity of people, their social activities, recreation, sport and other social contacts in the urban environment? Scientific development so far knows only methodologies for individual subjects of instruction, having taken as its basis the school organisation of education. A new challenge for research in adult education concerns methodologies for instruction in specific activities. The educational potential of vocational work and cultural activity is not yet realised. Given a suitable methodology, it is possible for other activities also to become educative.

Adult education, integrated into people's life and work, represents but a part of the entire learning process. It has certain advantages. Since it is carried on in the natural environment of other activities it is not likely to become dissociated from them in its content. The knowledge acquired in this way is of an inter-disciplinary kind, just as are the problems people are called upon to solve with their knowledge. Knowledge thus grows in its value for application, and in its transfer potential. External integration, or the integration of adult education with life and work, calls for research at the individual level (persons who are learning) and at the institutional level (work organisations, local units, families, societies). Work towards discovering ways for adult education to relate to life and work represents the foundation for the 'learning society'.

Functional evaluation of education - creating new criteria for evaluation

The valuing of education is derived from school experience and has been subsequently transferred into adult education. There is a deficit in research work on the evaluation of adult education in terms of the use of knowledge and the influences that knowledge has on people's overall activity. The lack of adequate criteria for the functional evaluation of knowledge, by means of which it would be possible to mark improvements made in the work and life of people, keeps the evaluation at just a symbolic level. Too much importance is still attached to the particular school which an individual attended, to certificates and diplomas, not enough to the knowledge itself and to how far this knowledge is in practice useful to a particular individual.

The transition from symbolic to functional evaluation will take a long time and requires continuous attention on the part of researchers. Transition to the functional evaluation of knowledge is affected by numerous restrictive biases and outdated views. Without scientifically worked out criteria for functional evaluation no step forward is possible.

Newly formed criteria for measuring changes due to the influence of new knowledge, as in performance, behaviour and functioning of a given individual, now provide opportunities for the evaluation also of informally acquired knowledge. Without this it is not possible to realise life-long education. Accordingly, we confront a wide range of problems. These only appear urgent when we realise how much precious knowledge was neglected; only formally recognised knowledge was taken into consideration. With an increasing need for more knowledge, all knowledge is precious as we strive for higher and higher rationality.

Thirst for Knowledge and the Developing of Motivation for Education

Motivation is a significant factor for the prospective integration of education into life and work. Acquisition of knowledge will start in a number of different ways as people feel the readiness for learning, and new knowledge. Numerous opportunities offered for learning through life and work may with motivation be readily seized; without motivation they are of little or no avail. With most people the thirst for knowledge as felt in early childhood becomes repressed during the school years. It is replaced by various secondary external motives, like earning money, changing job, social status and reputation, and other rewards. But these secondary motives are not of long duration. Before long they become extinguished, while continuing learning can be based only on suitable motivation (thirst for knowledge, need for knowledge, or primary motivation).

The development and preservation of motivation for education depends on numerous factors which are not yet fully understood. People tend to learn retroactively and not in advance: only after a need for certain knowledge comes up, when they come to feel gaps; not in advance, with the aim of acquiring knowledge as more permanent capital. It could be claimed that 'curative' education is predominant whereas there is very little of a 'preventive' kind. Curative education is stimulated by external impulses (secondary motives), while preventive education is related to the thirst for knowledge, the incentives of which are still insufficiently investigated and understood.

Increasing learnability, openness to the outside world, means considering both psychological (educational model, defence mechanisms, personality structure) and social (valuation of knowledge in the society, educational opportunities, economic conditions) factors which still require research.

The Study of Opportunities and the Developing of Ways for International Cooperation in the Accumulation and Use of Knowledge

No nation can remain in isolation with the amount of knowledge it has managed to acquire. The closing up of what is known and the closing off of what is known from others, can lead individual nations to decline into backwardness from which it would be hard indeed to escape. Knowledge is increasingly becoming a value in circulation, a value owned by mankind and not by an individual, an integrating and not a separating force. Words about and assessments of the position of knowledge and education in the present world are not simply wishful thinking; they are a consequence of the development, a part of the concrete actual relations prevailing in our economic, political and cultural life. They represent laws underlying the society which cannot be ignored. The science of adult education will have, through cooperation in international endeavours, to find how to circulate knowledge internationally.

The development of modern technology provides a realistic basis for international use of knowledge. Microprocessors and satellite transfer can provide linkage among computer learning centres and greatly increase the availability of knowledge and the adjusting of education to actual individual needs and to the search for knowledge in different social environments.

Also required is attention to cultural, economic, political and social handicaps. Constant watchfulness will make it easier to overcome these. Developing the field of adult education calls for hard, solid work; also it necessitates big changes as regards the work done so far. All this requires a basis of sound research work.

Conclusion

This paper is more about content and problems than about research methods and organisation. Attention should be drawn to the significant and extensive activity of ICAE in developing a suitable methodology for research. Participatory research has led to a special movement for a new methodology which makes it possible for persons engaged in education directly and actively to cooperate in research work: from starting a research project to final interpretation. The first concepts have already been topics at consultation meetings of researchers; technical publications have been issued, and a network of permanent collaborators from various continents has been formed. In our efforts for a still better organisation of participatory research we see not only a significant contribution towards developing a new methodology but also objective possibilities for close cooperation and for coordinated performance internationally. We could jointly decide which problems in the overall research inquiry are to be given priority and how to tackle them.

B. Panel Commentary and Discussion

Professor Rubenson set his comments in the framework of universities on the ground that though they are not the only or necessarily the main contributors of research they have been given a special role in this regard. He addressed two issues:

How should adult education research be organised within the university?

Professor Kranjc makes the point that adult education can and ought to be developed into a unified science. Her position is based on the observation that there are serious shortcomings in the development of adult education research where it is organised within the boundaries of pedagogy or where it rests on an interdisciplinary basis, that is the aspects of sociology, psychology, biology, economics etc. In the first case areas outside the formal system tend to be neglected and in the second case we end up with scattered knowledge that precludes a deepening understanding of the adult education phenomenon.

I share these concerns but am not convinced that the solution is to look for a unified discipline of adult education. To think of a unified discipline would be possible only if we reduce the territory to the area of learning-teaching and probably not even then. What about issues like the history of adult education, adult education and social change, just to mention two? I think it would be more fruitful to identify research problems and be less concerned with whether there exists a discipline or not. The fact that other disciplines do not systematically cover adult education should not be taken as the reason to abort the notion of an interdisciplinary approach. I consider that the underlying problem is a pragmatic one and not of an epistemological nature. By assembling various disciplines under an organisational umbrella of adult education many of the problems Dr Kranjc has identified could be solved. Traditionally adult education departments have been organised mainly from the standpoint of dissemination of knowledge, ie. professional training, and not from that of the production of knowledge. These two tasks are difficult to combine in one structure and a focus on building an interdisciplinary unit could be a solution.

Practice and theory

With reference to the somewhat hazy concept of research and development, adult education research has mostly been of the 'development' kind. Practice-oriented research aimed at solving an immediate problem is not necessarily negative. The heart of the matter is the lack of balance between practice-oriented and discipline-oriented research, where the purpose is to develop and test theories and lay the necessary foundations for applied research. Due to a lack of theory-orientation, practice-oriented research has become almost totally atheoretical. There are thus two inter-related problems facing adult education: the balance between practice and discipline-oriented research, and the atheoretical approach of applied research. The problem is not practice versus theory, but how to get the best of both. The sooner we realise this the more useful will the research become.

Dr Hall first suggested that the three positions described by Dr Kranjc as typifying different systems are in fact often held by people within the same country, institution or even small group. Secondly he offered a sceptical comment on such terms as educology, andragogy, andragology: "I hope that we are genuinely deepening our knowledge of adult education in the context of those people who need adult education the most, and not merely following academic traditions that insist on viewing the world through single disciplines such as sociology, psychology or anthropology".

He then turned to Kranjc's classification of research and offered another, complementary, classification:

Category I - research directed towards understanding of the mechanisms or means of adult learning itself, eg. studies of methods; alternative methods; delivery systems; motivation; perception.

Most of Kranjc's work as described would be found in this category.

Category II - research on the interaction of adult education and society, eg. the relation of education to productivity; the relationship of adult education to political consciousness; the relation of adult education to the needs of specific groups.

Category III - research in which people themselves, as members of popular classes, create **new** knowledge, eg. workers in Shanghai machine tool technical innovation; workers in an abbatoir in Montreal studying their health and safety conditions; farmers in Chile sharing ideas on new techniques; landless labourers in India creating knowledge about the law in order to regain their land; women restudying their own situation in order to lessen domination.

Hall argued that a full and articulated theory of adult education which was directed to transformation of societies would not emerge without giving substantial attention to all three categories. He closed with the poem attributed to the late Professor Jowett about an unnamed but distinguished university:

Here I stand
My name is Jowett
There is no knowledge
But I know it
I am the Master of this College
What I don't know is not knowledge.

Dr Maydl stressed the importance of considering the social context of adult education, looking for a wider context and set of issues than Kranjc's paper contained. Referring also to the shared reality and experience of the time in Shanghai, he alluded to three sources of experiences from the past decade: interdisciplinary studies, including the scientific and technological revolution and its social implications; the development of comparative studies by various agencies including ICAE; problem-oriented studies.

Five dimensions should be considered in addressing theories and methods of adult education research:

the **socio-economic dimension**, especially socio-structural analysis and its development in relation to demography, social classes, migration, social organisation and institutions etc (witness recent social change indicators in China);

the **temporal dimension**, including the concept of 'social time', at both individual and group level;

special **topographical or ecological** - administrative and territorial divisions, such as communes and districts;

activities of recent years with research as a **way of life** built into changing the organisation of work, developing new social and productive roles and relationships, etc;

and finally **social planning and perspectives** - creating social, including educational, processes relating to alternative choices for the development of the individual and society.

Such a framework influences and is influenced by all the elements of adult education systems. It was necessary to find ways of considering and coping with the total context of adult education in a particular society, time and place, if a science of adult education was to generate useful research.

In discussion, activists' scepticism about theory was directed clearly to theory which is unrelated to practice. Many 'theoreticians' were remote from practice and were not really theoreticians either. There was a related question about who controls knowledge for what purpose: often it serves the powerful and perpetuates the status quo. It was felt that the career structures and reward systems of universities had much to answer for in this respect. Practical translation and dissemination of research was important but often badly ignored.

Members of the Symposium were very conscious of Chinese interest in developing adult education research. Adult education research in China was the focus of one group's discussion:

> There are independent research units at the national and municipal or provincial level. Parallel to this, social research institutes conduct part-time research involving many adult educators. It was stated that Chinese research methods do involve the people. It was asked how much the Chinese experience had contributed to Marxist theory. The Chinese participants explained that Marxism was applied to the Chinese context. For example, Marx had not explained the ideas of armed struggle, the use of a rural base or the formation of a common front with other progressive forces. It was pointed out that although China has a long history of adult education, its experience in adult education research was small in comparison with other countries.

Chinese participants in another group confirmed that research was seen as having a very high priority. However adult education research per se would have little meaning or relevance unless it related to the practical application of knowledge to the complexities and diversities of experience in China, especially to work situations and to economic development. There seemed to be ground for criticising the typical adult education research in the west if it was too university-centred and theory/academic-oriented. "However, in organising and mobilising the more literate sections in adult education research, theoretical applications could certainly help."

> At present much of the materials used in adult education in China come from formal education. This needs change, and research in this area could help. Training of teachers in adult education was

another vital area for research and application of research.

Other areas of need for research included systems of management, and utilisation and rationalisation of resources, as well as psychological aspects of adult learning, including self-study.

Who should be doing the research, and should there be national research centres, linking teaching with research, or as separate institutions? How should research be coordinated? While this depended on the nature and purpose of the particular research:

> research should be concerned with decision-making with regard to resource allocation and utilisation, planning and programming, cost-benefits, and in terms of the special needs and characteristics of the learning population. In this context it could be nationally coordinated at the centre and carried out by appropriate support research institutions including universities, and duplicated in the provinces with the lowest level of research going down to the grass-root levels.

C. Structures and Working Methods of Chinese Research into Teaching in Adult Education

Wang Wenlin

[A special evening session of the Symposium offered two academic addresses to the large community of adult educators in Shanghai. The paper by Wang Wenlin took as its theme research into the teaching of adult education. As such it provides one Chinese response to some of the questions raised about the organisation of research especially in China, in the previous section.]

Adult education in China plays an important role in spreading cultural and scientific knowledge among the people, and in training personnel in specific fields. In order to carry out these tasks it is urgent to strengthen research on teaching, spread advanced teaching theories and teaching experience, and guide teaching affairs. Therefore teaching research must be taken seriously, its position and role rightly evaluated.

At present, the scope of adult education is getting wider and wider, the content of courses becoming richer and richer. For example, education for workers and staff members generally ranges from primary to higher education.

This developing trend is demanding a better teaching system: those who teach must be qualified and able to teach different courses; content of courses includes fundamental knowledge, natural science, applied technology, social science etc. Teaching should be versatile and diversified; there should be not only face to face teaching but also distance teaching. In view of the complex developing teaching tasks, education needs to be guided by scientific theories and the latest results of research into teaching.

Looking back in history, people have to recognise that the campaign to eliminate illiteracy at the beginning of the founding of the Republic has shifted to intermediate level cultural and technical education for adults. This influences adult education in our country greatly. At the beginning of the Peoples' Republic, the content of courses was at the primary stage; what people did mostly was to offer more educational provision. But now much more work must be done on the teaching aspect which is becoming prominent throughout the whole adult education system. This greatly changed situation requires people to strengthen research into teaching.

The position and role of adult education have now been recognised generally. In the final analysis, good teaching is the key. So, to undertake research on teaching, to improve the quality of teaching, to give education full play in the realisation of the Four Modernisations, to let education gain social recognition: these are very important factors for the future of adult education.

The Four Modernisations are being realised very rapidly. The whole economic front is experiencing reforms. The new situation has raised new questions and issues for adult education. Peasants' demand for agricultural know-how is increasing, the training of workers and staff is an urgent need, refreshing of scientists' and technicians' knowledge must be carried out immediately, enterprises are wanting administrative personnel badly. To cope with the needs, the content of courses and ways of teaching must be seriously studied. There should be a unified plan, with due consideration for present and future need. Without research, these needs cannot be well met. For instance, in the training of the entire workforce, should education be one-dimensional with members progressing together, or should it be multi-dimensional, considering different target groups, different subject-matter, different levels and different aims? How should content of courses be targeted towards the different needs of production? Without research, these questions cannot be answered scientifically. Unless these questions are correctly answered, adult education cannot cope with the programme of the Four Modernisations, and fulfil its role.

Because of the present status of adult education, strengthening research into teaching has also become a pressing matter. Adult teaching is much more widely scattered than regular education. So much needs to be done on a unified teaching programme, teaching plan, teaching quality and the maintenance of standards.

Teachers' status is far from ideal at present. Many teachers' teaching ability is weak, their level of knowledge is low, and most have not received formal teacher training. We cannot wait for an ideal teaching force. The only way is to strengthen research into teaching, and let teachers enhance their abilities through practice. Teaching research, whether on theory or on practice, appears as the key link in further developing adult education.

To carry out this research, an organisational entity with an assured establishment needs to be set up to explore theories, spread and apply the results of research, exchange information etc. To function well, the organisation must have the following features.

There must be a teaching network around it so that the research can be implemented easily on the one hand, and information can flow freely in all directions on the other.

Key members as researchers into teaching serve as a pioneer and mainstay force.

It must stay in close touch with administrative personnel and teachers in grass-roots units.

Heilongjiang Province has adopted the following measures. At provincial level there is a Worker-Peasant Education Teaching Research Department; at prefectural and municipal level there are Worker-Peasant Education Teaching Research Sections; at county and district level, the administrative staff of the Worker-Peasant Education Offices are concurrently teaching researchers of different subjects according to their specialisms. In a few counties and districts there are full-time teaching researchers. Where conditions permit in certain cities, for instance in Harbin, Worker-Peasant Education Institutes have been set up. The teaching centres in some large factories, mines and other enterprises also have their own full-time teaching researchers. Therefore in the whole province a specialised teaching research contingent has been formed. Teaching research 'backbone' members have been organised as well. At the same time a Provincial Adult Education Society and teaching Research Societies in various subjects have been formed. Those in charge of adult education in grass-roots units have been organised. A province-wide non-professional adult education teaching research contingent with large membership has been formed. Professional institutions and scientific organisations for the masses cooperate and complement each other. Thus a rational teaching research network has been formed, providing an organisational base to develop research.

Professional Worker-Peasant Education Teaching Research Institutions subordinated to Worker-Peasant Education Bureaux at all levels study the content of courses, teaching methods and scientific teaching theories, and give advice to administrative units. These institutions are essentially educational research organs. They have their own specialised fields. They are different from the educational administrative units. Thus administrative working methods cannot be applied to the teaching research institutions; routine work cannot replace research work. The quality of creativity, and seeking differences, must be encouraged among teaching researchers, to develop the range and quality of adult education research. Teaching researchers should not only have relatively sophisticated specialised knowledge but also be capable of doing research work. Secondly, such institutions are authoritative organs guiding teaching research and teaching. Teaching researchers at all levels have the right to direct and study the teaching of all subjects in all schools in the system, and teachers must respect their opinions. All documents and instructions from the teaching research units at all levels have statutory status and must be acted on seriously by the schools concerned. Certainly such authority is based on scientific research. In this respect the most acceptable authority is the scientific attitude in teaching research.

Teaching research institutions are responsible for:

research on teaching materials and teaching methods;
research into learning teaching theories for specific subjects;
guidance to teaching;
organising teaching research activities.

Research on teaching materials and methods and research into teaching of specific subjects are the core tasks for the teaching institutions. The two items belong to two levels of theoretical study. The research on teaching materials and methods has direct significance to guide teaching work. Teaching work directly concerns the suitability of the content of courses to the practice of production and life, the principles and design of teaching materials, the principles of teaching, the teaching procedure, and the specific characteristics of teaching methods consistent with the principles of adult education, etc. Subject research is more theoretical and higher level research; it provides directions for the research on teaching materials and methods. Vice versa, it absorbs the fruits of the research on teaching materials and methods to replenish and develop itself. Teaching research is in the category of scientific research. Without theoretical exploration, teaching research cannot be scientific. If the institutions of teaching research cannot produce work with theoretical depth, they cannot give teaching guidance. The last two items, guidance to teaching and organising teaching activities, may be called popularisation work. To give vigorous and convincing guidance to teaching at grass-roots levels, application should be emphasised in the theoretical research so as to serve teaching practice better. Thus theoretical research and teaching guidance can be made to dovetail. We should also actively organise various teaching research activities to assist teaching to develop smoothly. The institutions may hold lectures, organise viewing of model teaching, and spread advanced teaching experience to solve common problems in teaching.

Generally speaking the institutions at provincial and municipal level do more work on theoretical research, while those at county and district level do more on popularisation.

Teaching research is in the category of scientific research. Only through scientific laws and with a scientific attitude can the laws of adult education be discovered, and educational teaching theories fitting China's concrete conditions be established.

Study Theories, Master Methods

Besides having specialised knowledge, teaching researchers need certain theoretical understanding of some other sciences to carry out teaching research smoothly. A teaching researcher should consciously train him to understand: (i) some Marxist philosophy, using a dialectical and historical materialist point of view to guide thinking in teaching research; (ii) pedagogy, which they are required to try to master, especially psychology, on which pedagogy has been founded; (iii) other social science subjects related to pedagogy, such as sociology, human resources development and future study. With the help of this understanding they can enlarge the field of vision and scope of adult education teaching research.

Scientific method is a sharp weapon for teaching researchers. Without mastering scientific methods, it is very hard to obtain major achievements. Research can neither be speeded up nor made accurate on the basis of experience and intuition alone in the whole field of education. Adult education teaching research is largely uncharted; people are required to address it bravely with the actual conditions of adult education clearly in mind. Using systematic analysis, scientific experiments, statistical inference etc., people need to open up their research fields and increase their research ability.

Go Deep Into the Realities, Make Investigations

Once a research subject is chosen, researchers must keep realities in mind from beginning to end. Research subjects of significance are chosen from commonly existing problems. Only by analysing and summarising a large number of facts and discovering the essence behind the appearance can significant results be obtained. Information and data should be carefully accumulated, and quantitative as well as qualitative analysis should be attempted. Reseachers should be adept at processing data and information, grasping both quantity and quality, and guarantee maximum reliability and accuracy. Being practical and realistic is a matter of scientific attitude as well as methods. Many specific features of adult education are not fully known. Specific laws of adult education teaching cannot be discovered by the deductive method and inference from ordinary pedagogic principles alone.

Repeat Experiments, Spreading the Experience Gained at Key Points

Pedagogy is a strongly practical science, so teaching experiments are important. Researchers should be good at selecting subjects from real life and design the steps and processes of experiments according to real purposes and plans. It is better to take examples from a wide than a narrow range; it is better to do many experiments than few, continuously until satisfactory conclusions are drawn. Never spread immature experience. Encourage success, and at the same time allow failure too. Analyse failures scientifically. Do not negate a conclusion rashly.

The conditions of adult education are complicated, the range is wide. Different circumstances should be taken into account in spreading teaching experience. In order to understand fully the adaptability and effect of gains at key points, these should be tested in different teaching conditions. Thus a better effect can be obtained when they are introduced generally into teaching.

Combining Full-Time Effort with Part-Time Effort, Relying on the Masses

Combining professional full-time effort with non-professional part-time effort and relying on the masses are our life-line and precious heritage. Teaching research is of mass character. It needs more people to participate in it, more teaching researchers to be organised, so that we can draw on collective wisdom and absorb all useful ideas, work together and reap the benefits.

Professional teaching researchers should organise and rely on the masses on their own initiative. Teaching research societies of all subjects are good to maintain close links with the masses, so they should be well used. To know at any time how the teaching at grass-roots units is going on, researchers should have their own contact points and persons, visit classes with a definite aim, teach some courses if possible. We should not nitpick at suggestions from the teaching researchers of grass-roots units, but value them, initiate them, foster them enthusiastically, catalyse them to ripen early.

II APPLICATIONS

Chapter 4

Workplace Education and Technological Change

The Chief of the Workers' Education Branch of the International Labour Office, chairing this session, called attention to the persisting labour surplus and high unemployment which would continue in the OECD countries. This constituted an economic, social and political threat to every society in the world. Massive changes were taking place, especially technological change which was displacing people from the workforce. Recession, depression and the slow rates of economic growth had generated levels of unemployment previously intolerable. Poloni saw the role of technology as clearly bringing with it social and economic costs as well as benefits: jobs were lost or downgraded, plants shut down. Many workers moved to lower levels of skill and remuneration, in shops, businesses and communications as well as in industry. For countries suffering serious decline in traditional industries high technology was 'an oversold promise', for there were too few jobs to replace those lost through introduction of high technology.

Poloni asked, in his concluding remarks, how societies could prevent people from being trapped in a permanent labour-service underclass, and sought an answer through more career and learning ladders for upward mobility. A wide range of social and political decisions was needed leading towards leisure- and wealth-creating options; more active participation in political, cultural and social life was crucial for this.

Schütze too, speaking in a personal capacity and not representing OECD or the national authorities of any of the Member countries, stressed the major changes that had occurred in the workplace, even in those areas where jobs have survived. The 'second industrial revolution' of microprocessors and microcomputers would also undoubtedly shortly affect the Chinese workplace; now was the time to look ahead to changes a few years hence. Schütze noted the major disagreements which exist over the impact of technological change on skill levels and the possible 'further parcellisation of work'. Was machine-tending to replace skilled jobs? Or would greater polarisation of skills result? Or was there a general need for more skills? It was impossible to say confidently which was correct. Skills were commonly too narrowly perceived; some unrecognised workplace skills were actually crucial. Schütze inclined towards generic skills, especially general and computer literacy, and more encompassing 'technological literacy'. The ability and willingness to learn had become a major factor in keeping and holding a job.

Within the general purpose of training for broad skill areas Schütze identified three target groups: the unemployed, including women seeking to return to the workplace; workers in small and medium-sized enterprises which could not afford on-the-job training; and community-wide basic literacy and numeracy skills. This implied a key role for recurrent education. Adult education thus faced a much broader range of challenges than merely retraining for new technical skills; a basic strategy was required to enhance personal growth and equity.

Min Shufen's paper on the integration of higher education for working adults with production acknowledges Marx's stress upon the inherent relationship between education and productive labour. She spells out some experiences of the Shanghai Municipal Sparetime Institute of Technology before drawing out economic and social benefits of integration. The combination of ideological and principled commitment with practical and applied purpose in her paper echoed what was evident throughout the visits to workplaces and adult education programmes with which the Symposium started.

The third paper, by Michele Jean of Quebec, addresses the implications of technological change, throughout society rather than exclusively at the workplace, for the education of adults. The paper sits comfortably with that of Schütze in its stress upon wider than economic issues and in its anti-determinism, though it is more pessimistic about the effects of technological change, especially as it concerns loss of jobs. The three papers were considered in two separate plenary sessions; the reflections from these sessions are here for convenience drawn together as the fourth section of this chapter.

A. Adult Education and the Changing Workplace

Hans Schütze

Introduction

For the industrialised countries, the last decade has been characterised by major upheavals and great changes. The energy crisis, the modifications in the world-wide division of economic and industrial power, the emergence of new social aspirations and values, and the slow-down in economic and productivity growth, have created conditions in many respects very different from those ten years ago. Structural and technological change are profoundly transforming industries and occupations: while a great number of jobs have disappeared and others have been newly created, the workplaces of many people have undergone important changes as well. In many cases these changes in the workplace connote a major educational and training challenge as skill requirements are also changing.

This paper concentrates on these changes in the workplace and their implications for occupational skills, and on the consequences for adult vocational education and training. This is only one, albeit a very important, aspect of the need for continued learning and relearning during the adult years. Thus, the paper deals with the consequences of structural and technological change neither for initial vocational education and training nor for education in general, but is concerned with the worker whose workplace is affected by these changes. (The terms worker and employee are used interchangeably since it is not only the industrial workplace but the workplace in general that is the focus of the paper.)

Structural and Technological Change and the Workplace

Labour market developments

First a glance at the labour market in general. In recent years, the labour market in OECD countries has been characterised by a number of important developments, some of which have a direct impact both on the workplace and on job skill requirements. A few figures will suffice to illustrate these changes.

Although unemployment has risen in OECD countries to a level unprecendented since World War II (around 30 million people, or 8.1 per cent in 1982), the number of jobs has also dramatically increased over the last decade. The absolute growth of jobs between 1970 and 1982 totalled 33.5 million (or 10 million more than the entire population of Canada). This seeming contradiction - more jobs, but more unemployment - is explained by three factors: a demographic one (the total number of the working age population, people between 15 and 64 years, rose by 55 million, or 12 per cent, between 1970 and 1980); the fact that women have entered the workforce in increasing numbers (the general participation rate rose from 40 per cent in 1950 to over 50 per cent in 1982); and thirdly, the fact that the number of migrant (foreign) workers, immigrant workers in the case of North America, had risen steadily until the beginning of 1980 (with a total of around 5 million in the West European countries in 1982 and some 10 million immigrants in the United States and Canada between 1970 and 1980).

This overall growth in the number of jobs, however, was distributed very unevenly between the sectors of economic activity. **Agricultural employment** has shrunk and in 1982 accounted for only about 9 per cent of total employment (compared with almost 14 per cent in 1970). **Employment in industry**, which had risen by 3.6 million jobs between 1975 and 1979, began to decline in 1980 and is estimated to account for less than 33 per cent of total employment (compared with 37 per cent in 1970). The service sector was the major source of net job creation: its share of total area-wide employment was over 57 per cent in 1982 (compared with 49.2 per cent in 1970).(1) In other words, while between 1970 and 1982 some 9 million jobs in agriculture were lost in OECD countries, some 42 million new jobs were created in the so-called service sector.

Although the number of jobs in industry has remained more or less the same, the industrial sector has also been heavily affected. This becomes apparent if one breaks down the aggregate data further by industries. Thus, large-scale employment dislocations have occurred in the textile industry, basic iron and steel, shipbuilding and the motor vehicle industry. Due to a variety of factors, such as increased international competition, market saturation on levelling-off of growth of demand or productivity growth as a result of technical innovation in production, millions of jobs have been lost in these sectors, causing plant closures and large-scale dismissals of workers.(2) In addition, new jobs have been created in other industries, although not necessarily in the same geographical area where the closures occurred, nor at the same time. Recently the number of jobs in the manufacturing sector has dropped in some countries (in 1981/82 a loss of 1.4 million jobs in the Western European countries), which means that the expansion of employment in growing sectors, industries or regions no longer suffices to compensate fully for the loss of jobs in contracting sectors.

The impact of new technologies

The emergence and introduction on a large scale of a new

generation of production technology was mentioned above as one, although not the only one, of the factors behind present structural change. Micro-computers, numerically controlled machines (in particular, machine tools), industrial robots, CAD/CAM (i.e. Computer Aided Design/Computer Aided Manufacturing) and other high technology equipment and processes are having a profound impact not only on the number of jobs in the industries affected, but also on the content of jobs, work organisation and professional job and skill requirements.

In particular, the **employment effects** of these new technologies are a matter of great concern and debate. Accurate forecasts or projections are impossible to make, but even a quantitative assessment of the impact technological change has had upon employment until now is difficult to come by. Micro-processors and industrial robots are labelled 'job killers' by some, while others argue that these technologies guarantee high productivity and quality, and hence competitiveness, thus saving jobs which would otherwise be lost.

It is clear that new technologies lead directly to higher productivity and are therefore labour-saving, less clear what are the jobs that are being newly created, for example, in the industries producing the new equipment and in the service sector. Let us take, for instance, the employment effects of the industrial robot. A case study of an automobile plant in Germany found that, for each robot introduced, the loss of working places was an average of four workers over two shifts, whereas the number of working places created through maintenance and repair of the robot was 0.3, and the working places created in production of industrial robots were just over 0.5.(3) Other studies have cited the number of workplaces suppressed per robot as between 0.8 and 6.2, depending on the type of application. However precise these findings, they cannot indicate or explain the new employment effects of robots since they do not take into account the viability of a firm and its competitiveness due to an increase of productivity, which is in turn a factor in safeguarding jobs which would otherwise get lost.(4)

Experts engaged in the discussion about employment impacts fall into one of three categories: pessimists, optimists and those who believe that the impact of technological change is so closely linked to other economic variables, such as the compensation effects on the macro-economic level, that a quantification of the net employment impact is quite impossible.

The pessimistic view is expressed by Nobel Laureate Wassily Leontief, the Director of New York University's Institute for Economic Analysis:

> The computer and the robot are already beginning to replace the simpler mental functions of blue and white-collar workers. Man, a

factor of production, has only two aspects: physical and mental. Both are being replaced, ... Human workers will go the way of the horse.(5)

Pessimists emphasise the labour-saving effect of new technology, calculating that the creation of new jobs cannot offset the losses resulting from the redundancies caused by the new technologies. Thus, for example, France's World Centre for Computer Science and Human Resources estimates that 50 million people in the industrialised Western countries will be jobless by 1990 because of high technology.(6)

The optimists, on the other hand, stress that productivity factors and improvement of the quality of products and services will lead to an increase in demand and a concomitant increase in investment; in this way technology is expected, in the long run, to create more jobs than it replaces.

However, even if there continue to be employment compensation effects - experts point out that so far these have indeed prevailed - the problem remains that they operate with important time lags and imply a major disequilibrium of the labour market, as the employment created will not match the workforce made redundant, either in skills or in other characteristics.(7)

'New technologies' consist of a number of different systems and processes. To discuss their impact on the workplace and the employment structure it is useful to give a few concrete examples. Most spectacular is probably the **industrial robot**, i.e. "a reprogrammable multifunctional manipulator designed to move material, parts, tools or specialised devices through variable programmed motions for the performance of a variety of tasks".(8) Robots have penetrated particularly the manufacture of machines in the automobile industry where they are used for machine tooling, spray painting, spot and arc welding, die-casting, press work, forging, pallet loading, etc. While robots have primarily been allocated to do dirty, dangerous, unhealthy or boring jobs, thus generally improving working conditions, their implantation has resulted in a considerable restructuring of work skills, and where certain skill profiles, both high and low skilled, have disappeared (e.g. casters, painters, welders), new ones have been created, such as system operators or technical personnel for repair and maintenance.

Another example are the **Computer Aided Design/Computer Aided Manufacturing Systems (CAD/CAM)** which consist of computerised design, including graphic design, process planning and parts programming systems, numerical controls, and groups of machine tools interconnected and supervised by computers. Computer Aided Design Systems are used not only for product design but also for modelling and simulation, and direct linkage can be installed from the design system to the manufacturing system, i.e. the design can be automatically converted into instruction for a machine tool system. Computer Aided Manufacturing Systems are used for numerical control of machine tools, welding, spraying, etc., automated inspection and grading of raw material, inspection of machine parts, inventory control and automated warehousing.

A third example concerns **Office Communication Systems** which are increasingly affecting and transforming office jobs. Word processors, micro-, mini-, and mainframe computers, video display terminals, photocopying, microfiche, digital telephone, private branch exchanges and closed circuit television find applications in the preparation, storage and transmission of documents. Databanks, information networks, telephone line-based data retrieval and computer analysis, serve to retrieve, analyse and present information, and long-distance communication and mailings are done by means of electronic mail and teleconferencing.

Consequences for Workers' Skills

The hypotheses: upskilling, deskilling, polarisation of skills

What the introduction of new technologies means to the skill structure of the workforce is a matter of disagreement among experts. Some hold that as technology becomes increasingly more sophisticated, it will require more highly skilled people in order to operate the equipment and put it to its most productive use. Others believe on the contrary that computer-based machines will not only take over most of the intellectual elements of work (such as co- ordination, monitoring, product control, etc.) but also lead to further parcellisation of work. They assert that through automation, many of the skilled jobs, currently requiring long experience and training, will be reduced to easily learned, machine-tending jobs. If so, future jobs will not require considerable education and sophisticated training in computer-related areas, nor will the use of high technology upgrade the skill requirements of existing jobs.(9)

A third group argues that both upskilling and deskilling can be observed, different job categories being differently affected by technological change. While a minority of the workforce, in particular technical and managerial staff, is confronted with increasingly complex and complicated tasks, for the majority (mainly executive personnel and manual workers), it is argued, jobs become less challenging and these workers lose their initial skills or never acquire more than rudimentary capacities necessary to execute simple tasks.

Who is right? Obviously, all three hypotheses are oversimplified in order better to demonstrate the expected trends of the skill structure of the work force. More importantly, they use what seems to be too narrow a conception of human qualities in the work force, tending to concentrate on capacities that are recognised as 'skills' but which are in fact only part of the qualities which people must possess and activate in order to be productive, even in jobs with low formal skill requirements. To a large extent it is on such non- recognised skills and their mobilisation and efficent utilisation that the efficent use of modern technology will depend. Thus the impact on the skill structure of the workforce depends on two different, yet related, factors: the definition and concept of 'skills'; and the way these skills are utilised in the workplace.

Skills and qualifications

'Skills' are commonly understood as human capacities which are acquired through education and training and which enable a person to work more or less efficiently at different levels of physical dexterity, intellectual capacity and responsibility for the quality of one's own work and/or for the work of other persons.

Speaking of 'skills', we generally think of well defined capacities either embodied in individuals or incorporated in jobs (then expressed in terms of 'job requirements'). We have a clear idea how such skills are produced (through education and training) and how they are applied (through execution of work functions defined according to 'job requirements'). This vision may be quite useful in everyday life. However, it assumes at least implicitly that the skills acquired are actually **applied** in work and that existing work situations represent either the only possible or the optimal solution at a given time. Furthermore, such a vision tends to consider the relationship between skills and work as a **static** one, as if skills were learned once and for all during a limited period of education and training and then applied steadily throughout working life.

Experience shows that this is not the case; the interest in continuing education and training, as well as in changing approaches towards work organisation and management, testifies to the intuitive recognition by most people of a much more dynamic reality. Instead of the term 'skill', which carries with it certain mechanistic and static biases, it may therefore be preferable to use the term 'qualification' (used in German as well as in French) which is broader, including background, orientation and capacities in addition to the mastery of a technique. This implies a broader concept, expressing a **state** (Zustand, etat) as well as a **process**, and taking better into account the initimate interaction between the acquisition and the application of human capacities related to work.

The Impact of Work Organisation and Management

The deskilling, upskilling and polarisation hypotheses mentioned above are based on the notion that the skill requirements for those jobs where new technologies are being applied are predetermined by this equipment. Such 'technical requirements' do influence the skills required for performing a job, but there are a number of other qualifications (e.g. social skills such as communication, co-ordination, or analytic skills) which, together with the technical skills, form the skill profile needed. More important, however, these technical requirements are not predetermined by the equipment but depend to a large degree on the way they are utilised.

A recent study on industrial robots points out that the impact of robots on occupational skills of the workforce (i.e. those workers who are not made redundant or relocated elsewhere in the enterprise) depends on the choice made with respect to work organisation by firms when installing robots. For example, a decentralised production control structure which uses machine operators to maintain and programme robots on the shop floor would tend to use and upgrade existing blue-collar machine operators. On the other hand, greater centralised control of the production process would entail a greater role for white-collar workers in programming and machine-setting, and a subsequent reduction in demand for blue-collar workers.(10) The same is true for the office sector, and the service sector in general, where experts stress that the new equipment can be used to enhance or upgrade skill requirements or, conversely, in such a way as to downgrade existing secretarial and clerical skills.

Nevertheless, historical evidence suggests that the mechanisation of the production process has led to an increasing divison and parcellisation of work. The "scientific organisation of work" introduced by Ford and conceptualised by Taylor and his followers did indeed assign the workers too narrowly conceived, simple and repetitive functions, and thus made obsolete formerly required craft skills.(11)

The danger that the new generation of automated equipment can again lead to a massive deskilling cannot be easily dismissed; however a number of reasons make such large-scale deskilling not inevitable and in fact unlikely. Fordism or Taylorism may have occurred due to particular historical conditions which were different from those prevailing today. The beginnings of industrial mass production were characterised by industrial conflict, and the workforce employed in industrial mass manufacturing consisted to a large extent of non-qualified agricultural populations unfamiliar with the logic of industrial modes of production and corresponding patterns of social relations. Today, the traditional modes of work organisation based on Fordism and Taylorism (i.e. the increase in productivity of human work through the parcellisation of production work and the imposition of ever shorter work sequences) seem to have reached their limits in technological and economic terms. Productivity, which has grown steadily in the industrialised countries, has levelled off since the mid-sixties. The answer to this 'productivity crisis' seems to lie both in the rapidly increasing productivity performance of computer-based machines and in the development and utilisation of those human qualifications, such as initiative, creativity and sense of collective responsibility, which were neglected or, in fact, suppressed by Taylorist modes of production.

Secondly, Taylorisation has come to meet with increasing social resistance. The workers' concern for better and more human working conditions in factories and offices, and the quest for shared control and responsibility, on the one hand, and the concurrent interest of management to mobilise in the most efficient way the productivity potential of modern technology, as well as the productive and innovative potential of the workforce, on the other hand, has led to a number of important changes, sometimes experimental, in the field of workplace organisation, industrial relations and human resources management. These concern the development of new principles regarding the division of work within and between work units in production, management and engineering in order to increase the motivation and responsibility of individual workers and work groups, with respect to both products and the quality of co-operation within the enterprise. New channels of communication and co-operation, such as shop councils, quality circles, expression groups, etc., are intended not only to result in smoother co-operation on the shop floor but also to produce innovative ideas concerning the improvement of the work process and the quality of products.

A third factor which operates against further parcellisation of work as a consequence of new technology is the increasing need for production systems to be flexible, i.e. adaptable to frequent changes in the nature of products as well as the sequences in which different products are produced. While earlier mechanisation was conceived to produce great quantities of the same product, computer-based systems can be programmed to adapt to different work tasks according to changing product series. This, it is argued, requires a flexible workforce, i.e. workers whose skills permit them to adapt quickly to changes in the production process, rather than being confined to a narrowly defined and repetitive task.

It follows that although deskilling may occur in practice it is not an inevitable consequence of the introduction of new technologies in the workplace; skill requirements depend largely on the way human resources are managed and utilised. There is no technical determinism such that qualifications are a direct consequence of the technology applied; rather, there is a considerable margin of choice which is influenced not only by consideration of productivity and profit, but also by a number of other factors, that determine the particular socio-economic environment in which technological change occurs.

Qualification Requirements

What then are the qualifications needed for the jobs which are affected by technological innovation? Given the rapidity of changes affecting the workplace, it is impossible precisely to anticipate future job contents and hence qualification requirements. Generally, therefore, emphasis will have to be put on generic skills, in particular the ability to adapt and learn, rather than on narrow occupation-specific training.

A recent survey, commissioned by the European Community and based on a questionnaire to industry (12), lists a number of general qualities which industry believes will be required from the workforce involved with computer-based systems or equipment:

the capability for analytic thinking applied to different processes of work;
a sense of quantitative appreciation of different processes;
the ability to conduct dialogue with equipment;
a sense of responsibility and a capacity for autonomous work;
the ability to link technical, economic and social considerations in the appreciation of equipment and working methods;
a planned and methodical approach to work.

Many experts agree that 'computer literacy', i.e. knowledge of the computer as a tool for managing and providing access to massive amounts of information, is becoming equivalent in importance to basic literacy. Others think that even computer literacy is not sufficient to cope with the new technological developments and use the term 'technological literacy' to describe a level of understanding of technology in its various forms that goes beyond a familiarity with computers. A recent study of the U.S. Congress' Office of Technology Assessment suggests that technological literacy will indeed soon be required of all members of the workforce as broader and more extensive applications of information technology are made in offices and plants: basic electronics and informatics expertise will be crucial for the great majority of jobs, alongside with general capabilities, i.e. broad basic knowledge and skills, high ability to learn, flexibility, and thinking in terms of abstract, complex systems and processes.(13)

Other researchers are less convinced that these will constitute general skill requirements applicable to the whole workforce.(14) They point out, for instance, that in the U.S., manpower projections by the Department of Labour suggest that the growth of jobs for computer system analysts, data processing machine mechanics, and computer programmers will be relatively small in comparison with such unskilled or semi-skilled job categories as janitors, nurses' aides, fast food workers and waiters. However, these researchers too stress the increasing importance of a basic foundation in logic, analytical reasoning, expressive and communicative skills, and in general the ability to learn and to adapt to changing workplaces and production processes.

Education and Training of Adult Workers

The above discussion has shown that precise predictions about the skill requirements of the workplace are difficult to make, since they depend on a number of variables, such as the degree and the speed of the penetration of new technologies into the workplace or work organisation. It is however clear that an important part of the workplace is already affected by the introduction of new technologies and, as technological change occurs with increasing speed, the move towards microprocessor-based machines and equipment will continue, bringing about changes over the next decade in most of those workplaces still unaffected. It is also apparent that skill requirements have changed and will continue to change as a consequence of technological change. Although there is disagreement about both the upskilling or, conversely, the deskilling effect of this change, and the extent to which the labour force will have to possess basic computer or technological literacy, experts do agree that it is no longer feasible to acquire all the qualifications necessary for working life during a period of initial vocational education and training, and that, therefore, the recurrent training or retraining of adult workers has become increasingly important. While in the past vocationally oriented education and training for adults was mainly a matter of upgrading and thus upward career mobility or, to a far lesser extent, desired career changes, the present rapid and profound change of the workplace makes the ability and willingness to learn a major factor in employability, i.e. in obtaining and holding a job.

In a way, the question of up- or deskilling is deceptive since every workplace that is equipped with computer-based equipment will require skills that are partly **different** from those required before. Some will be more easily acquired than others. Concerning Computer Assisted Design Systems (CAD) it has been said that for a skilled draughtsman to get acquainted with the new system, "minimal special training is required and the best way to learn is just to play with the system in order to understand what each function does". Although this may be a gross understatement - the draughtsman will have to know quite a lot about hardware and software in order efficiently to use the system, to say nothing of maintenance, repair and programming - it is true that some of the ordinary skills to handle the new equipment can be picked up on the job rather than through classroom instruction. However, complex automated systems do need constant maintenance and adjustment, occasional reprogramming, and frequent repair in case of breakdown or malfunctioning. The notion of a workforce that is increasingly divided between those who work with the equipment without knowing anything about how it functions, and those who do the installing, programming, maintenance and repair, is more in keeping with the Taylorist organisation of work than with the modern workplace of computer-based machines and equipment. Studies in five major car manufacturing firms by OECD's Centre for Educational Research and Innovation show that most of the workers who stayed on in their job after the introduction of new technologies needed additional formal training (i.e. provided off the job) in order to cope with the new equipment. Thus, the following gloomy observation is correct:

> The world of work today is the product of one hundred years of 'deskilling' - why take the trouble to let people acquire the skills of craftmanship when all that is wanted is the patience of a machine minder? (15).

Although it is true that many of the old professional skills have lost their importance, the 'patience of the machine minder' is not what is required of the modern worker.

How then do workers learn these new skills which cannot be learned simply on the job? And who provides this training, in particular for those who are made redundant or are being displaced, i.e. those who no longer have a job from which to learn?

Continuing training and retraining of workers and, in particular, displaced workers, is, in many OECD countries, a major policy concern. A variety of programmes are run, sponsored or financed by government agencies. In addition, adult education and training institutions, both non-profit and for profit, play an important role in the provision of training. However, increasingly it is the workplace that provides the training. This is in some instances true even for those workers who are laid off. Training for redundant workers is sponsored by 'the last employer', sometimes jointly with the trade union. This takes the form of counselling, in-house training, and placement programmes to help workers get ready for opportunities that exist in the labour market. In some countries, such as Germany, France and Sweden, public funds are made available to the 'last employer' for this purpose.(16)

Much more important, both in terms of participants and cost involved, is employer-sponsored training for those workers and employees who stay on. Reliable data, however, are difficult to come by. An indication is provided by the money spent by firms for training activities. Even though outlays are difficult to assess, given the complex nature of the costs involved, realistic estimates suggest that this 'shadow education system' accounts for a major part of the total budget for post-secondary education and training. Thus, for example, in the United States the annual amount of money involved was an estimated $30 billion in 1980, which is approximately half of the amount spent for traditional higher education, not counting the wages and salaries of the trainees.(17) In the Federal Republic of Germany, the estimate for private sector outlays for continuing education and training - thus not counting the costs of initial, i.e. apprenticeship training - was DM 10-11 billion in 1979, which constitutes about 70 per cent of the sum spent on higher education.(18) The same order of magnitude applies roughly to France where the law stipulates that employers spend 1.1 per cent of the wage bill for the continuing education and training of their workers (failing which they have to pay a corresponding sum to a special public fund earmarked for training programmes).(19)

In-house training by industry takes a multitude of forms ranging from short introduction and familiarisation courses to substantial retraining programmes of twelve months or more. Although most are designed to sharpen job skills and to update on the state-of-the-art technology utilised in the enterprise, some are more broadly conceived and provide training aimed at developing analytical, managerial, and communication skills. However, in spite of the recognition that the modern workplace and the rate of future change will require a broadly based, adaptable workforce with polyvalent skills, the primary content of current programmes seems to lie in the traditional topics addressed in technical training, i.e. machine operation, maintenance, and safety procedures.(20)

Current in-house education and training programmes by industry focus very little on the basic skills, i.e. traditional literacy and numerical skills. Particularly problematic are those workers who have not even achieved mastery of the basic skills of reading, writing and arithmetic, let alone basic computer or technology literacy. Although school enrolment figures suggest in all the OECD countries that the level of schooling has increased to unprecedented levels, it has been discovered that important parts of the populations are more or less illiterate. In the United States it is estimated that one-fifth of the population does not possess basic reading and writing skills; and in France, normally considered a bastion of European civilisation and culture, some eight million people over the age of 15 are estimated to be incapable of reading, writing and understanding a short and simple text related to their daily life.(21)

As microprocessor and telecommunication technology has invaded all workplaces, or will shortly do so, so it has also reached education and training. Industry, especially those sectors with the most pressing needs for continuing training and retraining, is making increasing use of computer-based training systems. Such systems are equipped with video display and typewriter keyboards complemented by textbooks or videotapes, and courseware has been developed for a variety of fields such as computer programming, maintenance and repair, electronics, robotics and other high technology fields. The novelty is that there is only minimal face-to-face instruction and the trainee learns at his own pace.

> Lessons are presented on the screen in text, drawings and animated graphics, and the terminal prompts the student with information, questions and advice in an encouraging, conversational manner. The student responds by typing on a keyboard or by touching the terminal's pressure-sensitive screen. The screen flashes a response such as 'That's right' or 'No, try again'. The student can progress to the next lesson in the course only after demonstrating competence in the current one. Those who learn quickly and those with some previous training can move rapidly through the course, skipping the sections they do need.(22)

Learning centres equipped with such systems have been installed, for example, by the major United States automobile manufacturers in a number of their plants, and managers say that employees learn about 30 per cent faster than in traditional classrooms, while cost savings have been as much as two-thirds over traditional training methods. Increasingly, traditional educational institutions, including those which provide training and retraining programmes for adults, use similar equipment and course-ware for their students.(23)

Although employers have assumed a greater role than in the past in the training of their workers and employees, adult education institutions continue to have an important role to play. As training for broader qualifications, such as computer literacy, analytical, communication and learning skills, becomes increasingly important, institutions must be prepared to meet changing demands from adults. Demand for job-related yet broadly based education and training will come from those who are out of work and want to acquire qualifications that are marketable and sought after by employers, but increasingly also from workers and employees holding a job, in particular in small and medium-sized enterprises.

Among this latter group the category of so-called professionals will figure prominently, those who are highly educated and well trained, including graduates from higher education institutions. This means that universities and other higher educational establishments are called upon increasingly to offer short-term courses to update and enlarge the qualifications of professionals as well as to make regular programmes at all levels more accessible to adult students.(24)

A particular target group, mentioned above, is those adults who lack basic literacy and numerical skills which are increasingly prerequistites to finding or holding a job. The problem here is primarily one of motivation; the needs of this group cannot be met by waiting for them to come to an educational institution on their own initiative. Rather, appropriate facilities and programmes have to be made available and special incentives put into place for this group to take advantage of them.(25)

In view of the massive change in the workplace and the concomitant need of the great bulk of adults to adapt their qualifications to changing job requirements, the role of continuing education and training can hardly be over-rated. The concept of lifelong learning, permanent education or recurrent education originally conceived some ten years ago,(26) primarily as an emancipatory strategy to enhance equality of educational and social opportunity, is thus reinforced by the technical and economic development in industrialised countries.

As a matter of fact,

> it is difficult to see how this massive task [of managing the changes in the workplace] can be accomplished efficiently without the initiation of a comprehensive system of recurrent education. Such a system must be organised to provide a level of comprehensiveness and adaptability that will accommodate the inevitable demands for workers that are qualified to meet the requirements of the new technologies and work tasks. If such a system is not forthcoming, it is conceivable that severe bottlenecks in production and costly inefficencies in retraining will arise, since the present approach to continuing education and employer training is probably not adequate to anticipate and accommodate the enormous changes that lie ahead. For this reason concerns for future employment and productivity will be powerful stimuli for the development by both states and the national government of a systematic and responsive approach to the promotion and provision of recurrent education.(27)

Ten Theses in Lieu of Conclusions

(1) Although technological innovation has massively increased the

productive capacity of machines, human knowledge and skills are no less important than in the past; on the contrary, the development and application of automated and flexible systems, as well as the full realisation of their productive potential, depend on the way human resources are developed and utilised.

(2) Structural and technological change will not only affect the level of employment but also profoundly change the workplace, i.e. work organisation and the contents of jobs. Telecommunication and micro-electronics technology are expected to penetrate all sectors of economic activity, but technological change in the workplace will occur at different speeds.

(3) The way in which work organisation and job content are affected depends to a large extent on choices that are made by both designers and the users of the new technologies. There is no technical determinism, and the fear that a greater degree of micro processor based automation will inevitably lead, as in the early stage of mechanisation in the manufacturing industry, to an increasing parcellation of the work process and a reduction of work content, and thus a degrading of the quality of work, is not supported by evidence available so far.

(4) Due to the rapid speed of change in the workplace, workers must become increasingly flexible, ready and able to adapt their qualifications to changing job requirements.

(5) The new technologies at the workplace have an important impact on skill requirements; there is disagreement, however, about the extent to which such technological innovation will entail a general need for upskilling or, conversely, lead to deskilling. There is little doubt that certain skills, in particular some of the craft and technical skills, will lose their importance while others will be increasingly in demand. These include analytical, expressive, communicative skills and a basic understanding of the functioning of micro-processors and modern technology (computer literacy).

(6) The need of the workforce for flexible and adaptable qualifications means that specific skill training is no longer sufficient preparation for working life. Training programmes must develop human initiative, train the mind and enhance flexibility and the ability as well as the willingness of workers to adapt to change. The emphasis of vocational training will be less on knowledge per se, more on understanding of the automated production process, on decision-making, problem-solving, communication and ability to work in teams.

(7) Working adults will need additional qualifications in order to adapt to present and future changes in the workplace. Enterprises and firms provide a good deal of continuing training and retraining, primarily for their own personnel but in some instances also for workers made redundant as a consequence of new labour-saving technologies.

(8) Enterprise-sponsored training opportunities are not available for the great bulk of those out of employment, or for workers in small and medium-sized firms. Training for these groups must be provided by education and training institutions. Adult education must also cater to the specific needs of those adults who do not possess the basic literacy and numerical skills that are increasingly becoming minimum prerequisites for obtaining or holding a job.
(9) In response to this demand, institutions for adult education and training must develop appropriate programmes and courses that provide participants with broadly-based polyvalent and flexible qualifications. Government and the private sector must initiate policies and strategies with a view to creating mechanisms and incentives that enable and induce adults effectively to participate in such programmes. The use of new educational technologies will help to overcome some of the existing barriers to adult participation in continuing training programmes.
(10) Technological change at the workplace and the need for the recurrent adaptation of workers' skills are thus reinforcing the concept of lifelong learning and recurrent education. It must be stressed, however, that adult education embraces a far broader range of educational and social objectives than training for technological change; the concepts of recurrent education and lifelong learning must not be understood as mere instruments to adapt workers to the changing skill demands of the labour market, but rather remain basic strategies for the enhancement of personal fulfilment, development, and equal opportunity and life chances.

REFERENCES

(1) For all these data, see **OECD Labour Force Statistics 1969-1980,** Paris 1982; and **OECD Employment Outlook,** Paris 1983.

(2) For details, cf. R.B. McKersie and W. Sengenberger, 1983, **Job Losses in Major Industries,** Paris (OECD).

(3) P. Kalmbach et. al., 1982, "Robots' Effect on Production, Work and Employment", **The Industrial Robot,** Volume 9, No 1. March.

(4) OECD, 1983, **Industrial Robots - Their Roles in Manufacturing Industry,** Paris, p. 79.

(5) In **Time,** 30th May 1983, p. 52.

(6) Centre mondial pour le developpement des ressources humaines, Rapport a Monsieur le President de la Republique par Jean-Jacques Servan-Schreiber, Paris, October 1981.

(7) OECD, 1982, **Micro-Electronics, Robots and Jobs**, Paris.

(8) OECD, **Industrial Robots**, p. 14.

(9) H. Levin and R. Rumberger, 1983, **The Educational Implications of High Technology**, Stanford (IFG policy paper).

(10) OECD, **Industrial Robots**, p. 83.

(11) cf. H. Bravermann, 1974, **Labor and Monopoly Capital**, New York (Monthly Review Press).

(12) A. Sorge, 1981, **Micro-electronics and Vocational Education and Training**, Berlin, International Management Institute.

(13) Office of Technology Assessment (OTA), 1983, **Automation and the Workplace-Selected Labor, Education and Training Issues**, Washington, D.C.

(14) See Levin/Rumberger op.cit.; see also G. Bonham, "Some Questions about Science Literacy", **Change Magazine**, July/August 1980.

(15) E.F. Schumacher, 1977, **Good Work.**

(16) For details, see OECD, **Job Losses in Major Industries**, p. 80-81.

(17) Cf. R. Craigh and C. Evers, 1981, "Employers as Educators: The Shadow Education System", G. Gold, **Business and Higher Education**, San Francisco, Jossey Bass.

(18) F. Edding, 1982, "Financing of Continuing Education and Training in the Federal Republic of Germany", D. Kuhlenkamp and H.G. Schütze, **Costs and Financing of Continuing Education**, Frankfurt (Diesterweg).

(19) Cf. P. Caspar, 1983, "The French Law on Continuing Vocational Training", H. Levin and H.G. Schütze, **Financing Recurrent Education**, Beverly Hills, Sage.

(20) OTA, **Automation and the Workplace**, op.cit.

(21) **U.S. News and World Report**, 17th May 1982, and **Le Monde**, 15 January 1984.

(22) P. Samples, 1984, "Using Computers to Retrain Workers", **Economic Impact**, 84/1, Washington D.C.

(23) Op. cit.

(24) For example, Advisory Council for Adult and Continuing Education, **Continuing Education: From Policies to Practice**, Leicester 1982; and Federal Ministry of Education and Science, **Continuing Professional Education Through Higher Education- Perspective and Models**, Bonn 1983 (in German).

(25) For a thorough discussion of this problem, see J. Lowe, 1982, **The Education of Adults - A World Perspective**, 2nd ed., Paris (Unesco), Chapter 3; and K. Rubenson, 1984, "Participation in Vocational Education: A Research Review", OECD/CERI, **Recurrent Education: Participation, Cost and Financing**, Paris.

(26) Cf. OECD/CERI, 1973, **Recurrent Education. A Strategy for Lifelong Learning**, Paris; and E. Faure et. al., 1972, **Learning To Be**, Paris (Unesco).

(27) H. Levin/H.G. Schütze, 1983, "Economic and Political Dimensions of Recurrent Education", Levin and Schütze (eds), **Financing Recurrent Education - Strategies for Increasing Employment, Job Opportunity and Productivity**, Beverly Hills, Sage.

B. Characteristics and Benefits of Integrating Higher Education for Working Adults with Production

Min Shufen

Workers' education is both an outcome of large-scale production in modern society and an important means of reproduction of productive forces. It can rapidly convert potential into actual productive forces. Since the birth of New China and with the development of the national economy, higher education for blue and white collar workers has made notable progress. In-service adult higher education in Shanghai has also assumed a flourishing new aspect. There are 92 institutions offering adult higher education. Two are under the auspices of the municipal authority, namely the Shanghai Municipal Spare-time Institute of Technology and the Shanghai Television University; ten are run by district administrations; 58 are managed by various enterprises; and 22 evening and correspondence institutes are set up by regular universities. They currently offer close to two hundred disciplines, with a total enrolment of 120,000 students (50,000 registered for undergraduate and specialised programmes, and 70,000 for single subjects and short courses). In the last three years, the undergraduate and specialised programmes have had a total of over 31,000 graduates. The institutions offering adult higher education in Shanghai have a full-time faculty totalling over 4,000 members, with supporting part-time faculty. Beginning in 1982, the Municipal Bureau of Higher Education has been giving examinations for participants of the self-study higher education programme; a total of 36,787 have been registered for these examinations in the last two years.

The integration of education with productive labour was first proposed by Marx in the mid-nineteenth century, bringing to light the inherent relationship between these two. After the birth of New China, the government's education policy has been "to enable everyone who receives an education to develop morally, intellectually and physically and become a worker with both socialistic consciousness and culture". It has always maintained that the integration of education with productive labour should be one of the basic principles of education.

After more than thirty years of practice, our understanding of workers' education has deepened. The following are derived from experience gained at the Shanghai Municipal Spare-time Institute of Technology.

(1) In order to integrate education with productive labour, we must adapt ourselves to the needs of industrial development of Shanghai and adjust and rearrange our curriculum constantly. Our Institute started

out with 14 specialisms, but following various changes only three remained. The objectives of the specialised courses and their content have also been updated. To meet the growing demands of industrial production, a number of new specialised courses have been set up, such as Metallic Material Testing and Heat Treatment, Industrial Automation, Applied Computer Science, Plastic Moulding and Processing, Quality Control, and special courses for cadres doing political work. Further changes will accord with the needs of the new technological revolution and the results of the large-scale manpower forecast carried out in Shanghai.

(2) Since our students are working adults coming from different professions with varying demands, classes are conducted at different levels, with different standards and in various forms. Besides the twelve undergraduate specialised courses for systematic study, we also set up short-term refresher courses for workers and engineers, and courses in single subjects. We also have courses commissioned by or jointly sponsored with the various commerce and industrial departments, aimed at fostering specialists. Among these courses are the Japanese course for training interpreters, the Electronics course for the Baoshan Iron and Steel Complex, and the college level Electronics course jointly organised with the No. 1 Television Factory of Shanghai. At present, the undergraduate programme has an enrolment of 2,800, and the short course programme an enrolment of 3,700. Since the establishment of the Institute, a total of 3,800 students have graduated from the two programmes.

(3) For enrolments, we hold the principles of "voluntary application, institutional recommendation, entrance examination, and admittance according to merits". Upon graduation, the students are to return to work in their original units. The government has stipulated that working adults are to continue receiving full pay during study, and after graduation are entitled to the same status as graduates from regular universities and colleges in terms of qualification, employment and pay scale.

(4) In view of the fact that those enrolled in our education programmes often lack a systematic theoretical knowledge, we emphasise teaching of the basics so as to help students lay a solid foundation for improving their professional skills. Making full use of the fact that the students possess a great deal of practical experience, we stress practice, and endeavour to raise their ability to apply theoretical knowledge to analyse and solve engineering and technical problems. While offering specialised courses, we take into consideration the emerging new

technological revolution and the students' respective professions. When students are preparing their graduation theses, we require them to select as their subjects those engineering and technical problems existing in actual production, so that they will have a good command of knowledge and be more capable of solving problems independently.

(5) It is necessary to build up a faculty devoted to the cause of socialist education, and rich in theoretical knowledge and practical experience. At present, our school has a full-time faculty of 450. Of these 350 are middle-aged, with ten to twenty years' teaching experience. They love their profession and are very familiar with actual production. They constantly absorb the latest developments in science and technology and the rich experiences of students in production, to replenish and update their teaching. While teaching, they combine theory with practice and make every effort to guide the students to study for the purpose of application.

Following this short description of our practice and experience in combining education with productive labour, I will briefly analyse the benefits of integrating adult higher education for workers with productive labour. We hold that education is potentially an important element in production, and an investment in the development of intellectual resources. Such investment will bring economic as well as social returns. The economic benefits of in-service adult higher education may be summarised as follows.

(1) How much it costs to run an education programme is doubtless one criterion of its economic value. Recently, we surveyed the last two years' graduates from three schools offering various forms of in-service adult higher education and from one regular university. The results revealed that the total expenses incurred in training an adult in-service student and a regular college student (the students' pay and stipend excluded) are 2,627 yuan and 4,534 yuan respectively. Thus the former is much lower than the latter. Another distinctive feature of in-service adult higher education is that its students are both consumers of investments in higher education and producers who create wealth by transforming intellect into productive forces. For instance, a student at the Shanghai Municipal Sparetime Institute of Technology who came from No. 4 Loading District of the Shanghai Docks, applied the principle of mechanics that he learnt to modify the reel of the electric crane used by his unit, prolonging the service life of steel cables from five to six days to two or three months, thus saving more than US$30,000 in foreign exchange per year. Moreover, the greater part of the outlay for in-service adult higher education is borne by local authorities and various enterprises, making no demand for state appropriations.

(2) In analysing the economic benefits of adult higher education, two aspects should be noted. One is the emergence of a contingent of competent managerial personnel, and the consequently improved management. 1,273 out of 1,482 graduates from the Shanghai Municipal Spare-time Institute of Technology in the years 1964-66 have become either technical or managerial cadres, 85 per cent of the total. Among them, in the technical category, 15 are chief or deputy chief engineers, 341 are engineers, and 436 are technicians; and in the managerial category, four are managers, assistant managers or heads of department, 117 are factory directors or deputy directors, 430 are section chiefs, deputy chiefs or heads of workshop. They have played a major role in improving management and operations, carrying out technical transformation, and raising labour productivity, thus greatly enhancing the production of their enterprises.

Another aspect of economic benefits is that the investment in in-service adult higher education also pays off in the form of application of up-to-date technology to production. For example, two graduates from the Shanghai Municipal Spare-time Institute of Technology, making use of what they had learnt in the course, designed a set of micro-computer-controlled presses for punching electric motor hoods. In the past, compound dies were used, each costing 20,000 yuan, and hoods were punched on 100-ton presses. The new system uses a micro-computer to control a set of four four-ton presses in the continuous punching of hoods. The four dies needed cost only 2,000 yuan together. Thus the cost of production is greatly reduced. Besides, this system may be adapted to punch hoods of different specifications. The system has been recommended by the Ministry of Machine Building for popularisation all over the country. Graduates from the Institute in the years 1964-66 have accomplished research projects and made technological innovations, while at school and after graduation, totalling 5,073 items. Sixteen of these research findings, and innovations were awarded national scientific and technological prizes; 30 others won provincial or municipal prizes. This shows the degree of economic benefit derived from in-service adult higher education programme.

We have come to realise, through practice, the correctness of the principle of integrating education with productive labour. Compared with regular universities, institutions of higher learning offering courses for adults are in a better position to put this principle into practice, because their students come directly from various enterprises with a working background. They have accumulated certain production and management experience, and have a strong sense of purpose in learning. Education is combined with productive labour and this has a direct bearing on the quality of teaching. For all its soundness and accomplishments, the in-service adult higher education programme in

Shanghai, as it is, still needs constant improvement. Its specialisms and curricula, length of courses, syllabus, teaching materials and teaching methods are yet to be fully adapted to this special form of education. Its potential advantages ought to be brought into full play.

Premier Zhao Ziyang pointed out recently that: "economic vitalisation is dependent on scientific and technological advances. Science and technology must be oriented to economic construction. Market competition, in the final analysis, is a competition in science and technology, a competition of talents."

Generally speaking, the level of scientific research, the technological level of production, and the level of management in present day China still lag behind advanced world levels. It remains a major subject for we education workers in spare-time colleges for working adults to study how most effectively to integrate education with productive labour, and how to raise the cultural and scientific level of our workers. We enjoy many advantages. The government has already mapped out short-term and long-term plans for the development of the national economy; a nation-wide manpower forecast has provided much information; there exist extensive contacts and cooperation between in-service higher education institutes and factories; and the workers are most enthusiastic and diligent in their study for the country's modernisation drive. As long as we reform with determination, experiment and practise boldly, continuously sum up our experience and strengthen our theoretical studies, we are sure to achieve still greater success in carrying out the principle of integrating education with productive labour and pushing forward in-service adult higher education. We hope to strengthen our academic exchanges with organisations and scholars engaged in higher education for working adults from various countries and to learn from their rich experience, thus further promoting the development of our higher education for working adults.

C. Implications of Technological Change for Adult Education

Michele Jean

Introduction

Since prehistoric times, we have been developing science and technology to make our work and daily life easier. Until the last few years the main contribution of machinery has been motor power, which lessened the need for physical labour. But we are now passing from the era of simple machines to the era of elaborate machines which deal with information. This evolution, sometimes called the technological revolution, already affects every area of our life: in the factory, in the office, at home and in cultural pursuits. Slowly, work, education and recreation are being transformed. Every type of worker is affected in some way: executives, labourers and service personnel. Thus our reactions to scientific and technological progress - the ability of the human being to adapt and to make the best use of it - become particularly significant. For we are witnessing the dawn of a new era, greeted by some as one of great promise, while others warn of great danger.

The Impact of Technological Change

The impact of technological progress on human society has probably been the greatest focus for the energies of sociologists and anthropologists (among others) over the last decade. Perhaps the headiest promises and the direst predictions have been reserved for information and communication technologies, especially television and microtechnology. But all areas of scientific research and progress have been similarly scrutinised, by the prophets both of doom and of salvation. Each have given their point of view on the progress foreseen in physics (especially nuclear physics), biotechnology, and even medicine.

Modern technology has taken a giant step over the last few years. We have reached a point where micro-computers can endow common machines with artificial intelligence. This intelligence, while limited, nevertheless makes these machines self-sufficient to the point that they can substitute for human beings, or at least significantly help with a host of particularly fastidious or repetitive tasks.

Only in the last few years have we begun to see practical applications of the new technology in our factories, offices, and homes. We now have at our disposal personal computers, specialised networks providing access to data banks, video games, transactional and interactive services - not to speak of even more ambitious administrative technologies, robotics, and computer-assisted manufacture. It has become possible in the last few years to get a personal computer or an 'intelligent terminal' at a fraction of the cost one would have had to spend to buy a computer. We can see that prices will continue to fall over the next few years, assuring that microtechnology, telecommunications and associated technologies will expand at an unprecedented rate over the coming decades.

These machines are also becoming more and more flexible. Their memory banks can hold all the information we need to manage our personal affairs. They can offer access to data banks thousands of kilometres away, giving information on the widest range of subjects. Consider the potential of experimental projects in several countries that in a few years will allow people to deposit or withdraw money from a bank through their home terminals, go 'teleshopping', or make use of professional medical, commercial or scientific services. Alhough many uses are not yet commercially viable, the list of possible applications is virtually inexhaustible. Consider all the tasks technology could handle that have traditionally required hours of finicky work.

The predictive sciences have been active in drawing optimistic or pessimistic scenarios of our future: for everyone wants to know what his or her universe will be like a few years down the road. In Canada, as everywhere, reports proliferate on the expansion of technology, the speed with which it is brought into the workplace and the educational system, and the policies and legislation around it. We really are seeing a change in society. With recent scientific and technological progress, especially in the field of microtechnology and telecommunication, it is clear that human society will evolve within a framework dominated by technology. So we must examine the implications of such change, and what consequences may flow from it.

Potential and Challenges for Society

We sometimes seem to forget that all this change is brought about by and for human beings, not only to increase productivity but also to improve the quality of life. Nevertheless, with our brief experience in the field, we are beginning to get a clearer picture of the impact of these new technologies.

The stakes seem immense: will knowledge, and thus power, be concentrated, or spread? Will thought and culture become robot-like, or information be shared for a convivial society? Will private life and human relations be diminished, or will community life grow? A look at the past suggests the real risk that the most pessimistic scenarios will carry the day. Through the ages, technological progress has for the most part served to concentrate power and knowledge in the hands of the few. Certainly, one cannot deny that there has been progress in access to education, access to consumer goods, the spread of culture, and the improvement of general health. But the realities of human beings becoming alienated, dislocated from their environment and powerless in the face of change; of the real intellectual and material poverty of millions of people: these leave us sceptical over the potential for improvement offered by the new technology.

These changes also threaten to widen the gulf between North and South. The same thing happens among countries as within them: the vendors of technology impose their language and their culture, thus making it even harder for many human communities to maintain their autonomy and catch up to the rest of the world. We do not yet measure the social consequences of these changes very well: carried away with enthusiasm for the potential of technology, we tend to minimise negative effects. When one looks at the question from the point of view not only of States and the economy, but also of the individuals who will have to undergo the changes, the contradictory effects of computerising society become more disturbing. The computerisation of the office and the factory will wipe out a large number of jobs, and change the organisation and the very nature of work. Thousands of workers will face the de-skilling process, and a few will face over-qualification. Work at home will become more common. Teaching will be transformed.

The capacity of people in the future to appropriate this new environment will depend largely on the tools they have been given, especially in their early and continued education. It is not enough simply to ask what the consequences of technology will be. We must above all ask ourselves, given these consequences, if current formal and non-formal education of children and adults is adequate, and what educational planning strategy we should use. Once past the first wild spate of invention and spread of new machines, business and political leaders are beginning to realise more and more that **human potential is the touchstone of a successful technological revolution.** In a number of industrial sectors, and in many offices which began with indiscriminate computer or robot installations, people are now starting to use more humane and appropriate strategies and training. Here adult education, within a perspective of lifelong education, comes into play.

Implications for adult education

When adult education began in Canada at the end of the 19th century, it was a tool for thousands of workers to gain knowledge, especially in agriculture. Nonformal education, in particular, allowed them to keep up with developments in their field and learn new techniques. Later, with industrialisation, professional training in schools and in the workplace was developed for youths and adults. Adult education, over the years, has been a way for concerned client groups to cope with change. It has allowed several groups to prepare themselves not only for their work, but also for fuller participation in making social decisions.

The technological revolution does present us with change but also, in some ways, with continuity. As the American author Richard Bolles pointed out, when speaking of the future we should not paralyse people by speaking only of changes and not of those things which are, and will remain, necessary: the need to know how to read and write, to be innovative and creative, to have a critical awareness.

Education must be able to respond to the needs of thousands of adults for basic and professional training. Nations must take a chance on the development of human potential, which will involve adults in decisions on their own education. Thus, to avoid the trap of overly narrow and rapidly outdated professional training programmes, or of short-term reform, we must press governments for careful development and educational planning. Planning should tie into global policies, taking into account all facets of the life of adults which relate to education. Such policies must examine and coordinate all the educational initiatives necessary, not only for an improved work life but for recreation, culture and society.

Since the contemporary reorganisation of work life will entail shorter working times, we cannot reflect about work without considering leisure time as well. Such policies will allow projects to be oriented to society, and the adult population to take a hand in defining their future, as long as planners take the trouble to build consultation mechanisms into the process.

The 'educative society' we have been talking about for decades really must be put in place now. One result of the development of technology is increasing consciousness of the need for a real system of lifelong education. In Canada, in the space of two years, I have noticed enormous changes in attitude. Business leaders, executives and political men, having themselves had to face in their day-to-day work the inadequacy of their own training to use micro-technology, have to some degree experienced the fears and anguish they have put their employees through all along: the fear of losing one's job, of being underqualified; the lack of effective educational responses.

We must make education the pivot of the technological revolution. Starting from that point of view, we can build programmes to teach the new disciplines, and to adapt older disciplines to deal with change. Education has five main roles to play in this process:

- training qualified man-power, and re-training people in line with technological change;
- organising instruction in the new computer disciplines;
- introducing young people and adults to the computer as a tool for

action and learning;
adapting cultural models (ways of thinking and acting) to technological change;
training teachers to be able to introduce programmes and information into computer systems which are apropriate to a given culture.

In relation to this:

> In the sectors in which the new technology is being widely and rapidly applied, the determination of both early and continued education which the educational system should guarantee should not be based simply on observation of current processes of production and employment structures. Quite a bit of foresight is also necessary. Timetables for implementing adapted early education programmes may be inadequate for pressing needs. Continuing education offers the fastest way to introduce new training programmes, but these are generally too short, too expensive and too superficial to make up entirely for the lack of initial training...(Malan, 1983:3)

So we must take a different approach to the connection between work and education; we must see it as a process in which many elements besides training play a role: age, sex, social class, seniority, management styles, etc. This leads us to consider diversifying educational activities, and to pay more attention to the methods through which technology is transferred. Technological training alone is not enough: we must also ensure that the technological culture is appropriated, through the development of critical judgement and logical thought as well as the ability to communicate. We must therefore link social apprenticeship to technical apprenticeship, especially in countries which have to absorb foreign technologies:

> Apprenticeship should not be considered as a passive process depending solely on the level of the workers' initial training and the time spent in accumulating experience. In the progressive management of a system of production, the body of workers come to new know-how, to weave new information networks among their members, to create new reflexes and behaviours. Apprenticeship is an active and productive process. (Perrin, 1983)

Thus, in transfers of technology, one must take into account the specific technical skills of the workers, and apply them to familiarity with the technical structures of the recipient countries. Nowadays, as several studies have pointed out, technical know-how is no longer merely the result of individual action, but has become an ongoing collective creative process.

In any case, it is important to leave behind a compartmentalised approach to work/training/leisure, and to develop overall adult education policies which aim to link the economic, social and cultural life of the individual. Research should be undertaken to "spell out the connections between society and technology within the education system, considered in all its aspects, especially its cognitive, cultural and social functions" (Reiffers, 1983:1). For although the educational system must respond to needs for manpower, it must not orient itself solely to economic efficiency at the risk of satisfying only a very narrow spectrum of social needs.

We are thus brought back to the issue of social change. For adult education, this means that "if adults are not involved in developing societies of their choice, computerization, instead of being an enriching and liberating factor, will merely engender a growing dependence of individuals on machines, and will throw a large part of the population into a sort of 'social vacuum'". The role of adult education thus consists of equipping adults both to handle technology and to participate in decision-making about it. We must also look for ways to prepare adults for more free time, for methods of work-sharing. Study-leave policies must be developed which will serve both for professional re-training and to enlarge our cultural world. We must introduce trainers and adult educators to the new technologies and to research on adult learning.

The response to these possibilities depends largely on whether governments want to move towards a more equitable sharing of knowledge and power, or to a growing concentration. Our response to these questions will influence, for better or for worse, the future of the women and men who live on this planet.

REFERENCES

Institut Canadien de l'education des Adultes, and Centrale de l'enseignement du Quebec, 1983, "Negocier le virage technologique", proceedings of a seminar on tele-communications held in Montreal in February 1983, Montreal, pp. 267.

Malan, Thierry, 1983, **Politiques de developpement economique et sociale et planification de l'education en France,** Paris. photocopy, unpublished, 24pp.

Quebec, 1982, **Apprendre: une action volontaire et responsable,** final report of the Commission d'etude sur la formation professionnelle et socio-culturelle des adultes, Editeur officiel du Quebec, pp. 872.

Quebec, 1984,**Un projet d'education permanente, Enonce d'orientation et plan d'action en education des adultes,** Editeur officiel du Quebec, pp. 77.

Quebec, Ministry of Education 1983, **Rebatir l'avenir,** report of the working group on telecommunications in education (working paper), June, 1983, photocopy, 38pp.

Perrin, J., 1983 **L'apprentissage des savoir-faire industriels peut-il etre integre dans une planification de l'education,** Grenoble, photocopy, unpublished, 23pp.

Reiffers, J.L., 1983, rapporteur, report of working group I: **Les implications pour la planification de l'education des politiques de developpement technologique,** seminar of the International Institute for Educational Planning, Paris, October 1983, 6 pages.

Seaborg, Eric, 1983, "They have seen the future", **The Futurist,** October 1983, 78-82.

Trudel, Lina, 1982, **L'informatisation: pour le meilleur ou pour le pire,** paper presented to the conference "Towards an Authentic Development: The role of Adult Education", Paris, October 1982, 19pp.

D. Panel Commentary and Discussion

Farrell noted how both Schütze and Min Shufen had first necessarily defined the nature of the workplace, thereby describing the contexts for adult education in the workplace, which are markedly different. Both concluded that recurrent adult education has never been more important: in the case of China as a means to achieve the goals of modernisation; in the case of the older industrialised nations, as a way of coping with the changing workplace and job displacement resulting from introduction of new technology. Given these different pressures, naturally the resulting policies differ as between China and the older industrialised countries. The former is embedding the integration of education with productive labour in a way not achieved by the latter, even including the European countries most advanced in this respect; witness for instance the support given to workers to participate in such activities. In terms of access, however, many of the industrialised countries appear to show greater flexibility over entrance procedures.

Noting Schütze's stress on flexibility, and on qualifications (rather than skills) in describing educational needs, Farrell looked for some development of the idea in terms of implications for the curriculum. For example, should every worker have a theoretical as well as a skill-based knowledge of the new technology? Or does this imply a general educational approach more in the liberal tradition as described by Jennings? Views expressed by Chinese members of the Symposium suggested support for a curriculum requiring intellectual, physical and cultural learning rather than merely job skills. Turning to the scenario which included overall net loss of jobs through technological change, Farrell referred to the need for community-based educational strategies as a means of increasing workplace employment opportunities. There were indeed already examples of this, with educational and consultative support to people to start their own small businesses using appropriate technology. Reliance on large-scale enterprises to create employment seemed inadequate.

Finally Farrell noted the rapid proliferation of adult education providers related to production in China and other countries alike. While Schütze noted a shift towards the workplace, neither speaker has directly addressed the role of trade unions. And what, especially in North America, might the future hold in terms of unions as adult education providers beyond what is directed just at maintaining their own organisation?

Taking up Farrell's observations about the curriculum and emphasising rather curricula in the plural, Stock called for analysis into sub-divisions on the following lines. First, upgrading of the existing workforce within enterprises in both narrow and broader senses including the higher levels of continuing professional education; sandwich, or cooperative, that is to say full-time blocks of study, should be considered as well as part-time and spare-time courses. Secondly there was a need, which China too would have to face, for redeployment into new industries from those with declining labour needs; a prerequisite was much theoretical, technical and social analysis of new industry and also of categories of education, general as well as skill-specific, overseas study and experience as well as sandwich courses, etc. Thirdly, there was education for potential redeployment where labour market needs were unavoidably uncertain, including: Unified Vocational Preparation, based on analysis of the probabilities of new scientific, technological and social developments; work directed towards the creation of new support service work areas and jobs; and provision designed to assist older workers to move out of possibly redundant production roles into voluntary roles in which, supported by a pension, they could contribute creatively to society.

Horn agreed with the view that in developing countries adult education should initially concentrate all efforts on social and economic development, meaning the process which enables individuals and groups to meet basic needs particular to them, including food, shelter, education, and social, political and cultural participation. His own organisation, the German Adult Education Association, accordingly supported income-generating projects with African, Asian and Latin American partners, rather than projects of a more general educational kind. Cultural activities ought also to be relevant in income-generating programmes according to the particular context and environment.

Noting the connection between production-oriented education and the introduction of new technologies in the society as a whole, Horn observed that in most industrialised countries adult education was not to be considered only as a service to employment; other factors needed consideration, as a new dimension of adult education. New electronic technology made it possible for 60-70 per cent of all female and male workers to be 'set free' (a phrase chosen deliberately to foster change of attitude) in the future. Already the working day, week and life had shortened, and this would continue in the future still further. Paid educational leave would increase. Not only would the world of work change dramatically; the entire way of life would be influenced and changed by new technology. Adult education would therefore need to prepare people for new social and economic circumstances and thus avert social disorientation and friction. The key political question for the future was how to distribute the growth of national income among those in conventional work and those set free from this; also how to share more of the wealth of industrialised countries with the poorer nations. All this implied new concepts of adult education, and total restructuring of traditional education systems, putting the new technologies to the service of a learning society, rather than allowing societies to become slaves to these new technologies. A concept shift towards popular education was also needed. Adult education, and international cooperation in this field, had lost their popular character and become too abstract, hollow and technocratic.

Referring to Min Shufen's account of work in Shanghai, Al-Nassri found the teaching method she described too traditional, and unable to cope with the urgent needs. There was need for a well-defined and systematic faculty programme to ensure that educators of adults are themselves practically oriented and up to date with new technology. Were the conclusions pointing to enhanced productivity through adult education based on a large enough number of cases? A recent survey in Iraq involved over 2,000 engineers who had taken part in some form of continuing education, and an equal number of supervisors. Sixty-two per cent of participants and 49 per cent of supervisors felt that attendance at courses had increased productivity; 16 per cent of participants were promoted or assumed new responsibilities within twelve months. Other gains included dissemination of knowledge gained and social effects on those taking part.

Professional consultancy presented one mode of interaction between academic faculty and industry. Often this was left to individuals, was unorganised, and did not relate to academic duties. At the University of Technology, Baghdad, there had been success with the consultancy firm being a part of the University, yet financially independent. Profits are distributed to participating faculties according to their contribution of effort, while the firm competed with private firms successfully on an equal footing. Phyllis Cunningham concluded the panel discussion with a practical example of Schütze's theoretical approach in looking at part of the American system of work-oriented adult education, as follows:

> Both the public and private sectors are providers of educational programs for adults directed toward preparation for work. Publically funded programs are scattered throughout the federal bureaucracy including programs in the military, vocational rehabilitation, corrections, health, humanities, welfare, and commerce. The three largest labor power programs are Vocational Education (Department of Education), Job Training and Partnership Act (JTPA) (Department of Labor), and Cooperative Extension (Department of Agriculture). The private sector includes business and industry as well as continuing professional

education.

Vocational Education begins in the public schools, continuing into post-secondary institutions as technical education. Seventeen million students were served in 1980; four million of these are in adult programs along with an unspecified number of mature adults in post-secondary programs. Since public education is a responsibility of each state, the vocational system is highly decentralised, taking various forms within states. However, the occupational areas are generic and include agriculture, business and office, home economics, marketing and distribution, technical and trade-industrial. Adult vocational education is carried on primarily in 720 community colleges, 162 technical colleges, 504 area vocational schools and over 300 non-collegiate post-secondary schools. A few states also have four-year technical colleges. Each program area operates with local general advisory as well as craft committees, to keep the training relevant to the workplace. The entire system is supported by: 1) a National Research Center; 2) a consortium which regularly analyses curriculum to keep it current with task analyses done in the field; 3) regional curriculum centers to encourage innovation and dissemination; 4) a computerised career guidance and counselling service. Annual appropriations in 1980 were 587 million federal dollars, and about 6 billion dollars in state support.

Cooperative Extension programs assist individual farmers and agribusiness. There were 16,313 full-time equivalent adult education positions in 1982 at the county or state level, people who provided non-formal educational programs. Each state has a Land-Grant University which is responsible for research and technical assistance in the field. Loose coordination is attempted at a federal level. One-third of the funding is at the federal level (328.6 million in 1982) with the other two-thirds coming from the state and county levels.

JTPA is the newest labor power program. Although the name changes, essentially it can be traced to the civil rights Economic Opportunities Act of 1963. The target audience here is the unemployed and the under-employed; recently there has been attention paid also to structural unemployment. Federal funds flow to the states, where public officials and private industry in partnership distribute training funds either to private industry for job training or to post-secondary collegiate and non-collegiate as well as proprietary training institutions. Each local program works with a Private Industry Council to promote training for jobs available within the area. Federal funds in 1983 amounted to 3.4 billion dollars.

Business and Industry training programs have increased markedly in the past ten years. Currently it is estimated that over 60 billion dollars annually is spent on educational training service and products. One of the largest industries, American Telephone and Telegraph, listed their annual training costs at 1 billion dollars. This included 10,000 course offerings at which, at any one time, 10 to 15,000 adults would be engaged in formal learning averaging from 3 to 5 days' duration.
Another major business, International Business Machines, reported 10 million hours of training for its employees last year. The range of programs extended from entry level training to executive development. In a 1977 study of 2,798 companies with at least 500 employees, two out of five firms had full-time employees responsible for training. This section of adult education, called Human Resource Development (HRD), is currently experiencing great growth.

Continuing Professional Education (CPE) is also a rapidly increasing sector of adult education. Its size can only be estimated, but clearly its growth has to be measured in terms of a 100 per cent increase in the last 5 years (some say perhaps 200 per cent). Provision of services is through universities, professional associations, and private entrepreneurial groups. In 1978, some 16 professional groups were mandated by the state to engage in CPE as a requirement for practice. The provision and recording of CPE activity differs for each profession. The emphasis is on updating, upgrading, and improved performance at the workplace.

Issues

(1) Adult vocational education is overwhelming the field and contributes greatly to the professionalisation of adult education. This professionalisation of the field is not seen as a positive development by some.

(2) Vocational programs have in general highly behaviouristic orientations and curricula which are perceived by some as being antithetical to an informed, broadly educated public.

(3) Though 'affirmative action' programs for racial and ethnic minorities, women, and the handicapped are formally addressed on

publicly funded programs, increasingly the majority of these programs reinforce the dominant culture.

(4) Ideologically, curriculum development is being taken over by multinational corporations, which can be seen at best as reinforcing efficiency and effectiveness in production as the "bottom-line", or, at worst, as a monopoly on the social control of knowledge.

(5) Some fear that emphasis on development of pedagogical (andragogical) methods leads to emphasis on the technology of adult education and seriously weakens historical and sociological analysis within the field.

In general discussion the question was raised who really benefits from education for production, and the extent to which programmes are designed to make workers adjust to unsatisfactory conditions. One speaker, observing the large increase in private sector expenditure within the totality of higher education, specifically in France, asked whether the universities were to be completely reorganised in response to technological change, or to continue giving traditional education. A speaker from Eastern Europe pointed out that Schütze's concept frame was West European, and that a different frame was employed in the socialist countries not focussed simply on a flexible labour market and job skills.

At the conclusion of this discussion, both main speakers acknowledged the important role of trade unions, and the great significance of new technologies, socially as well as in terms of jobs and retraining. Schütze argued that change implied a need for more flexible and generic training; there was a need to specify requirements in each work area in great detail (for instance in welding robotics); at the same time broader skills were required to monitor changes and keep up to date, rather than narrow. Expressing disagreement with Cunningham, Schütze did not see higher education as necessarily a distinct field from adult education. While much of what took place in higher education was in fact skill training, the mission of higher education was wider than just preparation for employment.

In the discussion which followed the presentation of Jean's paper, Charles Wong suggested looking also at the direct impact of technological change on adult education, as distinct from its impact on society and thence on adult education. As to the latter, the discovery of tools had altered human life irreversibly, as studies of the introduction of the plough in China and elsewhere indicated. Science and technology had had a tremendous impact from the simple tools of prehistoric times; perhaps the introduction of micro- technology and bioengineering should be seen as simply further incidents in the same series. In his view we are not so much dominated by technology as dominated by others through technology. While work and living patterns have been drastically altered by technology we have on the whole adapted to these changes well; the failure is in managing the domination by others through technology.

Reflecting upon distance education and technology available for education in the sixties and seventies, we can recall that many people were buying audio and video equipment - tape recorders and VCRs - for education. Yet even now only a small proportion of new technology is being used for education. The new technology is not being put to good use. Education is still at the stage of cottage craft industry: now might be the time to consider what some at the British Open University call industrialised education.

A prerequisite to coping with technology is understanding it. Even simple household technical appliances like the washing machine are understood by very few people. Adult education has a significant role to play in seeing that people are not dominated by others through technology. Without addressing the difficult tasks of developing social awareness, independent thinking, the ability to make sound judgements, moral and spiritual education, the exercise of democratic rights, without genuine development in these areas, we will not be able to cope with the development of technology in all its implications.

Moro'oka reflected on the five previously identified areas of adult learning in terms of technological development. In the physical aspect it surely made work, study and recreation easier than before, while taking away much of the need for human muscular power. In the social aspect it gives effective means of communication. The telephone had reduced the need to write letters, contributing to the increase of illiteracy in some so-called developed countries. It did nothing to enhance face-to-face communication, nor to reduce discrimination and ethnocentrism. In the economic and productive aspect technological development surely contributed to efficiency of production, but the efficiency derived from the innovative means themselves rather than from those handling the equipment. Mechanised and competitive mass production also produced many trivial and useless things, and information only for commercial profit. Television also fostered inactivity, a reduction in direct handling and perception, a problem of expansion in surrogate or quasi- experience.

Moro'oka appreciated the possibilities presented in the cultural aspect of self-fulfilment, however, in modern fields of creativity such as music, where artists can express themselves in new ways, as with synthesisers. Here opportunities were widened. As for political decision-making, computers, data processing, modern transport etc. did enhance possibilities but did not guarantee quality in how they are used. There was a need to stress 'liberal education' more to counteract deficiencies in the uses to which technological development were put. The disciplining of the judgement, the enlivening of the imagination, the widening of the sympathy: these authentic human qualities could not be replaced by man-made tools and machines.

Professor Sichev, in speaking of adult education in the USSR from the perspective of technological change and the workplace, laid stress upon the importance attached to correspondence education which could be harmonised with the needs of production. Training and updating in science and technology had proved very successful using part-time and correspondence methods. Further improvement might be sought through intensifying individual work, improving the quality and control of instruction and study generally, enhancing the knowledge and skills of teaching staff, and expanding and strengthening the network of correspondence and part-time higher education centres.

In subsequent plenary discussion, Rubenson reflected upon adult education's 'uneasy relationship' with the workplace and with labour market issues, observing also that 'the long arm of the job' had effects outside the workplace. Polarisation of the workforce between high skills and deskilling implied totally different policies than seeking more generally qualified people across the board. We should beware of work going in one direction and adult education in another. Barrow echoed this concern in speaking against compartmentalisation: adult education must be integrated to contribute to total people's development.

Several speakers referred to the spillover effects of economic and social change from new technologies in the North upon the societies of the Third World. New cultural models were implied by the introduction of industry. Machines could not do everything: how can the old and oral cultures adapt to the new technologies? Adult education should embrace all, including industrial, technology. Each country, it was asserted, should find its own mode of adapting technology and its own culture, integrating these to protect the unique culture. This applied, for example, to the French Canadians of Quebec as well as to the Third World generally.

'Cultural fear of technology' was an almost universal phenomenon: 'the failure to understand one's washing machine'. Greater technological literacy was generally needed. It was suggested that workers' and their unions' concern should be and was increasing with equality of educational opportunity as a whole, rather than just with specific vocational and unionist skills: another echo of the plea to avoid compartmentalisation.

Group discussion of the relationship between education and scientific and technological change centred upon Chinese theory of the development of humanity and the development of technology: the history of civilisation was the history of technology. In general, science and technology should enhance happiness, but they could also lead to harm; education was needed to ensure the desirable application of developments. There was discussion whether this differed from the Marxist doctrine that the history of civilisation is the history of class struggle. Changes in social structure will affect the use of science and technology; it was a question of who controls education. If it is in the hands of the people, science and technology will be used for the people. Different Chinese views were expressed about the history of civilisation being the history of class struggle: for some they are the same thing: for others it is "one part in the long river of history". There was however clear agreement that the Chinese science and technology would not lead to unemployment and unhappiness but would, rather, reduce the drudgery of labour.

Chapter 5

Literacy: The Moving Target

Reducing and abolishing illiteracy remains a major objective, often the first priority, of adult education programmes and campaigns in many countries of the Third World. In addition illiteracy has been rediscovered, and is seen as a major problem, of large though disputed dimension, in many industrial and post-industrial societies. There has of late been much debate in the adult education journals about the 'fight against illiteracy': not to question the desirability of enabling people to become literate but to examine some of the assumptions and unintended, undesirable, side-effects of some of the strategies adopted. The use of 'league tables' of statistics to compare national progress towards total literacy has also come under criticism. The concept of attaining universal literacy is misleading since meanings and necessary levels of 'literacy' change with social, economic and technological development: literacy is indeed a 'moving target'.

In this chapter Carman Hunter, a leading authority on illiteracy in the United States, raises key issues, and Musare Al Rawi and Zhao Wenqing present sketches of approaches to literacy work in the Arab World and China respectively, the latter with stress upon the importance of post-literacy continuing education to build on the potential of becoming literate and to avoid relapse into illiteracy. Plenary and group discussion, as summarised in Section D, disentangled several important strands of the 'literacy debate', especially the effect of different political, economic and cultural factors on motivation and strategy for literacy work. The sessions clearly demonstrated the value of comparative analysis of experience across different places, times, and socio-cultural contexts.

A. Literacy: The Moving Target

Carman St. J. Hunter

The major purpose of this brief paper is to provoke discussion around some of the issues that underlie the 'literacy debate'. Perhaps no other apparently simple concept has created so much difference of opinion as the questions surrounding literacy. Everyone agrees that literacy is important, but beyond that affirmation, there are seemingly endless questions. And there is a series of myths which, though generally discredited by those most knowledgeable in the field, persist in different forms to cloud the discussion.

The Literacy Myths

It is commonly believed that it is possible to compare levels of literacy among nations on an international scale. Various world bodies publish statistics purporting to show the literacy levels in every nation of the world. The figures are quoted to prove a wide range of points by persons who ought to know better. Comparative statistics have no meaning unless they are based on comparable data. In the case of literacy, such comparable data do not exist. There is no set inventory of skills that is measured in every country of the world.

The second myth is that there should be such a set of absolute measures that would allow us to compare one nation with another. But literacy is a set of skills related to the coding and decoding of written language. The ability to code and decode is not an end in itself. It is used by people to accomplish purposes important to themselves within certain cultural and personal parameters. Depending on the level of social, economic, and cultural development, nations require larger or smaller numbers of citizens at different levels of proficiency to fulfil the current needs of the society. Therefore, the question of who needs what level of literacy skills to do what is a key question. This varies from one culture to another and, even, within cultures. An Indonesian villager and an urban Canadian will obviously require different levels of literacy skills. Therefore, even if there were a way to use the same inventory of skills to measure the literacy level of two persons so distant from each other geographically and culturally, the result would tell us very little. The reality is that desirable levels of literacy vary not only within and among nations but also over time. A person living in Paris in 1984 will require considerably greater literacy skills to carry on his/her daily work compared to the skills a Parisian needed in 1924, for example.

This leads us immediately to another myth. It is quite common to hear about the need to eradicate illiteracy. While it is quite possible that a nation could achieve universal basic literacy, that is, reach the goal of having every citizen able to write her name and read a simple passage or write a paragraph that would be intelligible, few, if any, nations have accomplished this task. However, as modernisation takes place, the person with those minimal skills would probably encounter great difficulty functioning in the society. Since literacy competence is not some absolute minimal level of achievement but, rather, a competence that is related to a set of demands that the society lays on those who wish to participate in it, then literacy is, indeed, a moving target. Once a minimal goal has been achieved, another will be required.

The Personal Dimension

In 1962 Unesco stated that:

> A person is literate when he has acquired the essential knowledge and skills which enable him to engage in all those activities in which literacy is required for effective functioning in his group and community and whose attainments in reading, writing, and arithmetic make it possible for him to continue to use these skills toward his own and the community's development.

Once literacy has been described in functional terms, as in this definition, it becomes almost impossible to think only about external measurement. A nation can set desirable literacy levels and measure them. China has at different periods defined literacy as the ability to read 1000, 1500, or 2000 characters. In the same way, the United States has set 4th or 6th or 8th grade reading levels as minimum standards. Employers also screen prospective employees according to levels required for specific jobs. However, these are external standards and apply to specific points in time. The Unesco definition, and others that are similarly broad, is more developmental. As conditions and ambitions change, individuals can only apply internal standards to judge their own levels of achievement. Who, other than the person concerned, can truly say whether he can "engage in all those activities in which literacy is required for effective functioning"? Who, other than the person concerned, knows whether he can "use his skills in his own and the community's development"?

Of course, literacy means reading and writing, but at what level? There is a sense in which the level can only be determined by what a person needs/wants/hopes to be able to do. A nation can set minimal levels that define literacy but these have little to do, in reality, with the objectives individuals set for themselves. Whenever participants in a literacy group are asked why they are seeking literacy skills at whatever level, the responses are very different. One wants to help her children with their studies; another hopes to write letters to a relative living far away. Some have ambitions involving further study and far-reaching vocational goals. Whether or not the minimal standard set externally will be sufficient to enable the individual to reach his personal goals is another sign of how the target changes, in this instance within individual lives. Minimum standards can be set, but are there any maximum standards? These are very personal.

But there is always a limit set, sometimes by the persons themselves and sometimes by conditions that they cannot control. Think for a moment about who the 'illiterates' are in any society. Are people poor because they are illiterate or illiterate because they are poor? This is one of the questions that has caused a great deal of controversy in literacy discussions. Generally it is easiest to avoid further discussion by saying that this is like the question of which comes first, the chicken or the egg. It is a complex matter about which there can be no absolute position. The evidence requires serious consideration.

The Economics of Literacy

Why is it true that the highest rates of absolute illiteracy are in the poorest nations? In China, prior to 1949, large landowners, government employees, and the small affluent class in general were not illiterate. Internal and external oppressions had kept the masses poor. Once the barriers to economic development were removed, a message of hope for the future was delivered together with the great literacy campaigns. Within industrialised nations, the poor (minorities, women, immigrants, older people) have the lowest literacy levels. Their options for development are few, therefore there are less demands for literacy in their daily lives, and, therefore, they have the lowest literacy levels. Economic development and the hope of participating in its benefits cause literacy skills to be more highly prized. Sometimes only the hope is necessary. Change begins to take place before the hope is fully realised. Where dramatic social and political change has occurred, literacy campaigns have had far greater success than in nations where there has been no such change. There is, of course, the possibility of serious problems for individuals and for the masses if hopes are raised and not realised.

All of this is to say that raising the literacy level of marginal people, those left behind in any society, requires more than the provision of an increased number of literacy programmes. Individual or group motivation is in direct relation to the degree of anticipation that the effort to achieve literacy skills will pay off in some tangible way. When economic and social barriers to full participation in society are removed, the motivation for and pursuit of literacy skills follow. When the desire to acquire literacy is present, how can programmes best be structured to meet the needs of adults long excluded from learning opportunities?

Conditions for Success

Just as existing barriers to participation in the full life of the society must be removed before there is a notable change in the desire for literacy, there is, built into the goals and methodology of successful programmes, the assumption that the learners will actually **be** full participants in the future. The following criteria have been developed by a group of literacy specialists: (1)

Learning programmes must emerge from the needs and problems of the learners themselves. Active, conscious, organised participation of the population in all levels and stages of the programme is fundamental.

Programmes must have credibility with, and inspire trust in, the illiterate population in order to motivate and mobilise them for the learning process.

Programmes must include both the study of theory and opportunity for practice.

Programmes should make use of animateurs who are integrated in the life of the local communities where the programmes are to take place.

Learners must have opportunity to participate in the construction of materials to be used in the programme.

At the level of literacy instruction, also, we can see that the target is a moving one. Good instruction does not see illiterate of semi-literate persons as a homogeneous mass to receive identical treatment. Methodology and materials must be shaped as closely as possible to the particular conditions, desires, hopes, and abilities of each group of learners. It is the unlocking of individual creativity and imagination that is at stake. Otherwise, to what end the cultivation of literacy skills? The ultimate target among all the moving targets is the literate individual freely contributing to the building of a better society.

Summary

Literacy does not represent a standard to be reached once and for all. Rather, literacy requirements change according to the opportunities for their use. They differ from one society to another and within any particular society. They also change over time. Motivation to acquire literacy increases as social impediments are removed and economic options increased. Popular literacy campaigns and literacy teaching have greater success when they are accompanied by policy changes in the larger society that move toward greater inclusiveness of all levels of the population in all aspects of national life. They are also more effective when methods and materials are grounded in the daily life of the people served.

REFERENCE

(1) The Commission on Literacy, International Council for Adult Education, meeting in Paris, October, 1982.

B. An Arab World Perspective

Musare Al Rawi

Literacy has always been a human target affecting the movement of societies and development plans. At the same time it has been affected by the changing targets of development plans and the ever changing needs of societies. To deal with literacy as a moving target from the Arab world perspective, this paper touches on the history of literacy in the Arab World and the status of literacy as a moving target.

History of Literacy in the Arab World

When we talk about literacy as a moving target in the Arab World, we have first to consult history about the Arab's contribution to the invention of writing. Samuel Kriemer, in his study **From Sumer's Slabs**, is of the opinion that the invention of the cuneiform writing in ancient Mesopotamia (Iraq) is the most important contribution of this region to the advancement of world civilization. Iraqi historian Taba Baquer asserts that the first form of writing was invented in Mesopotamia during the Warkaa era, 3500-3200 B.C. Edward Keier, tells in **On Clay They Wrote** how people of the Mesopotamia raised the slogan "Let's learn how to write". A clay slab, discovered in Babylon, reads "who will surpass others in writing on the slab, will shine like the sun".

After the fall of the Keldanian Empire in 535 BC the foreign rule (of the Romans and Persians) dominated most parts of the Arab region until the advent of Islam in the Seventh Century A.D. Islam made learning a duty for every muslim man and woman, and raised the slogan of life-long education. It provided the appropriate environment for continuing education without constraint of time or place. It called for learning "from cradle to tomb" and asked muslims to "travel and ask for knowledge even in China". Under the umbrella of Islam, Arab Society achieved the goal of the "Learning-Teaching Society", i.e. the full literate society, during the golden days of the Abassid state in Baghdad and the Ummayad state in Andalusia (1027 A.D.). Thanks to the widespread existence of nonformal education mediaeval society witnessed leaps in scientific thought, in writing and translation, and in literacy and cultural creativity.

This epoch of cultural influence and flourishing science in the Arab World died down and was replaced by successive periods of cultural darkness and destruction from the year 1258, which witnessed the fall of Baghdad, the capital of the Arab Empire, under the domination of the Tartars led by Hulagu. Since this barbaric invasion, the Arab World has not regained its cultural health. For centuries it suffered the natural results of its decline and fall - partition, dependence and foreign domination, and backwardness.

The Status of Literacy as a Moving Target in the Arab World

The twenty-two newly independent Arab states still suffer from the effects of Western colonialism. Illiteracy came at the top of the legacy of the colonial epoch. Despite the intensive efforts exerted by many Arab countries to eradicate illiteracy and provide education, specially primary education, the rate of illiteracy among Arab adults within the productive age-group (15-45) is still around 43 percent, which is much higher than the 28 percent world rate of illiteracy.

The concept of literacy went through a number of stages in the Arab region. While the concept of literacy was confined to teaching educationally disadvantaged adults the skills of reading, writing and arithmetic at the outset of the period of national independence, horizons were gradually extended to take into consideration the international experience in literacy, especially the concepts laid down through Unesco.

The following is a brief review of these concepts.

Fundamental education

This concept emerged after World War II. It meant providing illiterate people with the minimum educational assistance that enabled them to understand the problems of their communities, to recognise the rights and duties of citizenship, to raise their living standard with their own resources, and to participate in developing their social and economic environment. Fundamental education was meant to compensate for the lack of educational service.

Community development

The concept of community development was presented in the mid-fifties after the emergence of the role of the state in the Third World in activating the process of development. The concept aimed at improving the standard of living of the community as a whole, making use of the active participation of both citizens and governments in community development activities. This covered the fields of literacy, agriculture, health and child care. The concept of Social Education was related and aimed at bringing about a close connection between education and social development to promote overall development.

Functional literacy

This concept was presented by Unesco in 1965 as a transition from traditional concepts to the functional concept that connects literacy with overall development. Its basic premise was to provide selected productive workers' communities with intensive literacy programmes and to measure the economic return of literacy among them.

All these concepts were experimented with and even adopted in most Arab countries with the help of Unesco experts and the support of national ministries of education. However, the concrete results, as shown by evaluation efforts, were disappointing. The field studies carried out by the Arab Literacy and Adult Education Organisation (ARLO) in 1976 to analyse the status of illiteracy in the Arab World showed that the traditional approaches would take more than one hundred years to emancipate the present number of illiterates from the bonds of illiteracy.

In terms of quality, ARLO field studies of 1976 revealed that the efforts exerted were not up to the required level specially with regard to material and technological progress. Furthermore, literacy work was only concerned with the alphabetical aspect of the problem i.e. teaching the 3Rs. In a word, literacy work was considered a marginal educational activity in many Arab countries; the efforts did not correspond to the magnitude of the problem. Therefore the 'Arab Literacy Strategy', prepared by ARLO and adopted by the Third Alexandria Conference, introduced a new concept: the Cultural Concept of Literacy. This is a new Arab diagnosis of the nature of illiteracy. Illiteracy is nothing but a symptom of a serious disease. Backwardness is that disease. Illiteracy is, therefore, a complicated social phenomenon which must be dealt with within an overall process of social modernisation and political revolution. We have to fight the virus of the disease itself, and not merely its symptom.

Accordingly, the Arab Literacy Strategy adopted an overall confrontation approach to the illiteracy of society, i.e. its cultural backwardness, in a direct and definite way, by political decision and determined popular will. The objective of the Strategy is to emancipate Arabs from both alphabetical and cultural illiteracy by raising them to such an educational and cultural level as enables them to:

master the basic skills of reading, writing and arithmetic to a level that qualifies them to continue education and training; and

participate in the development and modernisation of the community by providing the cultural and social atmosphere which motivates the individual to continue with education.

With such an objective it is possible to go beyond the limited traditional concept of literacy which is mainly concerned with teaching the basic skills and is a marginal educational process. The new cultural concept takes account of the movement of the society, cultural progress, and accompanying social changes.

The Strategy is founded upon a number of basic principles:

the cultural concept of illiteracy;
the overall confrontation approach;
the importance of the political decision and the people's will in a comprehensive campaign;
elimination of the sources of illiteracy by generalisation of compulsory primary education;
the integration of formal and nonformal education;
continuous follow-up and evaluation of all stages, steps and objectives.

A good number of the Arab States have adopted the principles of the strategy and have launched national comprehensive literacy campaigns. First came the Iraqi pioneer campaign (December 1978) which compulsorily accommodated more than two million illiterates in literacy classes and then in popular schools to help them reach the sixth primary level. Afterwards, national literacy campaigns were launched - or planned to be launched - in Kuwait, the two Yemens, the Sudan, Somalia, Jordan, Syria and Bahrain. Other Arab countries are launching only regional scale campaigns due to lack of technical or material resources. In its endeavour to fulfil cultural literacy in the Arab region, the Arab Literacy and Adult Education Organisation (ARLO) is regaining the authentic Arab character, and the Arab world is reactivating its role and its contribution to human culture after a long period of absence.

C. The Relationship Between the Elimination of Illiteracy and Subsequent Continuing Education in Jilin Province

Zhao Wenqing

How to carry out continuing education after illiteracy has been basically eliminated? This question must be addressed to determine the correct direction for adult education. Such continuing education must not only conform to the laws of development of adult education itself, but must also be suited to economic development. So, after finishing the task of basically eliminating illiteracy, we have mainly promoted comprehensive cultural and technical education and developed adult education at many levels, in many forms, of many kinds and of many standards.

Jilin Province, located in the north-east of China, is predominantly an agricultural province: about seventy percent of the population is agricultural. So peasants' education makes up a great proportion of adult education. Over the years, this has been developed in two stages. The first was in the period when modern China was just founded. Because illiterates and semi-illiterates were more than 90 per cent of the total agricultural population, the task of eliminating illiteracy was very arduous. Under the leadership of the Party and the People's Government, with the spirit of being masters of destiny and the strong desire to be better off culturally, peasants threw themselves into the movement for eliminating illiteracy. The task was basically finished in 1958. At that time we also ran some spare-time primary schools, spare-time secondary classes, cultural make-up courses for workers and peasants, intensive middle schools for workers and peasants, etc.

Because we were not aware enough of the relationship between literacy and continuing education, and especially because of the ten-year turmoil, there was a man-made break in peasants' education. As a result, the achievement of literacy work could not be reinforced; instead, a new batch of illiterates was produced. The second period started in 1979. We gathered strength for a three-year crash programme to eliminate illiteracy on a large scale, during which 1,100,000 illiterates and semi-illiterates became literate. The percentage of illiterates was reduced from 18 per cent to 4 per cent and the percentage of literates in the province reached 90 per cent. We reviewed the experience and lessons of history, paid attention to the inevitable relationship between the elimination of illiteracy and continuing education and took some active measures. Thus we have not only reinforced the achievements of the literacy campaign but also had new developments in peasants' education. At present we conduct comprehensive cultural and technical education in many forms with 1,330,000 people taking part.

Secondly, we are carrying out formal full-time peasants' specialised education at secondary and post-secondary levels.

We are studying the question of the relationship between the elimination of illiteracy and subsequent education. The following points represent our preliminary understanding of this question.

Elimination of Literacy is the Prerequisite for Continuing Education.

Elimination of illiteracy is the prerequisite for raising the scientific and cultural level of workers and peasants. The four modernisations can't be realised in a country with many illiterates. When modern China was founded, the central government considered it an important task to develop workers' and peasants' education and to train new types of intellectuals from workers and peasants. Starting from the reality of our country, the government put forward the slogan of "starting a movement of learning to read and reducing illiteracy gradually", and took literacy education as the starting point in workers' and peasants' education. Later, elimination of illiteracy was put into the constitution as one of the basic policies of the country. In order to complete this task efficiently, the State Council formulated literacy standards for both individuals and organisations. According to the regulations of the country, the People's Government of Jilin province put forward - "unified programme, use diversified instruction methods, eliminate illiteracy within a definite time and check in batches" - as the guiding principle of this work, formulated regulations and made some mandatory rules. As there is difficulty and relapse in the elimination of illiteracy, the leadership was strengthened for literacy work. Personnel responsible for adult education have been established in education administrative departments of all levels. More than 2,200 staff have been provided in the whole province, fostering an administrative system from above to below. At the same time we have established a teaching force with full-time and part-time teachers (there were more than 60,000 peasants' teachers) to mobilise strength from all sectors. Every year since 1979 we have organised a work-force of 100,000 people to tackle illiteracy and organised about 1,000,000 people to take part in the study; besides, because adult education is usually on an accelerated basis, we have also started extensive campaigns.

Because workers and peasants have production tasks and housework, literacy work is limited by production work and household chores. This requires that teaching forms and methods and scheduling be flexible and diversified; they cannot be all the same. We followed the principle of "learning more in slack seasons, learning less in busy seasons and learning by oneself in rush seasons". We used many forms: centrally organised classes, neighbourhood study groups, study group at paddy fields, guaranteed teaching and learning, and so on and made use of the "pinying (romanisation) system of reading, recording of work points, using picture cards, real objects and literacy cards" and other methods in teaching peasants to read. Through all this we have achieved comparatively good results.

Our practice proves that the elimination of illiteracy has not only laid a cultural foundation for subsequent education; it has also trained a great number of teachers and cadres. This prepared for the development of continuing education in ideological, organisational and material terms and provided valuable experiences.

Continuing Education as the Inevitable Way to Develop Following the Elimination of Illiteracy.

To become literate means to acquire merely basic ability in reading, writing and arithmetic. To suit the needs of building the four modernisations, it is far from enough. Moreover, if one stops study after becoming literate, one will become illiterate again very soon. Continuing education after the elimination of illiteracy is not only very necessary; it also allows for no delay. Take Qiangang town in Nongan Country, for instance. This town paid attention to continuing education of all kinds after the elimination of illiteracy. The percentage of people who became illiterate again is lower than 5 per cent. In Chaigang where continuing education is not done well after the elimination of illiteracy, the percentage of people who became illiterate again is higher than 16 per cent after 2 years. Some findings also showed that some of the young peasants who took part in production after graduating from primary schools would become new illiterates or semi-illiterates, if they stopped their study. This is because study itself has the nature of being continuous. If you go on learning, you will make progress; if you stop learning, you will fall behind. The law of study requires that we should lose no time in the provision of continuing education after the elimination of illiteracy. In fact, they have a cause and effect relationship. The elimination of illiteracy lays a foundation for continuing education, and continuing education is the unavoidable way to reinforce and develop the achievements in literacy. If we do not eliminate illiteracy, we cannot carry out continuing education. On the other hand, if we do not carry out continuing education, we cannot really complete the task of eliminating illiteracy.

Those who became literate are eager to continue their studies. Since the Production Responsibility System was put into practice in the countryside, peasants' enthusiasm for in production has been running unprecedentedly high. They have a stronger sense of responsibility and have become much more open in thinking. They understand that to develop production they have to rely on science and technology, so they have a stronger desire to study. They were comparatively passive in the literacy campaign and were made to learn; now they have become active and they themselves want to learn. Many peasants are even willing to invest in human resources development. Thus we consider that continuing education after the elimination of illiteracy is the inevitable development of the objective situation and is decided by the law of adult education and learning.

The Content and Form of Continuing Education After the Elimination of Illiteracy.

To carry out continuing education after the elimination of illiteracy, we must follow the characteristics and law of adult education. Adult education should mainly be spare-time study with a clear purpose of being applicable. Adults want to study for the sake of application. This is also one of the characteristics of peasants' continuing education. The peasants hope that the content of their study can satisfy the needs of present production and life and open up new ways for them to become rich. They do not like pure cultural study, but show an eager desire to learn technology. So peasants' continuing education should combine culture with technology. That is: promote cultural education by technical education and help the development of technical education by raising the cultural level. Looking at the actual condition of our province, in 1982 there were 8,400 spare time primary classes and 160,000 people took part in study; by 1983 only about 4,000 classes remained and only 100,000 people took part in study. On the other hand, in 1982 4,780 spare-time classes in culture and technology were started and more than 180,000 people took part in study; by 1983, within only one year, the number of the classes increased to more than 12,000, and more than 520,000 people took part in study. This comparison shows that only by combining cultural education with technical education can it be welcomed by peasants. We conducted an investigation of 226 young and middle-aged peasants in the six production co-operatives in Yidan, Yitong county. All of them want to learn. Among them, 223 are willing to learn both cultural and technical subjects; only 3 express the wish to learn culture only. This shows that close combination of cultural education with technical education is required by the character of adult education.

Continuing education after the elimination of illiteracy must also be suited to the distribution of knowledge in the countryside and to economic development. Of the young and middle-aged peasants in Jilin Province, 1,300,000 have not reached primary level; 3,360,000 have reached primary level; 1,850,000 have reached junior middle level; 780,000 have reached senior middle level. Moreover, because different people have different experience in life and production, and different abilities in self-study and in summing up and absorbing others' production experience, the differences in technical levels are also very great. And because the countryside is changing from self-supporting and semi self-supporting to a commodity economy, many families in various special trades and exemplary families in science and technology have appeared. They have different particular scientific and technical require-ments. So the above-mentioned cultural and technical education must be comprehensive. Comprehensive education mainly means giving different-level cultural and technical education to peasants at different cultural and technical levels, and teaching different contents in education to peasants with different requirements in their study. Peasants' comprehensive cultural and technical education in Jilin province is carried out according to a "unified programme, measures suitable to local and individual conditions, and running schools in many forms". At present, the education can be roughly divided into two kinds: one is the non-formal, universal cultural and technical education which is the focal point of our present work; the other is formal specialised technical education with the purpose of raising standards which is in its trial period. The former is carried out by running peasants' cultural and technical schools in towns and villages, running cultural and technical classes, spare-time primary classes, spare-time secondary classes or night schools attached to primary and middle schools. Because of the increasing economic strength there are more and more towns and villages that run peasants' cultural and technical schools. Besides, use is made of all kinds of short courses, lecture tours, lectures by recording, broadcast schools, self-study groups and other forms to complement and coordinate this work. At the same time, we also start various activities such as reading newspapers and books, and recreational activities, using fully the cultural centres of villages, libraries and film projection teams. In terms of modes, we have half-time, seasonal, full-time, long, short and ad hoc courses. These forms all have their own strong points, so they can complement one another.

Formal and systematic specialised technical education is carried out mainly by running peasants' secondary vocational schools and peasants' colleges. We now have ten full-time peasants' secondary vocational schools and four specialised peasants' colleges for professional training in the province. To run these kinds of schools is one of the basic measures to exploit intellectual resources in the countryside, and to promote agricultural modernisation. Because these schools have relative superiority, they will become the bases and centres of peasants' education. Besides the task of training, directly, talented persons in agricultural techniques, they are also responsible for the comprehensive universal cultural and technical education of the counties where they are located, and for the training of technical teachers in all kinds of peasants' classes.

The Trend and Plan in the Development of Peasants' Continuing Education.

Through dozens of years of development, peasants' education in our province has formed an education system of four levels: literacy, comprehensive cultural and technical education, secondary specialised education, and specialised higher education. The elimination of illiteracy is the first period in peasants' education, but to some degree has already had the nature of primary cultural and technical education. Along with completing the elimination of illiteracy and changing peasants' cultural structure, its function will gradually become unnecessary and finally disappear from the peasants' educational system. So the elimination of illiteracy is only a transition phase in a certain historical period. Comprehensive cultural and technical education is the main part of peasants' education. At present, its main functions are: (1) to consolidate achievements in the elimination of illiteracy; (2) to teach elementary cultural and scientific knowledge; (3) to carry out basic technical education relating to experience, knowledge, and techniques of production. But because of the change in the economic structure of the countryside and the development of the two kinds of households, we have at present to provide a certain amount of specialised education in production knowledge and techniques. Thus the educational content of this period will naturally have the elements of secondary cultural and technical education. Along with the development of universal education and the reform in educational structure, secondary cultural and technical education will weigh more and more heavily in the future education of young peasants. Secondary cultural and technical education and specialised higher education are within the scope of formal education, and they are full-time studies.

The above-mentioned four levels are not discrete; on the contrary the four levels permeate one another. In particular, the peasants today will become new-type labourers who are both workers and peasants, both traders and managers. The fourth industrial revolution also puts new demands on peasants' education, so we have to adjust, enrich, and reform the management, the form and the content of peasants' education. How to establish as soon as possible a peasants' education system relevant to the national condition is the problem we are now trying to solve. In planning peasant education in our province, we insist on the following principles: make different teaching arrangements and use different forms of running schools, starting from peasants' needs and possibilities; handle properly the relation between seasonal technical classes and the systematic study of agricultural techniques, and the relation between learning of scientific farming and the learning of basic theory of agricultural production; handle properly the relation between the needs of local production and the needs of technical persons required by the development of agriculture, industry, commerce and other trades; and handle properly the relation between popularisation and raising of standards, between full-time formal education and spare-time, non-formal education.

For several years, peasant education in Jilin Province has promoted the development of production. In 1983, the province had a bumper harvest and had the biggest increase in the sale of commodity grain to the state. Besides the great power of the Party's policy in the countryside, this is also because scientific technique has played an important part. Huaide County, an advanced model in peasant education, is also advanced in agricultural production. This county has taken first place in selling commodity grain in the whole state for two years. The cadres in this county said: "Our bumper harvest depends, first of all, on policy and second, on science. But the foundation is education." The masses said it even more vividly: "it is the Party's policy that has united our limbs to develop production, and it is cultural and technical education that has given us golden wings to become rich". It can be predicted that under the leadership of the Party and the government, peasant education in Jilin Province will be certain to develop. No doubt it will play an even greater role in building a socialist countryside, in narrowing the difference between cities and the countryside, and in promoting the great change of agricultural modernisation.

D. Panel Commentary and Discussion

Apropos the industrialised countries and such concepts as 'essential knowledge and skills...for effective functioning in...the community', Jennings observed that not all those in advanced industrialised countries - even excluding recent immigrants and guest workers - have reached the necessary standard. In Britain some two million people are estimated not to be sufficiently literate to function effectively in that complex modern society. Over the past nine years about a quarter of a million people have been given some instruction in literacy and basic numeracy. However, the demands of modern society were becoming more complex all the time, so that the number of people needing assistance would grow: another moving target.

He posed four questions: to Hunter's assertion that 'when the economic and social barriers to full participation in society are removed, the motivation for and pursuit of literacy skills follow', he asked whether this applied to the nomadic herdsmen or tribal groups with a relatively self-contained economy and traditional way of life. Secondly, what are the ways of penetrating the consciousness of such peoples without violating their rights and traditions? What about the needs of parents to keep up with their children who may be at school? What about the value of reading skills in health care; and the obligations of citizenship? Thirdly, when 'functional literacy' is being considered, who decides which are the appropriate functions? Finally, how can we distinguish people held back from learning by apathy which is induced by exploitation, and those who are cheerfully self-deprived?

Dirus Dore spoke as Director-General of the Literacy Service of the Republic of Guinea, a former French colony concerned since independence with illiteracy. Despite the support of a determined national political will, the country had managed to produce schooling for only 35 per cent of its children. Seventy five percent of those enrolled were in urban areas, leaving the rural areas heavily deprived. In parallel with efforts for schooling the government began a widespread literacy campaign in 1962: illiteracy at the time of independence stood at 90 percent. The subsequent period fell into three phases. Until 1967 the government backed a voluntary literacy campaign intended for all adults without distinction. Teachers were poorly prepared and there was only a hastily prepared set of national alphabets; in these circumstances the few results achieved were due to the enthusiasm of escaping colonialism. In the first phase the national authorities gained some grasp of the scale of the work ahead.

From 1967 to 1972, thanks to Unesco's Work Oriented Literacy Programme and supported from 1968 by a National Literacy Service, literacy work shifted to a selective approach. The emphasis subsequently has been increasingly integrating literacy with rural development, health, agriculture and livestock production. Literacy centres were either 'staffed' or 'local'. Staffed centres operated full-time, generally in industrial settings or with large agricultural projects. The others were financed by the villages and operated in the agricultural off-season between October and May.

Most illiteracy is among the 4,500,000 children and adults living in 3,000 villages in relative isolation with a traditional economic base. The need for these people to communicate with the outside world through the written word is insignificant; moreover civil servants turn up only at tax time, which creates mistrust of townspeople. Public awareness campaigns are necessary for the authorities to gain acceptance for literacy programmes among village people, using the mass media and political organisations. Decentralisation of the National Literacy Service has begun through inspectors and literacy directors at all levels of regional and provincial administration. Women's centres have been created to counter sexist or discriminatory measures and traditions.

Guinea chose from the outset to teach literacy in the mother tongues, despite strong opposition from intellectuals. The eight national languages chosen had not however been written, prior to the literacy campaign. There were also strong differences in dialect within the languages. Written alphabets were developed by scholars of good will but with little linguistic training. A research institute, the Language Academy, was created only in 1972. Six of the languages for adult literacy are also those used for primary and secondary school instruction; here French is simply a subject. French remains the official language and the link between the different maternal languages. In this context learning to read and write in a local language creates a marginalised new literate.

Adult literacy in Guinea has several objectives. It is intended both to serve as a vehicle for scientific and technical knowledge and to educate citizens to know their rights. Collectively it seeks people's participation in social and economic development. The literacy primers are therefore in a way an extension of those for community development: vehicles for literacy and arithmetic but also for civic and political education, hygiene, the campaign against burning the fields, for raising livestock, and so on. All in all the difficulties facing literacy work in the rural areas are numerous. The people have little motivation to learn to read and write in their daily lives, and they are burdened by heavy physical labour. Literacy alone seems an irrelevant luxury, hence the concentration on adult education through health and agriculture projects.

The choice of language for literacy emerged in general discussion as an issue of keen controversy in a number of countries. Yao, responding to a request for clarification of the Chinese approach, first indicated his general agreement with Hunter. He stressed the great progress since 1949, but also the scale of work still to be done. According to 1982 statistics there were some 200 million illiterates, about 23 percent of the adult population. Literacy of all adults over 40 was the target by 1995, if not by 1990. The proportions of illiterate to literate had changed from roughly 80:20 to 20:80 since Liberation. Those now illiterate were scattered all over the country, some of them in remote and border areas including the boundaries of each province as well as on the national boundaries. While some minorities were very advanced others still had a low educational level and poor conditions. Sixty to seventy percent of the young illiterate were women and they were hard to make literate. Many languages were not in written form; this forced people into learning Mandarin Chinese before they could become literate. A single nation-wide campaign could not handle this, and more good new methods were needed. Different kinds of motivations and sanctions were tried, including economic and job incentives, and even in places a bar on marriage prior to attaining literacy. Voluntary effort and motivation were however very important, and great difficulties still remained.

Indian literacy programmes, it was noted, were conducted in the learners' spoken language, with the exception of very small (50-60,000) ethnic groups. Cadena spoke forcefully for teaching in minority languages and preserving these cultures.

Gajardo took up the question of social and political action, arguing that the eradication of illiteracy would derive not from partial educational programmes but from a universal educational approach in a context of social, economic and political transformation. In Latin America universalisation of schooling had proven necessary, the outstanding examples being Cuba and Nicaragua. It was necessary to examine the relationship between formal education and adult education practices in relation to the problems of daily living.

Al Rawi echoed the importance of social and political factors, to which the economic system was subordinate. This was demonstrated in the Arab World, especially the Gulf States, where great wealth co-existed with high illiteracy. Individual (alphabetical) illiteracy derived from societal (cultural) illiteracy. While modernisation and change were the key, economic factors were not **the** cause and obstacle.

Questions of primacy of motivation and the sources of 'development' also exercised the discussion groups. One asked whether, if as some hold illiteracy causes poverty, its elimination will cause automatic development. It was pointed out that changes of economic structure in fact provide motivation for literacy: people acquire skills when they see some hope of using them. A Chinese participant observed that while economic factors were primary, political factors could also be highly significant, such as the Cultural Revolution, which lowered literacy levels.

All groups sought to clarify aspects of the Chinese experience, especially the question whether the literacy campaign was formal or nonformal. It was explained that originally a wide variety of methods was used, under the slogan 'nationwide teaching, nationwide learning'; without popular participation there would be no success. Different examples were given, such as for example grouping for intensive instruction during the slack winter season, and 'each one teach one' between friends, married couples, etc. Nowadays the motivation of economic gain through 'sideline enterprises' was a significant factor for literacy and continuing education.

As the groups compared different approaches and experiences between their countries, and even within one country at different times, the importance of different specific contexts and circumstances became evident, as well as the complexity of many issues, such as motivation and methodology. The value of such comparative analysis, especially as between Chinese experience and the situation and needs of developing countries, led one group to recommend that ICAE organise a system of cooperation between China and Third World countries, as well as with selected industrialised nation universities, for comparative work in the areas of research and evaluation.

Chapter 6

Agricultural Development and Peasant Education

Chanida Chanyapate, drawing on experience of both governmental and voluntary sector work in rural Thailand, brings out the very different, contrasting perspectives of the urban minority which dominates, and the rural majority which is dominated, in countries of the Third World. Looking in turn at 'four actors' in the rural scene - the peasant, the official, the volunteer, and the businessman - she demonstrates how misplaced in the common faith in 'trickle down': that general economic development will benefit the remote and the most poor. Her paper constitutes a gentle yet very radical plea for 'preventive education' to assist peasants to retain and build on their traditional strengths. She draws out the connection between this and the Thai philosophy of khit pen, in turn anchored in Buddhism, suggesting that the conservatism with which khit pen is charged misses much of its point and strength.

In the subsequent discussion, summarised in the second part of this chapter, an absorbing dialoque mainly between other women from China and South Asia, together with Cadena speaking about Mexico, raises such issues as the role and credibility of governments in authentic people's development, and the possibility or otherwise of non-revolutionary change in a direction of greater equity. To some participants China and Thailand's experiences appear as two sides of the same coin; others saw Thailand - perhaps along with India, Mexico and other countries of the Third World - as in the situation of China before 1949, but China's pre-liberation adult education experience as therefore the most relevant to their present needs in peasant education and rural development.

A. Strategies for Agricultural Development and Peasant Education

Chanida Chanyapate

The Present Scene

All who have experience of rural development quickly discover that the various components of rural misery - poverty, ill-health, poor education - are interconnected. A nutritionist, for example, cannot get far persuading villagers to eat a healthy balanced diet if those same villagers simply do not have enough to eat. The literacy teacher finds that the constant nagging need to seize every chance of making a bit of money renders attendance at classes sporadic. School teachers might observe the effects of protein-deficiency in early life on school achievement (one reason perhaps why the 80 per cent rural population of Thailand provides only 7 per cent of university students).

A common response to this situation by development organisations is to focus on income-generating projects. Educational efforts are directed towards the teaching of marketable skills, or skills that may lead to self-employment. Or agricultural extension officers will concentrate on propagandising methods of raising agricultural production. With the extra income that, one hopes, will result from this, peasants might start building latrines or indulging in other 'improving activities' that require an initial bit of cash.

So far, so good. The problem is that it does not seem to be working very well. Otherwise we would not be talking about it as a problem still today. There is little evidence, for example, that the lot of the poorest peasants in Thailand has substantially improved over the past two decades, whereas economic indicators on a national scale indicate a steady, even impressive, improvement over the same period.

Actors in the Scene (1) - The Peasant

In looking around for somebody to blame for this quite remarkable non-improvement, I would dissociate myself from the chorus that commonly accuses the farmer. Blaming the victim rarely helps anybody. While it may be true that certain peasants are stubborn, or (from the eager development worker's point of view) lazy, and that communities may shy away from new technology in superstitious ignorance, you begin to think that the peasant cannot win.

What if the peasant does increase production, as has happened periodically in Thailand in the sugar-cane and pineapple industries? By the invisible hand of the capitalist market, prices slump, the peasant is virtually no better off for all his hard work, and pineapples get thrown into the Gulf of Thailand. The newspapers talk of 'overproduction' - and guess who gets the blame for that.

Actors (2) - The Official

Let us now look at other participants in the rural landscape who might also share the blame.

First the 'official' development agents. (In many countries, including Thailand, these are synonymous with government officials.) The most important thing is that the primary objective of such rural development workers does not directly concern the village where they may be working. Their viewpoint as government officials is, almost by definition, more directed towards their city-bound superiors. They may be sincerely striving for some kind of improvement in the lives of the local peasants, but the plans by which they work are drawn up and directed by their superiors; the budget that they dispense has been approved by some more central agency; even their very existence as salary-earners demanding the respect of the 'ordinary' peasants represents an intrusion of alien, urban ways.

Two important features of this situation must be stressed. First, the role of the development worker as 'helper', or 'facilitator', or 'adviser', becomes inextricably bound up with the function of 'controlling' or 'supervising'. One of the functions of local government officers in Thailand is to arrange for local elections for positions such as village headman. This seems to be a clear case of 'facilitating'. And after the election, the same officer must give his official approval to the community's choice for the results to be valid. A similar system of 'controlled democracy' (where the control is effective and the democracy largely illusory) governs agricultural co-operatives, a fact which some observers use to explain their widespread failure.

The second feature is that the policies that inform the actions of the local development worker are largely decided by a centralised (and, in Thailand, westernised) group of planners whose vision has national scope and who simply cannot afford to inquire after the details of the situation in each village. To these planners, rural areas in the mass are a source of 'rural manpower' in the mass, which must somehow be put to work increasing agricultural production. This will both increase the export of raw materials on which the country's balance of trade depends, and will allow peasants themselves to become consumers, thus fuelling an acceleration of economic growth.

So the problems of rural areas are viewed as national problems. More rice must be grown so that Thailand can increase export revenue, so that Thailand can pay for the importation of 'necessary' commodities, the most important of which is energy. The fact that these energy imports are used in the generation of electricity that does not get to the village, or in the gas tanks of cars that the average peasant will never own, is not a significant problem for the central planner - he has the national accounts to balance. But it is a problem for the individual peasant, waiting patiently for something, anything, to trickle down through the system.

One example of the 'national' view of rural problems is a yearly 3,000 million baht ($130 million) project called the Rural Job Creation Scheme. Under the guide of participatory community development, the government hands out sums of money to specially-formed local organisations called sub-district councils. These councils then decide how, in their locality, the money is to be spent. Commonly the money is spent on dry-season activities such as building roads, digging irrigation canals, sinking wells etc.

The two obvious purposes behind this scheme - to inject some cash into the local economy and to improve the local infrastructure - are in fact subordinate to a hidden third objective - to discourage the annual migration into the towns in the dry season. One by-product of this scheme has been accusations of misuse of funds and corruption at the local level. When critics point out that in many places peasants were being paid to build roads that were washed away in the rainy season, only to be rebuilt with next year's government handout, one Minister said that this was not entirely unsatisfactory, since at least the local population would be kept down on the farm, even if they were rebuilding the same road year after year. So this 'rural' scheme was quite clearly intended by the government to benefit the situation in the cities.

Among the various officials involved in development work, agricultural extension officers seem to be a breed apart. (I am intrigued by the use of the word 'extension' - what exactly is being extended?) The Department of Agricultural Extension in the Thai Ministry of Agriculture and Co-operatives has a specific mandate to increase agricultural production, on the assumption that increased production must ipso facto be beneficial to the peasant concerned. As we shall see, that is not necessarily the case, and so a tension arises between the agricultural extension officer, who has virtually no experience growing things himself, and for whom success is defined by the adoption of new crops or cultivation methods, and the peasant, who may not always agree, but who is often in a poor position to resist the influence of the government agent.

Actors (3) - The Volunteer

The shortcomings of the official development worker are of course quite visible, even to townspeople. This has spawned a number of small voluntary groups of concerned citizens: private, non-profit development organisations are established, which set out to work with rural communities on a limited scale. Most workers are well-intentioned middle-class young people who soon discover that they possess no skills or real understanding of the peasant's mind and economy. Their plan of action is sometimes little more than an eager and vague desire to help. Many learn that village life is not for them and become frustrated when things do not change as quickly as they would like. Those who stay involved in rural development sometimes resign themselves to cultivating their own gardens more for the sake of self-fulfilment.

Actors (4) - The Businessman

Another agent recently entered on the rural scene and of growing importance in Thailand is represented by agribusinesses. These companies are primarily concerned with monetary income. Their influence is towards greater mechanisation and market-oriented agrarian reform. Such efforts could be beneficial to the peasant, but the profit motive does not always coincide with greatest social benefit. Increased mechanisation may increase yields, but perhaps at the expense of rural workers who are left landless. Market-oriented production often impels the peasant into producting cash crops, which will not keep him alive and which offer only an unstable monetary return.

Agribusinesses also have an unpleasant side-effect in siphoning off some of the governmental development effort. Highly trained but poorly paid university experts on poultry are commonly under retainers to a major chicken and egg-producing company in Thailand. Similarly, plant specialists are being lured away by cigarette manufacturers and breweries to work on their tobacco and barley crops. Individual peasants directly employed by, or under contract to, these agribusinesses often enjoy a better than average standard of living. But the effect of commercialised agriculture is to concentrate scarce resources of knowledge and expertise into exploiting areas already favoured in terms of soil conditions, communications and ancillary services.

The Effects

Past development efforts seem to have been largely predicated on the assumption of national or even global interdependency. The effect has been to neglect subsistence culture in favour of producing a marketable surplus of agricultural goods to be exchanged (generally at an unfair rate) for consumer goods from the city factories.

A recently completed research study paints this picture of life in the poorest area of Thailand, the north-east. Rice yields have started to decrease. The soil has always been poor and the application of chemical fertilizer, which has consistently been encouraged by agricultural extension officers, is no longer effecting any increase. In fact a ceiling has been reached, with the soil being left in a depleted state, so that increasing use of fertilizer is needed just to maintain present yields. The large-scale use of chemical fertilizers has overshot the absorption capacity of the environment. The ecological balance is shifting, producing a marked change in water quality. Fertilizer-related pollution of water has resulted in widespread destruction of aquatic life, which traditionally served as a major protein source for the local population. Since the expenses of farmers have risen, the debt burden has also steadily increased, so land is being confiscated or sold off cheaply. Thus there is a rise in tenant-farming and share-cropping, to match the situation in more fertile areas. The incentive for quick profits in cash crops, such as cassava, has led to massive deforestation by capitalist enterprises. Effective official reaction has been negligible, with local officers turning a blind eye, or even conniving in the practice. The loss of forests, apart from any ecological disadvantage, also removes a source of additional non-cultivated produce for the peasants' own consumption.

The effect of current development efforts in such cases has been to make the poor peasant worse off than he used to be. Half the population of the north-east of Thailand has sunk below the poverty line. Increasing numbers of rural people are forced to migrate to the cities, to live in slum and squatter areas, to undertake unskilled casual labour or factory work at extremely low wages, and in the case of young rural women, to go or be forced into prostitution. Similar situations are repeated throughout the third world as international agencies consistently report a growing gulf between the largely urban haves and the normally rural have-nots in many countries.

The Old and the New

A number of concerned individuals have become so disillusioned with the effects of development efforts that they advocate that we should all leave the peasant alone. The peasant community survived for centuries before the advent of development workers; maybe the peasants would be better off if left to themselves. Before we countenance such radical strategies of benign neglect, we should however look at the agricultural and community practices that allowed peasants to survive in self-sufficiency in the past, and at the factors that have intervened to upset the even tenor of their lives.

In many developing countries the rural population still heavily outnumbers the urban, except in terms of power. Living in small communities spread over the arable land in relative isolation, peasants represent the cultural tradition and identity of the land, in contrast to their westernised, consumer-oriented city cousins. This traditional culture has been one of subsistence. Activities are geared towards providing life sustenance in terms of food, clothing and shelter for the family, and to maintaining a spiritual identity. The source of all wealth in this system is land. Families produce for their own consumption and also gather from surrounding non-cultivated land. Skills are passed on from parents to children. The existence of communities allows specialised functions to certain members, such as spiritual leaders and midwives. So a certain amount of interdependency is evident, but this is largely limited to within the community, with relatively few needs being met from outside the immediate village.

The main force in such communities, given the Buddhist ethos prevalent in Thai society, is towards harmony both within the community, where individuals would seek to provide for themselves and each other all their material, social and spiritual needs, and between the community and its natural surroundings, such that dependence on outside organisations is at a minimum and each community was virtually self-sustaining. Such a situation of harmony or balance can be upset by disruptive forces from both within and outside the community.

Forces of Disruption

Within the community the pressures of increasing population have strained the ability of the land to provide sufficient wealth. A change of this sort, however, takes place relatively slowly, allowing peasants time to make adjustments. In rural Thailand, the most common adjustment has been to send the surplus manpower of sons and daughters into the cities for seasonal work. Outside the community there are other forces which are largely beyond the control of the peasant and which directly and dramatically affect his ability to subsist.

Mass destruction of forests, for example, is making rain-fed rice farming an even more precarious business in a cycle of drought and flood. It also removes a source of fuel and a supplementary supply of food that was traditionally gathered by the peasant. Commercial goods, produced by a growing industrial sector supported by government policy, are invading rural communities and changing peasants' consumption patterns. Modern education in schools alienates the successful schoolchild from the agricultural background and contains a powerful hidden curriculum which teaches that jobs in the service sector, with their relatively easier way of life, should be the goal of an academic career. The aspirations of peasants have been raised without any corresponding increase in the likelihood of their success, causing frustration.

Changes in agriculture are generally in the direction of capital-intensive methods. However, the average peasant has no capital. He would therefore have to risk substantial debt in return for what must be an unpredictable return, given the artificially depressed price of rice, the high cost of fertilizer and pesticide normally needed in new methods, and the producers' vulnerable position in the market. On the other hand, those few farmers who already enjoy a financially more secure position may well be able to benefit from such a situation, thereby widening the gap between themselves and the poorer peasants, and further destroying the harmony of the community. The one modern service from outside that can directly and immediately improve the quality of life for peasants - curative medicine - has been applied in a haphazard and disappointingly inadequate way; today Thailand can boast of more Thai doctors working in the United States than in rural Thailand.

The forces that disrupt the peasant's traditional self-sufficiency in a subsistent system of agriculture are mainly from without. Many peasants have tried to resist them. They have, often wisely, shown great reluctance to invest in new technology, to move from staple to cash crops, to increase production substantially when there is no realistic guarantee of return, or to exacerbate their dependence on the market. This conservatism is fortified by an attachment to the land that will, for example, see farmers accept two or three years of non-productive drought and the resultant crippling debt before they would think of relinquishing their land to become tenant farmers or hired labour elsewhere.

It seems safe to predict, however, that unless conditions change markedly, the forces of disruption are slowly going to demolish the self-sufficient harmony of the community, forcing peasants off their land and thereby allowing agricultural production to be taken over by larger economic units. While such a shift in the socioeconomic structure might be beneficial to national prosperity in gross terms (though there are reasons for doubting this), it is difficult to see how this would improve the lot of the poor peasant of today. It therefore seems that if we are interested in helping the poorest of the poor, we should be helping the peasant to resist a changing situation that can only lead to his demise. We can best do this by helping people to do what they do best, ie. working on the land, meeting their own minimum needs, storing by the occasional surplus to meet emergency cash needs, and thereby maintaining the ecological balance and living in harmony with each other and their surroundings.

Meeting Minimum Needs for Self-Sufficiency

Any attempt to help peasants meet their minimum needs must begin with the belief that the peasants themselves know where their problems lie. This translates into the development worker going directly to the individual peasant, his family and his community, and trying to gain a real picture of the situation. Before any decisions are made as to what advice or assistance to give, a thorough survey must be carried out of factors causing problems and the availability of resources for solving these problems. These assertions could come from the first chapter of dozens of development manuals. The ideas are widely endorsed by experienced development workers. Yet they are regularly ignored.

Many agencies go into the field with ready-made decisions incorporating assumptions that may not be shared, or at least should be questioned, by the prospective 'developee'. This may be a necessary consequence of centralised standardised bureaucracies. The Thai government, for example, invariably sets objectives and activities for officials to implement in any development programme, and programmes themselves must often be carried out on a nation-wide scale, irrespective of local differences.

There seem to be numerous areas in which assistance could be given to the peasant to help maintain or re-instate self-sufficiency. For example, look at what has happened to the wing bean, whose varieties constitute one of the most important and high-protein 'fruits of the forest' in many areas of Thailand. In the wake of deforestation, this significant supplementary food source is fast disappearing. Yet there has been virtually no official interest in research on wing beans in Thailand, from either the agricultural or nutritional aspects, since these plants have never seriously been cultivated.

A local breed of chicken, naturally adapted to the existing environment and serving basically as a device for turning household and farm refuse into a source of eggs and meat for the peasant, has been wiped out in certain areas of Thailand by diseases introduced by commercial poultry breeds that require, and get, close veterinary care.

Primary medical care can have a substantial influence on reducing the level of human misery in rural areas. Preventive health measures themselves constitute a form of self-sufficiency by reducing the likelihood of the peasant's need for outside medical assistance. Further research into the efficacy and proper use of herbal medicine would also reduce the peasant's reliance on outside sources of medication.

Education for Self-Sufficiency

The peasant needs no direct educational input to enable him to achieve self-sufficiency; he has been doing this for generations. He does however need new skills to be able to manage the outside influences that threaten his subsistent culture. In other words the peasant must learn to protect himself and his community from advice, information, material goods and commercial propaganda that may disturb the balance of self-sufficiency by creating dependence on goods and services delivered from outside, and hence beyond the control of the community or the individual. Skill in evaluating the likely implications of communications from outside the community is clearly needed.

Such an educational philosophy might be termed 'preventive' education, education that aims to enable the peasant to avoid the unpleasant consequences of unthinking acceptance of new ideas. The parallel with preventive medicine should be obvious. Preventive medicine would presumably include attempts, by legal force or persuasion, to protect peasant communities from the candy bars, cheap cosmetics and addictive proprietary drugs that are touted from the cities where they already cause unnecessary illness and disease. Similarly, preventive education would seek to establish a protective barrier of healthy scepticism against the worst excesses of ill-informed advice from 'experts' with only a superficial understanding of actual conditions, and with a mandate to apply the same panacea in every locality. From behind his barricade of critical questioning, the peasant would view such experts, be they government agricultural workers, private community development workers, commercial travellers, or even the purveyor of preventive education himself, with a respectful and reasoned distrust.

A raising of peasant suspicions seems to be closely related to the 'khit-pen' concept that forms the philosophical basis for current basic literacy programmes in Thailand. 'Khit-pen' means, literally, the ability to think. In brief, the process involves taking learners through the steps of problem-solving, from identifying problems and their causes and effects, to formulating alternative solutions, and finally to decisions made by the peasants in the best interests of harmony within their society and with their environment, as they see it. At each step, the teacher may inject new information, perhaps in the form of 'what the book says', followed by an invitation to the learners to react in the light of their experience and to explore other factors in their social, economic and cultural environment. Often the chosen solution will go against what the book says, but this has no importance compared with the fact that the peasants themselves understand the reasons for their decision.

'Khit-pen' has been criticised as being counter-productive to development and non-progressive, legitimising fatalism and allowing reasons to maintain the status quo. Such criticisms are of course only valid when it can be proved that change is necessarily beneficial. Much the same criticisms have been made of Buddhism. This is no coincidence, since 'khit-pen' has been developed in a Thai Buddhist context. Buddhism emphasises inner peace and harmony, and considers that happiness is achieved not through the satisfaction of every desire, but from the limitation of desire to the basic needs of food, clothing, shelter, and medicine - almost a definition of self-sufficiency. Strong emotions, such as greed, anger and obsession, are to be eliminated by choosing a middle path between extremes and thereby maintaining equanimity and harmony.

Well-meaning workers in agriculture, health and community development may be able to create an environment conducive to the preservation or re-establishment of self-sufficiency by practising 'khit-pen dialogues' with the peasant communities where they work. There must be mutal respect for each party's opinion, and each dialogue should be a learning event for both sides. No outside proposal should be accepted without thorough discussion and evaluation of its implications by the community. In creating a discriminating barrier to outside ideas, preventive education is not entirely negative in its approach. One of the reasons why outside influences on subsistent culture have been so strongly subversive is because the flow of information has been controlled and imposed from above. New ideas generally arrive in a village reinforced by the authority of the central power which delivers them. A more reliable and trustworthy flow of information might be horizontal between communities rather than the current vertical direction. Information passing by this route will increase peasants' confidence in their own judgement in dealing with problems and in making conscious and informed decisions.

A second side to the concept of preventive education concerns those involved in intruding into peasant communities. Many of those now responsible for destroying the ability of the peasant to subsist are acting more out of ignorance or indifference than malice. The formal education curricula have so neglected the issues of development that it is quite normal for even the educated Thai city-dweller to be unaware of the mechanisms by which the government artifically depresses prices at the farm gate for the benefit of urban consumers and to the disadvantage of the farmer. Development workers themselves appear occasionally to suffer from a woeful ignorance of the effect of their own activities. It has been reported that agricultural officials urging the adoption of high-yielding varieties of crops were blissfully unaware of the implications such adoption would have for the farmer in the way of necessary dependence on fertilizer and pesticide, for example.

Implications

An emphasis on subsistent agriculture and away from marketable surpluses will have a direct impact on the unproductive urban minority. An easing of hardship in rural areas may imply imposed restraints on urban consumption, especially in the form of realistic food prices and a more conservative use of imported energy.

Government policy toward rural development must undergo a shift of strategy. Instead of directing all efforts at stimulating economic activity by the poorest farmer while allowing the freedom of the market-place to large and economically powerful units such as agribusinesses, it would be wiser to allow the peasant to work towards his own salvation behind the protection of strict government-imposed limits on the use of corporate forces.

Every step along the road towards localised self-sufficiency entails a loosening of central authority's control over social, economic and political matters. While some may fear that this represents a move towards anarchy, it should, rather, be interpreted as a strengthening of a democratic way of life, and an orientation towards a more equitable economic system.

B. Panel Commentary and Discussion

In introducing a paper drawing on experience of seeking to eliminate illiteracy and build universal education in Hunan Province, Ning Xin echoed many themes from Zhao Wenqing's earlier paper (see Chapter 5), especially the need to 'strike while the iron is hot' and build on illiteracy work with universal and continuing education. Her paper especially stressed the importance of prevention - though in a different sense from Chanida's 'preventive education', quoting sayings such as 'the more illiteracy eliminated, the more illiterates born', and slogans like 'rather prevent ten than eliminate one'.

Ning Xin commended Chanida's paper as deserving close attention. The peasant majority in rural societies generally suffered low levels scientifically, technically and managerially; their education was a serious and difficult problem. In China three purposes were generally manifest: to contribute to socialist civilisation in rural areas; to promote the drive for modernisation in the society generally; and to help peasants in their efforts to be better off. Illiteracy was still widespread in Asia, especially, and its elimination constituted an urgent task. She sketched the combination of strategies which had proved successful in China (while, like Zhao Wenqing, pointing out how much remained to be done): prevention through good basic primary education; elimination of existing illiteracy among young and middle-aged adults; and consolidation by means of concrete follow-up steps, since even a year's neglect caused a 50 per cent relapse, and two years lost meant the whole job has to be done again. Among lessons distilled from experience in Hunan were included: attending to the practical needs of the peasants; attending to their economic interests; integrating traditional and modern approaches in agriculture; combining popular with more academic education; combining moral, cultural and scientific education; and combining formal with nonformal systems of education.

Ning Xin referred to the popularity of adult education in the form of schools run by the peasants, and the crucial importance of government supporting and encouraging such adult education effort of the people especially in rural areas. It was also important to help people directly apply what they learned, since this greatly enhanced motivation; research into teaching methodology, staff development of teachers, and improving teaching materials, were all important here. From the Chinese perspective, strengthening Government leadership was important. Ning Xin wondered whether Chanida was not calling for less government intervention. She noted the diversity of situation between countries and circumstances, and the impossibility of imposing generalisations on all: it depended on the form of government and in whose interests the government acted. In China, enormous progress had been made through government leadership.

Cadena, in congratulating Chanida on her analysis, presented 'three acts of the same drama' common to the majority in the Third World, as they took form in Mexico.

In Act One, during the Second World War when the economies of developed countries were oriented to military production, the ruling class in Mexico decided:

> to launch into full-scale modernisation of the country;
> to orient this towards industrialisation and urban development on the model of the industrialised countries;
> to assign to the peasants the three roles of - producers of primary commodities including food to the cities at cheap prices; - providers of cheap labour for industrial work; - providers of cheap labour to the privately-owned modernised farms in order to produce primary commodities for export which would in turn pay for importation of machines and foreign technology.

This was on the premise of a modern competitive nation active in world markets, with 'strategic' accumulation of capital in some regions making it possible to absorb the labour driven from the countryside by modernisation.

In Act Two, over the following twenty years, Mexico saw a large increase in production and productivity, and a large export of primary commodities in accordance with the economic strategy of 'comparative advantage' as determined by the transnational corporations. There was also growth of a middle class ideologically oriented to the consumption of material goods, and widespread peasant migration resulting in intensive growth of the cities. The government maintained the prices paid to the peasants at the same level throughout these twenty years. There was also a large increase in foreign investment, and significant enriching of a minority of the population.

In Act Three, starting about 1970, there has been a productive structure totally dependent on external technology, finance and commerce. Urban growth has produced many critical problems which have no short-term solutions. Eighty per cent of agricultural production is dominated by transnational companies, with loss of self-sufficiency in production of basic foodstuffs and importation of 40 per cent of basic foods. For the campesinos the situation is worse than it has been for forty years: less food each day; less money and goods each year; less control over the processes of production. In the economic crisis of 1982, the minority which grew rich early sent out of the country in only six months more money than did the imperial Spanish in three centuries of colonial occupation.

Cadena concluded by recalling President Nyerere's words to the 1979 Rome World Conference on Agrarian Reform and Rural Development:

> The principal cause of the failure of rural development programmes is not the lack of finance or technology. It is fundamentally a problem of power: of the real capacity of rural producers to decide the development which they want.

He reinforced Chanida's challenge for adult education with peasants: to strengthen **their** mechanisms and organisational processes. This did not necessarily mean strengthening the traditional political structures, such as parties. Rather, adult education should reinforce power within the various structures of the working class which is fully integrated with the satisfaction of day to day modes of working people. "In other words, as a number of popular educators said in 1981 at a meeting in Colombia concerned with a new literacy: 'people must be able to read the world, in order to write history'".

The third panelist, Kamla Bhasin, began by telling what an Indian peasant once told her: she was not afraid of wild animals, but she got nervous when she saw any educated person coming to the village - 'they come only to rob us', she said. So much for the role of education and educated people.

Bhasin found Chanida's a very good description of the Thai situation, in the first part of her paper, and true for many Third World countries, certainly for South Asia.

> In these countries which have a fantastic cultural heritage there now exist extreme poverty, inequality and exploitation. More than half the population lives below the poverty line. Conditions of living are inhuman for the majority but a small minority which controls resources and decision-making lives in great luxury and obviously does not want any basic changes. With the help of foreign military powers they resist and clamp down on all attempts radically to change the status quo.

In such societies, Bhasin found, where a small power elite is interested only in short-term and short-sighted development to suit narrow self-interest, state-sponsored programmes for development further marginalise and pauperise the poor. They lead to landlessness, rapid destruction of forests, land and other natural resources. Education of all kinds also becomes a tool for exploitation and domestication of the masses.

Bhasin had problems with Chanida's suggested solutions, following her realistic description and analysis of causes of the present situation: "what she describes is cancer but she diagnoses it as simple non-malignant growth and prescribes an aspirin for treatment. I am afraid the cancer of inequalities, exploitation, injustice, needs something stronger than aspirin, maybe an operation!" Bhasin did not agree that those responsible for the condition of rural areas acted out of ignorance rather than malice. Nor did she believe that the exploiters could be persuaded to leave the rural areas alone: the exploitation was calculated and vicious "and if they stop exploiting the masses their islands of vulgar luxury, their five star hotels, their colour TVs, their private schools, will all merge in the sea of poverty". In India it was said that animals which have tasted blood do not voluntarily become vegetarian.

The main issue for Bhasin was one of control:

> control over the means of production, decision-making, mass media, etc. The present balance of power needs to be tilted in favour of the toiling masses. So the peasant education we require is that which will help the peasants become critically conscious and get organised to fight for their rights and to control the means of production - to become subjects of their own development.

The kind of education required and the rationale for it was outlined by Cadena (see chapter two). In addition, popular education, as well as raising consciousness and leading to organisation, should work for improvement of agricultural production, people's health and education. And special issues for women should be an integral part of popular education. Separate organisations for women were in fact needed within mass organisations:

> we cannot wait for the revolution to take place and then deal with the question of women's oppression. Without the liberation and mobilisation of women no revolution can take place.

If governments represented only the interests of minority power elites then clearly government programmes could not be expected to initiate a process of genuine popular education. The challenge had to be taken up in these circumstances by non-governmental organisations, whether trade unions, political parties, independent activist groups, or women's organisations. Links needed to be created between all such progressive forces.

Although the overall situation is grim there are also candles of hope here and there. In every country of South Asia groups are working against great odds, at personal risk to initiate popular education among peasants, to help them get organised and improve their living conditions. Examples of countries like China are a source of strength and inspiration for us because the task China successfully completed in 1949 is the task we face now.

Bhasin therefore found the experiences of peasant education of pre-Revolution China the more relevant. While one could learn from everywhere, the actual programmes for peasant education and rural development could be developed by the local people "in the context of their concrete socio-economic, political, cultural situation"; it was neither advisable nor possible to provide generalised strategies for all societies and communities. The objective of peasant education, to reiterate, was "to help peasants liberate themselves from hunger, drudgery, exploitation, patriarchy, and to make them subjects of their own development, writers of their own future and fate".

In the subsequent general discussion, Poloni referred to ILO Conventions 141 and 149 on peasants' freedom of association as being essential; although, as was remarked, many signatory counties do not honour these Conventions. It was for adult educators to accept and work within the parameters of peasants seeking self-reliance, organising voluntarily, escaping dependence, actively shaping their communities; these provided the framework and springboard for peasants' adult education.

Another speaker observed that development strategies had mostly increased rather than reduced inequality; there was a need to look at how peasant economies worked in different contexts and see what organisational forms were supportive in each.

Dame Nita Barrow, speaking from WHO experience and of the Chinese success with barefoot doctors, noted that Chanida and Ning Xin were presenting two sides of the same coin. The Alma Ata agreement of 1978 signed by 158 governments called for health for all by 2000. It drew directly on Chinese experience. By 1983 not one government had actually turned its health care around to implement Alma Ata: clinics were still in big buildings, doctors still in power. The challenge to adult educators was to find 'how to make governments honest'.

Al Rawi noted from Ning Xin's address how developing agricultural production in China meant education in science and technology. Here the Government did rule in accord with the people's interests, advocating peasant education and calling on them to learn. Here people also organised schools by themselves, with the support of government.

Montenegro of FAO, as chairman, noted that there was agreement over peasants' participation at their own level in their own development. Big costly intergovernmental projects had failed to reach people's needs.

Many 'experts' were sent to identify needs; they came from different realities, and used different languages. Foreign money and expertise was employed to carry out projects planned externally. They worked separately from the locals, completed the project and left. The buildings left behind were equated with 'development'. Local people however lacked the know-how and commitment to follow up, so the project really was all over. FAO since 1979 sought to build people's participation into all its projects officially, difficult though this was, from the philosophical clash with conventional 'expertise'.

Chanida sought to conclude on an optimistic note. All governments should desirably represent the people. One difficulty was that government officials were generally trained in western agriculture. She was not opposed to government intervention in principle, but they should study the situation more closely and relate to it better. She did not, apropos Bhasin's remarks, see armed struggle as the only way forward. One could also work with peasants to organise them and influence the government to change its behaviour: the Thai Government was certainly trying to help the people there.

III SYSTEMS

Chapter 7

Policies and Organisation

Rubenson's lead paper on industrialised country policies and systems stressed the major expansion of the sixties which had ground to a halt in many countries during the seventies. Meanwhile adult education had moved from marginality towards centre stage. Reasons for this were to be found in the economy; in the expansion of schooling for the young; with the inter-governmental organisations; and with political radicalisation in favour of equity. Rubenson analysed structures of provision in terms of remedial, general, and work-related education, the last of these breaking down between education as a labour market instrument, employer-sponsored training, and trade union education. In reality most workers received on-the-job training or else no training at all. Despite the great increase of the sixties and early seventies adult education had not become part of national policy in most industrialised countries, and had been squeezed with the economic recession and cut-back in public expenditure. Harmony could not be assumed in respect of priorities, and general adult education was most at risk. Rapprochement between the humanistic lifelong education philosophy and the skill development movement was now timely. Some of these issues were explored in subsequent panel and plenary discussion, as summarised in B below. Guan Shih Xiong's panel comments appear in this section; part of his tabled paper appears separately as section C, which is followed by the second lead paper - Bordia's on the organisation of adult education in rural societies - and the summary of discussion following that paper.

Bordia, with a strong background in the Indian nongovernmental adult education tradition, was also a key architect in India's massive National Adult Education Programme (NAEP), possibly the largest and most ambitious such programme outside the post-revolutionary planned societies. His paper is thus anchored in practical experience. It considers the rural milieu and key characteristics at least of the Indian sub-continent. Bordia see political commitment as crucial for organising, and adult education experience as essential for good management and planning, including mobilisation and coordination of different parties and sectors within and outside government at all levels. The paper, which concluded with five key issues for consideration, generated lively panel commentary and discussion, which is summarised in section E, ranging from the inherent limitations of top-down planning to important forms of 'meta-learning' likely to be overlooked in formal evaluations.

A. Adult Education in Industrialised Countries: Perspectives and Approaches

Kjell Rubenson

Introduction

Adult education is not a new phenomenon but has occurred in different forms during history. In many of the industrialised countries essential parts of the present system emerged in the latter part of the nineteenth century. However, it is only in the last twenty years that adult education has become a major topic of public policy. The growth rate of adult education in both number of students and creation of new forms of institutions remained steady until about 1960. Thereafter followed fifteen years of spectacular growth that came to a halt, at least temporarily, when the economy started to falter in the latter part of the seventies.

The changed role for adult education should be understood in terms of the major social, economic and cultural changes that occurred. As a result of these changes adult education moved from being a remote activity pursued by individual persons and voluntary organisations with the aim of achieving their own goals to become an instrument for different levels of government in their overall public policy. The new status for adult education is reflected in the promotion of adult education by major inter-governmental organisations like OECD and Unesco.

While the general development is the same throughout the industrialised world, there are still vast variations between individual countries. These are due to differences in political and economic systems, demographic and geographic factors as well as historical developments in the education sector. In fact, to a certain extent there are greater similarities between some of the developing and developed countries than between countries within the same category. This is especially true on issues like the overall ideology of adult education which is closely linked to political ideology. Thus the goal of adult education in Tanzania has much in common with the goal in the Nordic countries.

Within the framework of this paper it is not possible to make systematic comparisons between different countries or provide descriptions of individual countries regarding functions, organisation and content of adult education. Instead the approach will be to present general trends in the recent development as well as some salient issues with which adult educators and educational planners around the industrialised world are still struggling. The discussion will start with an analysis of the forces behind the 1960s expansion of adult education.

There follows a description of the structure of adult education, and the paper ends with comments on some of the critical issues facing today's and tomorrow's adult education in the industrialised world.

Societal Forces

Several coinciding factors brought adult education to the fore; changes in the economy, expansion of primary and secondary education, internationalisation of educational planning, and the political radicalisation.

Economy

The human capital thinking that came to dominate educational planning in the 1960s had a profound effect on adult education. Investment in human capital was proclaimed an important source for economic development. Dennison (1962) in his famous **The Sources of Economic Growth in the United States** found that investment in education and research would be three times as profitable as investment in real capital. According to Schütze, increase in earnings per worker could be explained from investment in human beings, which greatly increased not only their productive capacity but also the wage and salary shares relative to that of interest and profits (Sobel, 1982). Not only was investment in human resources seen to lead to economic development but it would also be expected to result in more equal income distribution. Schütze contended that the best way of achieving greater income equality was by increasing the availability of free or low tuition education programmes provided by the state, as well as by developing new types of institutions designed to reduce the opportunity costs of achieving post-secondary education (Sobel, 1982:56). The idea of providing increased opportunities for education was given more nourishment by another general thesis of the time, namely that the structural changes in the labour market raised considerable demand for educational investments to meet the need for well-educated manpower.

Ten years after the enthusiastic reception of the human capital thinking it was obvious that the relationship between investment in education, equality and economic development was more complex than the prophets had proclaimed. Heavy investment in education has not generated the expected economic growth, and worse, more and more schooling did not necessarily solve equalisation of excess to available goods and services in society.

Note that the scepticism of the early 1970s concerning education was directed solely towards the expansion of secondary and higher education. In fact, it was partly out of this disillusionment that adult education came to move to the forefront of public policy. The costs of expanding the education system had led to acute problems, and further expansion had to be restricted. The need for a closer connection between educational planning and labour market planning was expressed. Further, there was a general awareness of the difficulties involved in assessing the future need for qualified workers in an ever more rapidly changing society and labour market. The answer to these and other problems facing educational planners was recurrent education, proposed by OECD as a master concept for organising the education system (OECD, 1973). The concept of recurrent education was based on the principle that education opportunities should be spread out over the individual's lifetime and that there should be an alternation between education, work and leisure.

Expansion of primary and secondary education for youth

For a long time schooling in most European countries was dominated by a highly selective and hierarchical system of parallel schools in which those well situated financially and/or socially received very different a very different education from those less fortunate. After the end of World War II there has been a change in many countries towards a uniform comprehensive school system in which all pupils receive at least nine years' elementary schooling and in some countries twelve years of schooling including upper secondary school.

The rapid expansion forced educational planners and politicians to attend not only to intra-generational inequality, which always has been at the centre of educational discussions, but also to inter-generational inequality. The problem became especially acute in countries where only very few had continued beyond seven years of school. In Norway, for example, seventy-five percent of those over 40 had only seven or less years of basic education as measured in 1965. The estimate for Sweden at the same time was that by 1980, nearly seventy-five percent of people who were 40 would have had only elementary school unless more resources were created for adult education (OECD, 1973:37). Policy-makers did not see adult education only as a solution to the between-generation problem, but also as a way of partly solving intra-generational imbalances. Despite an expanded youth education there still remained large differences, and adult education was seen as a way of giving the disadvantaged a second chance. Thus despite the expansion of the school system, adult education could not give up its remedial function.

The other effect of more people going through education has to do with the well-known 'snow-ball syndrome': the more education a person receives the more they will strive for. Thus with larger groups going on to post-secondary education, an increased consumption of adult education will follow.

Intergovernmental organisations

The major intergovernmental organisations like Unesco, OECD and ILO have come to have a profound impact on the reconceptualisation of adult education in industrialised countries. Concepts like lifelong education (Unesco), recurrent education (OECD) and paid educational leave (ILO) form the foundation for current discussions of adult education. One of the reasons why the intergovernmental organisations became so important was the lack of any developed policy on adult education in most industrialised countries. In fact, one criticism that can be made today is that most countries have contented themselves with participating in the creation of broad policies at the intergovernmental level while doing little or nothing at national level.

One outcome of the transnational pattern of adult education policy-making has been increased impact of Third World countries on thinking in the so-called developed countries. This can be found in areas like literacy, which for a long time was seen as something solely for the developing world. The whole discussion on non-formal education has certainly been instrumental in shifting the focus from education to the broader concept, learning. Finally, many adult educators in the industrialised countries feel familiar with the social change aspect that comes across in much of the writing on adult education in the Third World, and can relate this to early developments in their own countries.

Looking at different levels of the adult education system, it seems that the adult educator identifies with and promotes Unesco's principle of lifelong education which is humanistic in nature, while governments seem to be more closely associated with the economic and social planning philosophy as outlined by OECD.

Political radicalisation

By the mid-1960s it was clear that the course of social development which generally had been presumed to be conducive to greater quality was tending to perpetuate inequality instead. The fact that, despite steady economic growth, vast differences still existed between racial and/or social-economic groups gave cause for great concern in many of the industrialised countries, and contributed to a radicalisation in society. The effect on adult education was particularly strong in the Scandinavian countries where it was linked to the trade unions' increased power resources and their demands for economic and industrial democracy (Hoghielm & Rubenson, 1980). The crucial point is that the unions' request for far-reaching reforms in the working life included the area of adult education. The interest taken by workers in adult education questions is connected partly with a growing educational requirement entailed by the realisation of reforms in working life. However, the increased activity in educational affairs may imply that the growing collective resources for workers have led them to generate renewed demands for cultural democracy. In fact there are clear parallels between the arguments put forward by the Scandinavian trade unions in the 1970s and the thought which prevailed in the European labour movements around the beginning of this century. In other countries there are similar trends, if not as visible as in the Scandinavian countries. In the United States, for example, one can point to the link between the civil rights movement, 'the war on poverty' and the establishment of adult basic education classes.

In summary, the movement of adult education into the major arena of public concern can be traced to the combined effect of two major forces: efficiency concerns linked to labour market considerations, and the striving for a more equitable society. The relative impact of these forces on adult education varies between countries and reflects the existing balance of power between the major collectives in society; it governs the structure of the adult education system.

Structure

To talk about the structure of adult education in industrialised countries may give the impression that there is a more or less coherent system across countries. However, one of the few things that is more or less universal is the lack of a clearly visible structure of adult education. Freidrich Edding expresses the situation in the following way:

> We did find in all the western countries we investigated (and in the available information on eastern countries too), a multitude of institutions for adult education and training. They had public or private or mixed financing. They offered full-time or part-time courses, degree or non-degree courses, on almost any imaginable subject, some were partly under public control, depending mostly on the share of the costs borne by the taxpayer. Others were not at all controlled by public authorities or subjected to any legal regulations: private firms, professional organisations, unions of employers and employees, churches and political organisations acting in their own interests and in those of their members or followers. (Edding, 1981:118)

To make comparisons between countries or even describe the situation within a specific country is further complicated by the lack of adequate statistics on adult education. However, despite the diffused character of adult education, a few generalisations can be made so long as it is understood that the specifics may vary considerably between countries.

The provision of adult education can be classified along various dimensions not, public or private funding, national or local provision, the primary purpose of the organisation, functions of the education offered, etc. No attempt is here made to create a uniform system of classification; there are too many variables involved to make it meaningful. Instead the presentation will be built around three broad areas of adult education: work related, remedial and general adult education. These categories are not mutally exclusive; thus remedial education is really a form of general education. Some examples from specific countries illustrate the case that is being made.

Remedial education

Almost all industrialised countries provide some remedial and basic education for those who have not profited from school or who have left school at an early age. In Canada for example all children have a right to a basic education defined as Grade 12 or its equivalent. However an estimated 20 to 25 per cent of students in primary and secondary education became dropouts. There is a general understanding, at least in principle, in Canadian society (e.g. among different levels of governments, industry and labour) that action should be taken to provide adult education to this group (Employment and Immigration, Canada, 1983). The same position can be found in most industrialised countries.

Recognising that the educational system has been given the role as a selective social screening mechanism one would have to consider at what points this process occurs (Farrell, 1981, 42). To continue with the Canadian example, the intention is that everybody should get 12 years of schooling. Remedial education can thus be seen as correcting a too early selection which violates the existing code of equality.

Equality of education is not a uniform concept but one that has been given different meanings. Farrell (1981:43) differentiates between:

> equality of access - the probabilities of individuals from different social groupings getting into education;
> equality of survival - the probability of individuals from various social groupings staying in education to some defined level;
> equality of output - the probabilities that individuals from various social groupings will learn the same things to the same level at a defined point in the educational system;
> equality of outcome - the probability that individuals from various social groupings would live relatively similar lives subsequent to and as a result of education.

In this context remedial education can be seen as equality of survival and is commonly regarded as the responsibility of the state.

While most adult education programmes not provided by the employer contain a remedial programme offered without cost, there are, however, often other costs involved - lost income, books, travel, baby-sitting - that participants will have to carry themselves. In some countries a certain number of students can get all costs covered, but nowhere is this a general right. Remedial education is generally provided locally by school boards, community colleges or similar institutions. In rare instances, e.g. Britain, there have been specific literacy campaigns similar to the ones in developing countries (Jones & Charnley, 1978). One specific function of remedial education is to provide courses for the socialisation of immigrants. Many countries provide a certain amount of free education for foreign workers.

To define remedial education from the standpoint of equality of survival raises serious problems. Accepting the principle of lifelong education as many governments do, at least in their rhetoric if not in concrete actions, one can question the usefulness of using only one reference point in time, years of youth education. Due to early socialisation, education and later life changes, intra-generational differences will grow wider and wider. The crucial question is, to what point should policies be guided by the notion of equality of survival, and at which point should equality of access take over. Further, one has to ask if the other more demanding criteria like equality of output and equality of outcome have any relevance - that is, to what extent is adult education aimed at an equalisation of living conditions? The outcome criterion calls for an increased understanding of the circumstances under which adult education can be an instrument for social change.

General education

When describing adult education in developing countries it is common to distinguish between formal, nonformal and informal education. Nonformal education is any organised, systematic, educational activity carried on outside the framework of the formal system. Formal education refers to the highly institutionalised, chronologically graded and hierarchically structured, education system spanning lower primary school to the upper reaches of the university (Coombs and Ahmed, 1974).

According to an OECD survey of adult education in its member countries, nonformal education is nothing more or less than adult education as it is widely interpreted in industrialised countries at the present time (OECD, 1977, 19). However, this is only partly true; it fails to recognise that the distinction between formal and nonformal education in the industrialised world is less clear than in the developing world. In fact, the formal system plays a greater role in the industrialised countries, by providing various non-credit programmes that sometimes resemble what is categorised as nonformal education in the Third World. Discussing the situation in the industrialised world it thus seems more relevant to talk about formal and non-formal systems than formal and non-formal education.

Looking back over the last 25 years, the relative importance of the formal system has increased considerably, as a result of two significant developments: the creation of special distance learning institutions within the formal system; and the opening up of the formal post-secondary system for adults.

The trend towards greater involvement by the formal system in adult education can be exemplified with the following data from the U.S.A. At the beginning of the 1960s about 36 per cent of adult students in the U.S.A. participated in courses sponsored by community organisations, and 21 per cent in college and university sponsored courses (Johnstone & Rivera, 1965, 61). Since then the relative role of community organisations has decreased while there has been a rapid growth in adult participation in formal educational institutions. According to official U.S. statistics participation in community organisations constituted only 9 per cent in 1982, whereas 40 per cent attended colleges and universities. Between 1970 and 1980 the number of college students under age 25 in U.S.A. increased approximately 22 per cent, but the enrolment of students 25 years old and up increased nearly 100 per cent.

The ambition of diversifying the path to higher education had led to a change in admission procedures in a growing number of countries. Among the criteria introduced with the aim of offering adults a chance to compete with traditional applicants in the admissions, the recognition of occupational experience is the most important (Unesco, 1978). The change in access, with increasingly heterogeneous student groups in post secondary education, has led to discussion how to change traditional educational institutions. A common criticism is that the particular needs of the adult student are being both neglected and rejected. The risk of such an exclusion is particularly large in a system characterised by traditional academic values and outlooks concerning curricular content, instructional forms and examinations (Abrahamsson et al., 1980). However, the adaptation of universities and colleges to a broader and more heterogeneous student clientele is not simply a question of study organisation and education frames. Another important aspect is the confrontation between two traditions of knowledge, the information assimilation model and the experiential model.

The other major structural development is the utilisation of educational technology, especially telecommunications, for establishing systems of distance of study and for creating open learning situations. Many countries have established special projects within traditional institutions. Most projects for 'distance teaching' have prospered, especially the Open University in Great Britain, which has become an unparalleled success (Peters, 1981). The criticism from 'adult education' of the Open University and similar institutions is that they have concentrated on offering purely university degrees and have not been used in different levels of adult education (Titmus, 1981:92).

The 'Open Learning Institutions' have their origin in discussions in the early 1960s of how television could best be used. Educational broadcasting via radio had been fairly successful and the new medium was seen as opening new avenues. At present we are just entering a new phase of 'open learning'. The combination of breakthroughs in microelectronics and telecommunications forms the basis for the information revolution. Policy-makers have been quick to proclaim the new technology the panacea for access to adult education. So for example it is the opinion in Canada that "the population must become user-friendly with computer managed and assisted learning becoming the norm" (Employment and Immigration Canada, 1983:123). The great danger with this is that it seems to assume that people are capable and motivated. In fact, it relies on self-selection to an even greater extent than traditional adult education. An approach to adult education that takes for granted that the adult is in possession of the instruments vital to making use of the available possibilities for adult education and that relies on self-selection will create wider educational gaps in society. Further, the new information technology is not only a mode for delivering education and culture to a wide spectrum of society; it could be used as well as a toy, or just another way of spreading commercialised entertainment.

Development towards the relatively greater importance of the formal system implies that the dominant culture has taken a firmer grasp over adult education. This raises a problem with regard to what kind of adult education is offered, and how groups outside the dominant culture get served. One of the reasons why the equity effects of adult education are so small is the way in which individuals' demands determine the adult education organisers' supply. One strategy to change the existing link between supply and demand is to finance adult education taking place in the non-formal system, e.g. in various voluntary organisations. This could give different interest groups power to control the content and method, and allow their educational programmes to reflect their ideology. The Scandinavian experiences show that the voluntary sector and especially social movements when supported by public financing can be very successful in providing non-formal adult education.

One major problem with regard to financing general adult education, regardless of whether it is provided by the formal or nonformal system, is the extent to which the organisation must rely on student fees. In the local competitive situation, organisations which direct their attention to serving the demands of the already well educated will have a 'market-leading' position. If an organisation started to act solely with an equity purpose, it would soon lose a great deal of the foundation for its activities.

Work-Related Education and Training

Work-related education and training is the single most important facet of adult education in industrialised countries (Peterson et al., 1982:171). We focus on the three major areas: labour market education, employer-sponsored programmes and trade union education.

Labour market instrument

Most industrialised countries have well established systems for manpower training. In fact this is often the most developed sector of adult education. Labour market training arose out of the need to act swiftly against imbalances in the labour market that could upset economic stability. The system is aimed at helping the underemployed and unemployed to improve their employability in occupations with better opportunities, and further to increase the supply of skills in industries where a shortage of suitably trained personnel tends to exacerbate inflationary pressures. National manpower training programmes tend to have not only economic goals to operate as anti-recession instruments and to respond to labour market shortages (see Peterson et al, 1982). This is especially true in the European countries, e.g. West Germany, where they are intended to facilitate upward mobility and to pave the way for women to enter the labour market.

A recent, and yet not fully accepted, motive for labour market training is the role it may play in reducing unemployment. By providing education for employed persons at any point in time the intention would be to create job openings for those outside the labour force, and thus to secure a more equitable distribution of work. This strategy is, due to the frightful unemployment figures, receiving increased attention by policy-makers as well as unions. These discussions are linked to strategies for work-sharing and the active integration of manpower training into a system of recurrent education (see Emmerij, 1983). To a large extent manpower training is nationally regulated and state financed. The courses offered vary in duration and level of qualification. Some are short introductory courses designed to activate participants to working situations outside their experience; others are one or two year courses, some at post-secondary levels. Most training takes place in regular educational institutions like community colleges, and is financed through varying combinations of special subsidies to the institution and special grants to the individual. In other instances the training is done in special 'Manpower Training Institutions'.

Employer-sponsored programmes

Relatively little is known about the vast and diverse educational enterprise that has been developed within industry and civil service. Its main function has traditionally been to adapt previously acquired general knowledge and skills to the needs of the job and to compensate for the deficiencies of both general and vocational education. Accelerated technological change has created a demand for employer-sponsored upgrading. The education and training offered is almost totally determined by the employer's perception of what measures could increase productivity, and equity concerns seldom enter the discussion. The traditional and still dominant form of employer-sponsored education is informal on-the-job training. The more organised education can consist of individual or small group instruction held in classrooms at the work place, or programmes located outside the work place at an educational institution often involving some form of tuition aid and paid time off (Smith, 1983:116).

It is almost impossible to get any exact figures on participation rate or total expenditure in this kind of education. However, available information very clearly reveals that participation is very unequally distributed across the workforce. The findings in Smith's (1983) survey of the situation in the U.S.A. are representative of the situation across the industrialised world. Educational opportunities were provided by 80 per cent of the large firms but less than 50 per cent of the smaller firms. Among those larger firms about 20 per cent of the workforce was involved in education during any given year, with a much smaller proportion for all industry. Education for broader skills and general knowledge (as distinct from company or product oriented) was rare and generally directed towards managers and other white collar skill groups. Manual workers received mainly on-the-job training and got a very small share of the organised education.

Not only do those in higher positions get more opportunities through their work to take part in institutionalised forms of education: they also have by far the best chances to learn new things on the job itself. A Swedish study found that while only 25 per cent of the unskilled workers had possibilities to learn new things on the job, over 80 per cent of the senior salaried employers reported that they had that possibility (SCB., 1981:51). This and similar data reflected the polarisation that occurs in working life; that is, the differences existing among various groups entering the labour market become more and more pronounced throughout the life span.

The class differences in employer-sponsored education have been questioned by the trade union movement which demands formal establishment of general availability of the right to educational leave. This demand was adopted by ILO in 1974 when the famous Convention 140 was passed. According to article 2 of this convention, each member country should promote the guarantee of paid education leave for the purpose of:

training at any level
general social and civic education
trade union education.

So far most of the paid leave systems are for vocational training and the greatest problem has been to introduce general education into the range of facilities offered.

Trade union education

In the industrialised nations, especially in Western Europe, the socio-economic systems have been moving increasingly towards widespread agreement between the state and employees' and employers' organisations (OECD, 1976, 20). The change towards greater worker participation in decision-making within firms has led to a need for education to prepare the workers for their new responsibilities and functions (Schuller, 1981). It has also forced the unions to take a new look at who participates in trade union education. Traditionally the main purpose of this education has been to enable a relatively small number of working class teachers to further their education. With the shift to industrial democracy it becomes essential to reach the entire work force. In Sweden the "1977 Codetermination Law" resulted in a massive education campaign to give union members a solid background in union affairs and other social matters, as well as information and training on the various labour statutes.

The increased pressures on the economy stemming from rapid technological progress have spurred an interest in building a more elaborate and at the same time more flexible system of work-related education and training. The strict separation between labour market training, employer-sponsored education and trade union education is beginning to disappear. The development is towards financing and institutional arrangements which lie somewhere in the zone between the state and that which is purely private (Clement, 1983). Examples are the Industrial Training Boards in the U.K., and the French and German system for paid educational leave. These so called parafiscal funds are not to replace state and private provision of education and training, but they could form the main part of the total provision. One favourable characteristic of this financing formula is that it could encourage individual choice, personal development and general education within the framework of work-related education, and could bring the two sectors closer together.

Concluding Remarks

I have outlined the development that brought adult education to the centre of public policy and described the structure of the system. Despite the phenomenal growth of adult education most industrialised countries never developed a comprehensive national policy, which explains in part the critical situation that adult education is facing today. The economic recession in combination with a change in economic policy has led to attempts to reduce public spending on social programmes. Despite lack of hard data, it seems that adult education is getting relatively harder hit than the rest of the education system, and that there are dangerous developments under way for adult education. The first has to do with the declining public support for what has been described as general adult education. The second is the way in which the structural changes in the labour market will govern the future of adult education.

Underlying the present situation was the conviction (evidently entertained by planners and adult educators alike) that adult education could evolve as a 'harmonious model' without the need for a more distinct definition of priorities. Developments have shown that it was a mistake to suppose that in a situation characterised by limited resources, adult education could be developed without sacrificing harmony. Thus the present economic crisis has accentuated the conflict regarding the distribution of educational resources, not only between different socio-economic groups but also between young and mature students.

Anything more radical that may happen in the area of financing adult education is likely to be linked to developments in working life. It is quite possible that in the last part of the twentieth century the industrialised countries of the world will be facing a major educational and training challenge as labour force growth slows and technological change accelerates (Levin & Schütze, 1983). There is an apparent danger that the actions taken will be based solely on labour market and economic efficiency considerations and neglect the equity aspect. In order to avoid this scenario there is a need for closer coordination of educational policy and other social sectors, especially labour policy and social policy. What is called for is a coherent approach not to one issue, skill development, but to the complex of interrelated problems that the industrialised world is facing - skill shortage, high unemployment, polarisation of the labour market, and insufficient worker and social participation. In this perspective one should consider a rapprochement between the two different forces promoting adult education, lifelong education embedded in humanistic philosophy, and the human capital thinking that is behind the skill development 'movement'.

REFERENCES

Abrahamsson, K., Kim, L. & Rubenson, K., 1980, **The Value of Work Experience in Higher Education**, Stockholm, SIE Report 1980.

Clement, W., 1983, "Intermediate ('Parafiscal') Financing Schemes" in Levin, H. & Schütze (Eds) **Financing Recurrent Education**, Beverly Hills, SAGE Publication Inc.

Coombs, P.H. & Ahmed, M., 1974, **Attacking Rural Poverty**, Baltimore, ICED.

Denison. E, 1962, "The Sources of Economic Growth" **Occasional Paper No. 13**, Washington, D.C., Committee on Economic Development.

Edding, F., 1981, "Economic Approaches to Recurrent Education" in Jourdan, M. (ed). **Recurrent Education in Western Europe**, Darville House, The NFER-Nelson Publishing Company Ltd.

Emmerij, L., 1983, "Paid Educational Leave: A Proposal Based on the Dutch Case" in Levin, H. & Schütze, H. (eds), **Financing Recurrent Education**, Beverly Hills, SAGE Publications Inc.

Employment and Immigration Canada, 1983, **Learning & Living in Canada**, Ottawa, Minister of Supply and Service Canada.

Farrell, J.P., 1982, "Educational Expansion and the Drive for Social Equality" in Altbach, P.G., Arnove, R.F. & Kelly, G.P. (eds), **Comparative Education**, New York, Macmillan Publishing Co., Inc.

Hoghielm, R. & Rubenson, K., 1980, **Adult Education and Social Change**, Lund, Gleerup.

Johnstone, J.W,C. & Rivera, R.J., 1965, **Volunteers for Learning**, Chicago, Aldine.

Jones, H.A. & Charnley, H.A., 1978, **Adult Literacy, A Study of Its Impact**, Leicester, NIAE.

Levin, H. & Schütze, H., 1983, "Economic and Political Dimensions of Recurrent Education " in Levin, H. & Schütze, H. (eds),

Financing Recurrent Education, Beverly Hills, SAGE Publications Inc.

OECD, 1973, **Recurrent Education**, Paris, OECD.

OECD, 1976, **Developments in Educational Leave of Absence**, Paris, OECD.

OECD, 1977, **Learning Opportunities for Adults** Vol. 1., Paris, OECD.

Peters, O. "Foreword" in Jourdan, M. (ed), 1981, **Recurrent Education in Western Europe**, Darville House, The NFER-Nelson Publishing Company Ltd.

Peterson, R.F., 1982, **Adult Education and Training in Industrialised Countries**, New York, Praeger Publishers.

SCB, 1981, **Social Report on Inequality in Sweden**, Stockholm, Official Statistics of Sweden.

Schuller, T., 1981, "Common Discourse? The Language of Industrial Democracy" **Economical and Industrial Democracy**, 3, 2, 261-291.

Smith, G.B., 1983, "Employer-Sponsored Programs" in Levin, H. & Schütze, H. (eds) **Financing Recurrent Education**, Beverly Hills, SAGE Publication Inc.

Sobel, I., 1982, "The Human Capital Revolution in Economic Development" in Altbach, P.G., Arnove, R.F. & Kelly, G.P. (eds), **Comparative Education**, New York, Macmillan Publishing Co., Inc.

Titmus, C., 1981, **Strategies for Adult Education**, Milton Keynes, The Open University Press.

Unesco, 1978, **Consultation for the Preparation of a Study on Access to Higher Education in Europe**, Bucharest, CEPES.

B. Discussion

Schütze, while generally agreeing with Rubenson's analysis, pointed out that recurrent education as evolved by OECD postulated alternation of learning and working. Intermittent education could enhance flexibility of educational provision to suit individuals' needs; promote equalisation of opportunity, especially between generations; and enhance motivation for education by linking it in concrete and applied ways with working and life situations. It was a concept advocated by great practitioners as well as by educationists. Flexibility and individual freedom had been the motivators within OECD. Recurrent education had not initially been advanced to enhance manpower planning and combat unemployment although its effect in the relatively free labour markets and economies would be in this direction.

Schütze noted that different economic systems generated different approaches to labour market forecasting and educational planning - labour market projections were the basis for educational planning in China, for example. To Rubenson's general and vocational educational objectives Schütze added civic education - education for active citizenship, fulfilling one's social role and attending to both rights and duties. In West Germany for instance, over sixty per cent of paid educational leave courses are for civic educational purposes, even though general and trade union education also include elements of this. This was crucial to the ideals of democracy, assisting as it did the control of public authorities and participation in the political process.

McNie took Rubenson's points about access to university and college systems: the changes to admission procedures to diversify entry into higher education, and the strong resistance encountered to these changes. Changes generally involved three considerations:

recognising occupational experience as an important criterion for admission;
granting credits for work experience;
revising curriculum content, forms of instruction, and examinations.

These proposed or actual changes had produced classic confrontation between two traditions of knowledge: information assimilation, and the experiential.

Granted diversity over access of adults to higher education across countries, institutions and disciplines, McNie held that the concept of equitable access was valid universally and deserved closer scrutiny.

One should ask, for instance, whether a country's educational institutions had admissions criteria and procedures for adults which reflected its often lofty educational aims. Do examinations test the memory of teenagers rather than the abilities of mature adults? Are examinations being reduced to multi-choice questions for technical convenience rather than sound educational reasons? Does 'integration' of adult education with the regular school system mean accommodating or overriding the distinctive needs of adults? How much interest is there in the adult applicant's creativity, integrity and experience?

McNie referred to the experience of the McMaster Medical Centre in Hamilton, Canada, which enrols many adult students each year from diverse backgrounds and achieves outstanding results both on course and as manifested in subsequent professional practice. Admissions criteria, course programme and teaching methods together constituted a model for progressive medical education. Nevertheless the programme was looked upon with suspicion by the academic medical establishment. Another example was the credit given by the Canadian Government to returning veterans after the Second World War of one year of school, which could be applied to interrupted secondary or postsecondary education. Many educationists were shocked: some of those affected had been out of school for five years and many had left school with poor grades to enter military service (where however they often took on difficult and intellectually demanding work). In the event not only did most veterans perform extremely well; they also changed much of the course content and the way courses were taught in the process. The only serious casualties were among the faculty and the younger students who found it hard to cope with highly motivated, no-nonsense, questioning students.

Chinese leaders of the pre-symposium study visits had stressed the access of peasants and workers to Shanghai's various educational facilities, with justifiable pride. It was to be hoped that such trends would go further, further enhancing access, perhaps on the McMaster Medical School lines. In such matters there should be a sense of urgency, of challenge to meet the needs of real people as well as the demands of national development.

Commenting on Rubenson's paper, Guan Shih Xiong found many similarities with issues facing China during its modernisation; at the same time China had much in common with the Third World of which it was one of the industrialising parts. He referred to China's two legs policy in making the distinction between adult and regular education and commenting on the status and functions of both for China's social development. They were equally important: two sides of the same coin. Adult education also needed to be formal, rather than informal: it was simply the education of workers, peasants and cadres, with great strategic significance for modernisation. Something like a half of

China's qualified and talented people were being produced through the adult education system. Social groups legalised by law and also private organisations provided adult education, as well as the government-run institutions.

It was important to guarantee the quality of teaching in adult education and introduce parity of standards: gradual formalisation of high quality which did not adopt the models of school education. Curriculum materials and teaching methods could incorporate some school features along with distinctive adult education approaches. Distinctive features included the in-service style for working people, the spare-time dominant scheduling, and the reliance on self-study. It should be relevant, focussed, applied and practical. Guan then sketched the essential features of the emerging Chinese system, as described in his tabled paper, which appears in part below. In the system as it was emerging the Government provided for the equivalent of up to 1.5 per cent of salary to be spent on adult education, with authorised certificates having equal standing for pay, work grades and promotion as those of the regular school system. The goal of adult education was to produce people both red and expert, to serve proletarian politics, serve the needs of both material and cultural civilisation, and to raise the qualifications of workers in both respects.

Hall, commenting on the impact of economic recession, identified a decline in democratisation of adult education, reduced emphasis on the 'forgotten adults' who featured in Unesco discussion at Tokyo in 1972, in the practices of the western industrialised nations. Access had been significantly reduced, he judged, in the early eighties. In Canada, for instance, the National Training Act shifted financial training resources from basic level training of adults to those with a minimum of Grade 10. The priority was placed on advanced skills training at the cost of the educationally disadvantaged. Western adult educators needed to stress transformation, as had happened in China, if they were to approach their ideal.

Maydl echoed a familiar symposium theme - the diversity between regions and nations - in explaining how Socialist Europe differed from the systems sketched by Rubenson. While closer to what Guan had described, there were still big differences between Czechoslovakia, for example, and China. By Czech law adult education was completely integrated with the rest of the education system; and in Eastern Europe all formal education was more and more 'adult-educationalised', and nonformal adult education more formalised. The different social structure and political ideas of Socialist Europe produced greater integration and mutual influence. Maydl posed the question how in these circumstances different systems could be compared - a question answered, in considerable measure, by the dialogue which characterised the whole symposium.

In ancillary comments to the same general theme, Li Li echoed Guan's emphasis on regularity and formalisation, with clear purposes and effects throughout, pointing out that for her, 'nonformal' connoted lack of discipline, and disorganisation. Krajnc asked about actual outcomes when an integrated system is established: does this mean that big fish eat the little ones? We should seek to list those factors and conditions which can improve the outcomes of integration.

In response to comments, Rubenson distinguished the ideology of recurrent education from its application: the latter was much more closely linked to labour market concerns. China's good exchange value for adult education attainments compared with those in the regular system was important for equity. Equity remained a crucial issue. In the West there had been a shift in human capital thinking: initially a change was expected in terms of pay structure as a result of training: the talk was now, rather, of highly specialised further education which went with a tendency towards polarisation between the highly skilled and the unskilled. Rubenson also issued, and Jean, chairing the session, echoed, a call for integration between different policy sectors such as social welfare, labour market, education and training. Jean observed the destructive effects of fragmentation and departmentalisation, but recognised that coordination presupposed both willingness and ability to work together from different power bases. An implication was the need for the continuing education of our organisations and enterprises themselves.

C. Developing a Socialist Adult Education System in China

Guan Shih Xiong

[Extract from a tabled presentation "The research of a socialist adult education system with Chinese characteristics".]

Adult education in China dates back to the 1920s, when the Chinese Communist Party started workers' night schools and peasant movement institutes. It has continued on a much larger scale through the 30-odd years since 1949, when new China was founded. It has thus built up a fine tradition ... There is a close connection between the development of adult education in other countries and adult education in China. Now the world is in the midst of a new industrial revolution brought about by modern science and technology. Scholars in the west call this the Information Revolution, or 'the Third Wave' or the fourth industrial revolution. This new technological revolution, international in character, will as a great moving force give an extraordinary impetus to our modernisation. It has made all the more important the development of intelligence and the mastery of advanced science and technology. Cadres and workers in China are therefore required to raise their level of scientific, technological and cultural knowledge, and to follow closely and understand well the development and latest achievements in science and technology. This has made it necessary for China to train a large group of qualified specialists to master modern techniques and modern managerial knowledge, so as to accelerate China's modernisation and bridge the economic and technological gap between China and the developed countries. In meeting the challenge of the new technological revolution, science and technology are the key, and education the basis. We must develop not only general education but also adult education. Adult education in China is the product of modern mass production. It is an important means for development of intelligence, training of personnel and raising the quality of cadres and workers. It is not primarily leisure-oriented or recreational in nature. The focus is on raising the economic benefits of enterprises. With flexible methods it offers on an extensive basis and at all levels training in culture, technology, management and professions of various kinds. By drawing all staff members into various training programmes, we will be able to equip millions of labourers with sound scientific and technological knowledge and good skills, and train large numbers of qualified specialists to meet the demands of modernisation in China. Here are a few suggestions as to how a socialist adult education system with characteristics peculiar to China could be established in the light of the actual situation in China.

(1) An adult education system with Chinese characteristics is

established in accordance with education policy, i.e. "education must serve proletarian politics and be combined with productive labour". China is a socialist country. Our adult education undertakings, such as professional schools, peasant schools and cadres' schools, should be places not only for imparting scientific and cultural knowledge, but also for disseminating patriotism and communism. The Ten Years of Turmoil, 1966-1976, caused great damage to the political life, economy and culture of this country. However, over the past few years our political life has been stable, the country's economy rehabilitated and developed, and cultural life diversified. As a result people's socialist consciousness has been enhanced. Participants in adult education acquire scientific and cultural knowledge with the intention of serving socialism. The objective of learning is to help build socialism, not merely to obtain a certificate, or to seek 'self-development', 'self-perfection' and 'individual advancement'. The kind of specialists socialism needs are those who can keep pace with the times, associate themselves with practice in socialist modernisation, and meet the needs of material and cultural civilisation of the broad masses. Therefore various adult education schools must follow a comprehensive programme that combines political, cultural and technological education. Political and ideological work should be conducted to help students become conscious workers with lofty ideals, moral integrity, cultural, scientific and technological knowledge, and a strong sense of discipline.

(2) The adult education system with Chinese characteristics has a relatively independent management structure. At present, adult education takes various forms, with many disciplines, various levels of learning and different types of trainees. It is entirely different from the anti-illiteracy campaign and spare-time education of the 1950s. It has its own management system and enjoys a guarantee in personnel, funds and material supply. As well as the Department of Adult Education Office in the Ministry of Education, various provinces, municipalities and autonomous regions, and various districts and countries, have corresponding adult education offices staffed with professional officers. All big enterprises, companies, factories and mines have their education divisions; medium-sized and small enterprises have education sections or appoint professional personnel to do the job. Adult education in industry, agriculture, finance and trade, science and technology is the responsibility of the respective fields. As a result, the policy of "strong leadership, unified management, division of responsibilities and full coordination" will be implemented. This comprehensive system of leadership is conducive to the promotion of adult education. In Beijing, adult education bureaux have been set up at all levels, from the municipality to the districts and countries. Four

years of work have proved that this system is of great advantage to adult education.

(3) The adult education system with Chinese characteristics also means incorporating the development plan into the national economic plan and the national education plan. Because of the Ten-Year Turmoil, the universalisation of primary education suffered great setbacks, and new illiterates have appeared. Besides, the number of secondary vocational and technical schools is very small. In the secondary schools there is a lack of variety in structure. Although things have begun to change, we are still short of vocational and technical personnel. The cultural level of cadres and workers is uneven. The lack of cultural, scientific and technical know-how is strongly felt in the rural areas. In order to meet the needs of personnel for modernisation, to meet the needs of vigorous economic development in the next ten to twenty years in quadrupling the value of total national output, government offices at all levels have started to pay special attention to intellectual investment, and to incorporate adult education into national economic and national education plans.

Various departments and units are all now engaged in forecasting manpower needs; and on the basis of these forecasts they will work out training programmes for all staff. Training requirements of existing staff and workers, the reserve labour pool, and the expected inflow of college graduates of secondary vocational and technical schools up till 1990, are being projected. While training will be compulsory for all the staff, attention should be given to the different training needs of different people. Leading cadres are to learn management, and key members in production new techniques, new technology and new knowledge. The present situation is that the cultural, technical and managerial level of our cadres and workers is low; and technical personnel are out of balance in that intermediate-level technical personnel are scarce. In our current endeavour to change this situation, major efforts should be devoted to workers' secondary vocational and technical education, i.e. secondary technical education. While this is the basis of our main effort, the training of advanced technical personnel is the most important. At the same time, the training of the reserve labour pool should be strengthened, and we will rapidly reform our apprentice training system. Recruitment for apprenticeship will be mainly for training, and jobs will be offered only to those who did well on the training programme.

With regard to the level of culture, technology and management, the situation in the countryside is even worse. The majority of illiterates are in the rural and mountainous areas. Take Beijing for example: in the age group 13-40 of its rural populations, illiterates still amount to 9 per cent; and in the mountainous areas the percentage is up to 10-20 per cent. While the main task of adult education in those areas is still to eliminate illiteracy and consolidate the results in the anti-illiteracy campaign, "three types of schools and two kinds of course" should be energetically encouraged: county-run peasant technical schools to focus attention on the training of cadres of communes and districts in management, and agro-technicians for districts, communes and production brigades; commune-run spare-time technical schools to train mainly cadres for brigades and teams, and technicians for teams; brigade-run peasant technical night schools to popularise knowledge in agricultural science; various production departments to run special technical courses to train technicians and to offer specialised knowledge to families engaged in particular occupations; and ordinary middle schools to run agricultural classes to train chiefly junior and senior middle school graduates who have returned to their home villages.

Only in this way can the needs of industrial and agricultural development be matched appropriately to the new era of importing new technologies and technical innovation.

(4) The adult education system with Chinese characteristics features a formal adult education programme in order to guarantee teaching quality. Adult education requires the establishment of an education system which suits the characteristics of adult learning. Though related to full-time regular school, it has its own distinctive features. The formalisation of adult education requires its own rules and regulations. The programmes should be well planned, teaching regulated and management systematised, thus forming basic elements of working rules for adult education. This will eventually lead to legislation for adult education.

A strong leading body, competent teaching staff and necessary equipment, are the guarantee for the formalisation of adult education. Teachers for adult education at different levels should go through a rigorous selection process, training, and advanced studies. Apart from the necessary cultural knowledge, the teachers should learn pedagogy, psychology, sociology and teaching methodology, and they should learn to make full use of modern teaching aids, for instance, radio, television, audio and video recordings. Teaching by radio and television should be combined with tutorials and teaching by correspondence. In places where conditions are right, educational radio and television stations may be established.

The formalisation of adult education does not exclude diversity of teaching. In diversity there is formalisation. There may be three types of enrolment: those with strict entry requirements, semi-open, and open. The strict type requires strict unified entrance examinations, and admissions based on the selection of a limited number of best candidates. The open type does not require any entrance examinations, but the students go through many examinations during the course of study. They either continue with their study when they find they have learned a lot or they drop out when they do not. Open education is suited to the characteristics of adult learners. Therefore we must run programmes with strict entrance examinations but also undertake other forms of open education: for instance, working and studying alternately, remedial courses, and tests for self-learners, thus gradually establishing a flexible system. Beijing Radio and Television University offers courses in 16 disciplines including electronic machinery, Chinese and economics. Thirteen thousand students have graduated, and current registered students number 20,000. Distance teaching through radio and television is suited to Chinese conditions and will develop further. The Higher Education Certificate Examination for Self-Study learners has been in existence for three years in Beijing. The cumulative total of applicants for examination numbers 120,000. More than 40,000 single discipline certificates have been issued. After passing the various examinations a number of students have become qualified college graduates. This open examination programme has opened up a new path for those engaged in self-study, and is helpful in the formalisation process.

How to establish an adult education system with Chinese characteristics is a large subject that requires long practice and continuous study. With correct theory for guidance we are now engaged in continuous practice to deepen our understanding. Situations vary from country to country. Methods employed will naturally be different. In spite of the differences we can surely find common grounds.

D. Organisation of Adult Education in Rural Societies

Anil Bordia

Introduction

Rural society is a complex system. Evolved over centuries as a result of economic stratification reinforced by religious belief, rural society also has numerous manifestations of the inherent creative genius of the people. The most conspicuous illustrations of this creative genius are the economic occupations developed by the people, the crafts and cultural forms, and the intricate value system. Progress in education, technology and science have had very limited impact on the rural systems due to the latter's isolation, caused by distance and lack of means of transport and communication.

The function of adult education for rural societies is to penetrate the masses to enable them to recharge their creative capabilities and critically to understand the ways in which rural institutions and relationships obstruct development. Obviously each country, indeed each community, must decide the ways in which adult education should be organised to serve this purpose. Here we first indicate a few characteristics of rural society, then refer to policy and planning of adult education as well as its management, and finally give a brief summary and points for discussion.

The Rural Milieu

Comments in this regard relate only to developing countries, and among them mainly to the sub-continent comprising Bangladesh, India, Nepal, Pakistan and Sri Lanka. A cradle of civilisation, religions and ancient culture, this region is also marked by extreme inequalities and widespread destitution. Some of the significant characteristics of rural societies particularly of this region are as follows:

Dependence on and problems connected with land

The principal source of income is agriculture, practised in a technologically outdated and arduous manner. There is a tremendous depletion of the environment - soil erosion, dwindling forests, disappearing pasturages.

Poverty and destitution

In India persons who do not get the bare minimum nutrition are estimated to be 50 percent, the proportion being worse in Bangladesh. As is natural, there is widespread unemployment and under-employment. The poorest sections are also generally deprived of essential social services like drinking water, education and health-care. The poor lack organisation and are often given to abject fatalism. Past efforts at amelioration of the conditions of the poor have had very limited success; often the rich and powerful sections of society corner the investment intended for the poor.

Antiquated technology

Advances in science and technology have had little impact on the work and life styles of the people. Consequently, productivity from land and industry is low and life is full of drudgery. There are attempts to import technology from industrialised countries, but not much attention is paid to development of technology which may be appropriate to the cultural background and development goals of these countries.

Lack of modern communication media

The environment is not conducive to modern media. Books, journals and newspapers are a preserve of the small proportion of the educated; television and films as educational media are yet to make an impact; and although transistorised radio can be seen everywhere, its use is for music and entertainment. India has launched its own space satellite, which has potential as a means for instruction, but the ground arrangements for its educational use and the software support are slow in coming up.

Rich cultural heritage

There is a rich oral tradition of learning as well as a fine sense of discrimination - in behaviour, design and day-to-day living. There is immense richness in folklore, amazing skill in handicrafts and a great deal of capacity to cope with harshness of environment and living conditions.(1)

These factors result in a deep realisation among the people of the futility of hope. Referring to this milieu the great Bengali language poet Rabindranath Tagore has said that the challenge of adult education is

> To instil hope in the hearts of people accustomed to despair
> To create articulation among people inured to silence.

Organising Adult Education Programmes - Indispensability of Political Commitment

Political commitment is the most important thing about the organisation of adult education programmes. It determines, first of all, **whether** programmes will be organised. There are several examples of acclaimed programmes which remained on paper only, mainly because they were not backed by the political leadership. Adult education programmes require forethought, indication of their place in national priorities, allocation of resources, and several types of linkages - ultimately all political issues. Political commitment also determines the nature of adult education programmes: whether the programmes would galvanise incoherent voices in order that they are heard; or be instruments in active and effective participation of the poor in the process of development; or be a facade, a concession to national and international opinion, but not necessarily meant to facilitate transformation of the learners.

In countries which have brought about, or are in the midst of, fundamental socio-economic changes, education of workers and peasants is essential for their politicisation. It is through education of the masses that these countries aim to release the latent energies of the people. The situation is rather different in countries which have chosen the path of gradual improvement in living conditions of the people. Some of these countries have further chosen the system of parliamentary democracy, which has a complex system of checks and balances. Whatever the form of government and the ideology of the leadership, political will is indispensable if large-scale and meaningful programmes of adult education are to be organised.

Political commitment cannot, however, alone result in the organisation of effective development-oriented adult education programmes. This calls for a thorough understanding of the problems of planning and management of adult education.

Planning of Adult Education Programmes

A good deal of how the programme would be implemented depends on the extent, nature and methods of planning. It is most desirable to involve, at the stage of planning itself, all agencies which may have to take responsibility for the various aspects of implementation of the programme. Some of the important aspects of planning are discussed here.

Critical analysis of past experiences and the contemporary situation

Most countries have significant experience of adult education. These vary from ancient and folk traditions of learning through informal methods and learning which may have taken place during the struggle for liberation to comparatively recent experiences. While planning India's National Adult Education Programme we found that the new programme could be planned on the basis of a systematic evaluation of past programmes. Such an evaluation can help in avoiding past mistakes.

Analysis of past programmes should be supplemented by an analysis of the contemporary socio-economic and socio-cultural situation. This would naturally include an analysis of the demographic situation, and first the extent of literacy and illiteracy for different age groups in rural and urban areas. An analysis by regions is also of importance. This often shows that people living in remote, hilly and desert areas suffer from educational disadvantages in comparison to people in cities and in rural areas which are well connected by means of transportation and communication. The third aspect of analysis should be with reference to economic and social groups. It will be found that working classes, minorities and ethnic groups are less privileged in regard to access to education. Also, almost invariably literacy and education among women will be found to be much less than among men. A fourth dimension of the demographic analysis is attainment of education by stages: that is, the proportion which has had primary, secondary, or higher education.

Defining the strategy

Countries which have brought about fundamental social and economic transformations in the wake of revolutionary change of government have almost invariably emphasised the role of literacy and adult education as the means of political education of the masses, and have tended to use education for improving the capability of the people to benefit from the fruits of revolutionary change. These countries also favour 'formal' courses of continuing education, as in Vietnam and China. On the other hand, countries which have opted for gradual change have to face the choice between organising well-planned selective programmes or mass programmes of campaigns. While the idea of mass campaigns is tempting and has the sanction of Unesco and important conferences sponsored by the International Council for Adult Education,(2) there are certain inherent difficulties in planning of mass programmes. Campaigns are necessarily the result of political determination, and such determination is not always visible. While planning India's National Adult Education Programme we opted for selectively planned mass programmes with strong resource support and close monitoring.(3)

In spite of great differences in political systems, there is in all cases enormous scope for spelling out the overall strategy. Countries which have had revolutionary socio-political transformation have to determine the way in which limited financial resources can be invested in order that the development needs are best served. Likewise, other developing countries must assign a well-defined place to adult education programmes. They have also to delineate the manner in which linkages will be established between adult education and other developmental sectors. An area which calls for particular attention is post-literacy and continuing education. The importance accorded to these activities depends on the extent to which formal education programmes bear fruit, and also whether education has an impact on socio-cultural development and economic uplift.

Mobilisation of Organisational and Instructional Agencies

A national programme of adult education presupposes active involvement, at the stage of planning itself, of all agencies having the capability to contribute to the programme. By and large, the agencies which can play an important role in implementation of adult education programmes include the following:

Political parties

Since adult education programmes inevitably have political overtones, and since genuine mass mobilisation is an act of political participation, it is obvious that political parties and their mass organisations of women, workers, peasants, youths, etc. should be actively involved at all stages of planning and implementation of programmes.

Government departments

It has to be understood from the beginning that development-oriented programmes of adult education cannot be the exclusive concern and responsibility of Education Departments. All Departments concerned with different aspect of development must be associated. These will include Agriculture, Animal Husbandry, Industry, Mining, Science and Technology and several others. Those Departments must make education of adults one of their essential activities.

Educational institutions

Universities, institutions of technical education, as well as secondary schools, should plan the role they will play and courses they will organise. The facilities available in the education system should be made available on a big scale for education of adults. Wherever possible teachers must be involved as instructors and community leaders.

Local Government structures

Countries which have effective local government structures often rely on these for running adult education programmes also. Communes and Production Brigades in China, Municipes in Brazil and **panchayati raj** institutions in some provinces of India have successfully shouldered responsibility for adult education. They are decentralised, viable and effective.

Voluntary agencies

Although these may not be an important agency in several countries, their role is very significant in some countries. The quality of voluntary workers, possibilities of organisation of flexible programmes, the contact many such agencies have with the local community, and the tradition of innovation in their working, make voluntary agencies eminently suited for taking up adult education programmes.

In addition to identifying organisational agencies it is also important that the planners arrive at reasonable clarity regarding the instructional workers. Different categories of people have been used in different countries, generally for good political and practical reasons. These agencies have included teachers, students, voluntary workers, rural development functionaries, etc. The important thing is to spell out the precise role of the instructional agency and to prepare them for playing the role.

Resource Development

By resource development is understood the technical and pedagogic resource support needed for an adult education programme. This includes curriculum development, preparation of instructional material, training of personnel, evaluation and research, etc. Needless to say, this is a very important input in all programmes of adult education, and should be an essential part of the process of planning. An initial exercise should be undertaken to see whether existing institutional arrangements could serve the purpose. Where new and large programmes are to be started, it may be necessary to establish fresh structures. Generally speaking, it is desirable not to have big institutions for resouces development, but to rely on short duration or task basis secondment of persons possessing the needed capabilities. Resouces development structures should have functional flexibility to experiment and innovate. It is also generally not enough to have one resource development centre for a very large geographical area or population size. Decentralisation in resource support is of the essence.

Delineation of a few model curricula is necessary at the planning stage. These curricula are generally required to be tested before they are finalised. Similarly well evaluated instructional material should be designed well before the launching of the programme. Preparations should also be made well in advance for training of personnel - from instructors and supervisors to people in leadership positions. Effective evaluation and research support is of importance in large national programmes. Energy spent on setting up such arrangements is always rewarded.

Management of Adult Education Programmes

The importance of management in large adult education programmes can hardly be exaggerated. In evolving a management system administrators always have several dilemmas: the extent of centralisation or decentralisation to be built into the management system; excessive bureaucratisation versus ineffective and superficial administration; the role of politicians, professional adult educators and field workers and the nature of their inter-relationship; and finally, provision of financial resources and how to ensure adequacy. While these issues remain important, we give below some indications on the basis of experience so far.

The local level

All countries which have notable adult education programmes have given special importance to the local level (country, commune, district, etc.). It is at this level that instructional personnel are chosen, supervision organised, and effective coordination established with the various local level functionaries. Coordination at this level can be facilitated by the setting up of a committee which would ensure the contribution of various government departments, credit institutions and media agencies. It is important to decentralise financial powers and give administrative autonomy at this level. Experience of a number of countries shows that lack of such authority.

The provincial level

In all large countries this level is very important, particularly so in countries which have federal systems of government. Since this is also often the effective level for administration of various development programmes, the problem of coordination needs to be tackled at this level. Establishment of a Provincial Board or Committee of Adult Education is known to facilitate coordination and improve management. Such a board or committee should have senior level representation of the departments and agencies which can contribute to the effectiveness of adult education programmes.

Decisions regarding the administrative apparatus are also generally taken at provincial level. We may emphasise in this connection the need to have an independent administrative machinery for adult education. Such machinery should not be top-heavy but should be designed in such a manner that positive cooperation of the political wing as well as of the other agencies is built into the administrative system. Stress should also be laid on the importance of appointing women at all stages of management. This may help in the involvement of women as learners in adult education programmes.

The national level

The overall responsibility for policy planning and implementation of the programme rests at the national level. It is also at this level that the political commitment is manifested. It is, therefore, necessary to impart visibility to this level that could ensure permeation of the political temper down the line. Equally important at the national level is broad coordination, by involvement of the mass media, armed forces, trade and industry, national organisations of workers, peasants, women, youth, etc. For this it is essential to establish a national board or committee at the national level.

Financing of adult education programmes

An important aspect of the management of adult education programmes is financing. This relates to all levels: local, provincial and national. At the local level it is important to emphasise the need for popular contribution. This can be in the form of voluntary work, provision of facilities and some monetary contribution. The local bodies can be expected to make a modest contribution to support the programme at their level. At the provincial level, too, responsibility has to be taken for making financial provision and for setting up procedures which are decentralised and at the same time well controlled. Broad policies regarding costs and sources of financing have to be made at national level.

We may reiterate the need to provide **adequate** support. Often there is a tendency to do adult education cheaply, forgetting that most learners in the developing countries are people who have had no formal education; sufficient funding is necessary to sustain the motivation of learners and to make learning effective. The other thing that needs emphasis is delegation of powers - at the adult education centre level and at local level. The assessment of the Experimental World Literacy Programme has shown that, generally, financial provision was not sufficient, but in several cases even the provision made could not be used in the field, due to lack of delegation.(4)

Monitoring and evaluation

The traditional systems of monitoring and evaluation - which view them as the last activity in a cycle which begins with planning, goes to implementation and finally to evaluation - have now been given up. In monitoring and evaluation emphasis now is on their being development or process oriented, to build in mechanisms of appraisal, feedback, diagnosis and remedial action at all stages of the programme - including the stage of planning, implementation and assimilation. In this case evaluation ceases to be cyclic and begins to cut across all phases of the programme.

In this context we may specifically refer to the monitoring system adopted in India's National Adult Education Programme. This system begins with an appraisal of the environmental setting in which the programme is to be launched, evaluates the inputs and processes - both managerial and pedagogic - and goes on to evaluate the outcomes as well as the long-term impacts of the programme.(5) An interesting aspect of this system is a scientific flow of information from the adult education centre to the local, provincial and national levels, and step-by-step feedback.

Summary and Major Issues

We have attempted to spell out some characteristics of the rural milieu, particularly as they relate to what is known as the Indian sub-continent. We have mentioned that while there is a rich tradition of learning, and a discriminating value system, the economic and social ethos discourages 'formal' learning. Adult education, being a means for awakening the masses, is essentially a political activity; we have stressed the importance of political commitment. While discussing issues pertaining to planning of adult education programmes we have underscored the need for a systematic analysis of past experiences and of the contemporary socio-economic situation. It is on the basis of such an analysis that a strategy of adult education has to be decided. We have, then, discussed the possible implementing and instructional agencies, and the need for giving importance to technical resource development. In dealing with the management of adult education programmes we have made brief reference to some of the management issues at local, provincial and national levels. We have also referred to the issues of financing, monitoring and evaluation, which cut across the three levels of management.

The imperative necessity of relating adult education with the development perspective of the country implies that the system in each country should be separately designed. There are, however, some questions which must concern the planners in all countries:

(1) **The extent of centralisation/decentralisation** - While some countries, with centralised planned economies, tend to lay down the entire structure through governmental instructions, several countries are emphasising non-formality and local relevance. In some countries the experience of overall central direction with decentralisation at the local level has proved to be effective.

(2) **Comparative emphasis on formal/nonformal methods** - Closely related to the first issue is the extent of emphasis on formal and nonformal structures, methods and accreditation, due to the convenience involved in such a system, and evidence of the importance they give to adult education programmes which are no different from the system of formal education. On the other hand, in countries such as India, Thailand, Brazil and Kenya, greater emphasis is laid on local autonomy and organisation of courses which are chosen by the local community.

(3) **The problem of popular involvement** - Here again the situation differs between countries which have brought about fundamental changes in social and economic relationships and countries which have chosen gradually to move towards greater equality of opportunity. In the countries of the former category literacy and adult education become a means of people's education and their involvement in socio-economic reorganisation. Problems of participation are, however, very acute in countries where the people are not inspired about development and are its passive subjects.

(4) **Problem of coordination with development programmes** - While interdependence between adult education and development programmes is universally accepted, few countries have been able to establish effective methods of coordination between the two. Tanzania made a particular phase of adult education programme subordinate to a thrust for improved agricultural production or better health-care; India and Bangladesh prefer to deal with the problems of coordination by introducing functionality in the content of adult education programmes. It would, however, be true to say that in practically all countries of the world effective coordination between development programmes and adult education continues to be a problem calling for study and innovative approaches.

(5) **Post-literacy and continuing education** - While the importance is recognised, opportunities for retention of literacy and numeracy skills, and for application of knowledge, continue to be insufficient. As the recent literature emerging from China shows, astonishing varieties of subjects relating to culture, science, occupational development, etc. are available in that country. However, most countries need to do a lot more in this sphere. A particular need is for provision of continuing education programmes for those who have completed primary education or literacy programmes.

REFERENCES

(1) See Myrdal, Gunnar, 1968, **Asian Drama: An Inquiry into the Poverty of Nations,** Vol I, Pantheon, New York.

(2) Bhola, H.S., 1984, **The Promise of Literacy,** Nomos Verlagsgesellschaft, Baden-Baden, 1983, and Paul Fordham (ed), **Cooperating for Literacy,,** ICAE.

(3) For an elaborate description of India's National Adult Education Programme, see Bordia, Anil, 1982, **Planning and Administration of National Literacy Programme: the Indian Experience,** International Institute for Educational Planning, Paris.

(4) Unesco, Paris, 1978, **The Experimental World Literacy Programme - A Critical Assessment.**

(5) For a detailed description of this model see Dave, R.H., 1980, "A Built-in System of Evaluation for Reform Projects and Programmes in Education", **International Review of Education,** XXVI, 4, 1980.

E. Discussion

Colletta, from the World Bank, owning to a 'healthy scepticism' toward economics as a predictive science, suggested that none the less Symposium deliberations generally had made scant reference to the economics and financing of adult education. He posed three questions:

> **on economics**: What do we know about the relative costs and benefits of various adult education strategies in meeting desired objectives, such as increasing the productive forces of the nation? Should we be concerned with measuring the internal efficiency, external effectiveness, and quality of adult education programmes?
>
> **on finance**: What are the sources and use of financing for adult education? What should be the relative share of the burden as between the institution and the adult learner?
>
> **on political economics**: If equity in access to and distribution of adult education is a desired goal, what should be the allocative mechanism for scarce resources to accomplish this goal?

Allowing for sympathy to the role of adult education in promoting critical thinking and social consciousness, these objectives had to be seen in their complementarity to the reproduction of productive forces in a changing society. China appeared to be seeking a balance between 'politics in command' and 'economics in command'; reaching and maintaining this balance would be critical to development.

Turning specifically to Bordia's paper, Colletta applauded its systematic approach, though more as an account of planning than of organisation of adult education in rural societies. Organisation implied more consideration of, for example: inequalities in the ownership and productive control of land; the effects of increasing demographic pressures; under-utilisation of labour, and stagnant wage incentives; and institutional reform and infrastructure requirements.

In conclusion, Colletta asked about linkages between adult education in the rural environment and in the urban context. Were there any functional relationships here? If so, what were they, and where was the interface between worker and peasant education? Discussion swung between one and the other, apparently implying no connective tissue.

Chanida described Bordia's paper as systematically laying a blueprint for organising national adult education programmes which, since he was talking on a national scale, necessarily involved macro-level planning. As another government worker in such a system, that of Thailand, she found the points raised towards the end of Bordia's paper unavoidably troubling to anyone who uses "this kind of national, top-down system of adult education organisation". Two problems could be selected to show that they were inherent in any such system, whether in India, Thailand or elsewhere.

Popular involvement

This will obviously remain a problem if the nature of programmes, curriculum content, and so on have been decided for the people at a high level of planning, where it is difficult to take into consideration different local conditions and needs. Could we not, in particular, find some way to use the 'rich tradition of learning' and the 'inherent creative genius of the people' to which the paper referred? This would mean adding one more important group to the list of agencies to be involved in planning adult education: the representatives of the people who are supposed to benefit from the planning.

Coordination among development programmes

If there is a number of development programmes each with its own personnel, technical resources, monitoring and evaluation systems down to the lowest level, as in the situation described in India, then there would clearly be a problem of coordination, simply because all the grassroots functionaries answer to different masters, and the programmes are handed down from different sources.

A related problem not explicitly named in Bordia's paper was that of duplication. As many countries seek to expand their adult education programmes to include agriculture, health and so on, which are seen as essential for rural development, they often find it difficult to arrange satisfactory cooperation from the responsible agencies. The result may be two or more agencies running their own programmes for the same target group.

To these points from Bordia's paper Chanida added another: the problem of management, which Bordia had observed was a matter of importance that "can hardly be exaggerated" in large-scale adult education programmes. This unfortunately seemed to translate into merely multiplying the numbers of managers of adult education. Third World governments suffered badly from bloated bureaucracies, and adult education was no exception. Could we not seek to reduce management to a minimum? The Thai national literacy campaign, mainly for practical reasons, had been forced to operate a system where there may be no direct management of teachers, teaching methods, materials, curriculum etc. Direct involvement from the top is limited to publicity to get the campaign going, and the granting of literacy certificates after an examination.

If these problems were inherent in top-down, macro-level planning systems, then the way to solve them was to look for an alternative method of planning. Even a top-down system like Thailand's had come to recognise that local organisations had to be strengthened to do their own planning, to run their own management programmes. Micro-level planning seemed to have the potential for solving many of the problems mentioned by Bordia. Popular non-involvement ceases to be a problem, since local people are involved in planning from the beginning. Overlapping would similarly disappear. It was a matter of government being prepared to be flexible in distributing its funds, reorganising the management of rural development, and allowing more decisions to be made outside the offices of the ministries.

Gao Ben Yi of East China Normal University emphasised the importance of helping the rural population to raise its educational level. He largely agreed with Bordia's analytical approach, noting however that the circumstances - social, political, economic, historical and cultural - of each country vary and the management problems also vary in consequence: one had to start with the concrete reality of each specific place and time. The management of schools and authorities in adult education both resembled and differed from the management of regular schools. Managerial problems in adult education were produced for example by the different work and learning circumstances of the students, and the great diversity of teaching staff. Different kinds of institutions had different goals. In China the study of scientific management for such circumstances was currently weak.

Management was especially important for adult education for rural areas. Bordia's analysis was essentially of the management of administration, not of the schools, which was important in the Chinese context. School management touched on coordinated leadership, a guaranteed organisational system, motivation of students, and supervision. Gao's tabled paper on correspondence education at university and college level demonstrated the labyrinth of variations contained within a unified whole, which his comments also stressed. At present schools and colleges displayed a great diversity of success and failure in respect of adult education, much of it to be put down to quality of management; adult education as an independent system would develop its own management theory in the future.

Wijetunga, reflecting in plenary discussion upon the Indian experience, asked about the qualitative as well as quantitative success of the Indian programme and the basis for carrying it through in terms of legislation, penalties and rewards (compared with China, Iraq and Pakistan, for example). Was not the bane of all such efforts the fact that the officials were more highly motivated than the intended beneficiaries? Gajardo, referring to the experience of another very large country, Brazil, asked whether the Indian NAEP approach had any effect on, or was blocked by, the apparently very strong class structure of Indian society.

Saez, speaking from the perspective of an old industrialised society, commented on the decline of the formerly important rural societies in such countries. He also spoke about the importance of civic education especially in a rapidly changing world and the difficulty of planning for and providing it within the one system. Who was to be responsible for such systems? This and other contributions to the discussion tended to imply an emphasis in the Third World upon transformation of society, in China upon economic and skill development for modernisation, and in the post-industrial societies for civic education.

Thus Bordia, responding to earlier questions, expressed sympathy with the call for radicalisation of society in the face of an intransigent class system. Whereas the Chinese Government did, the Indian Government did not, represent the people. On the other hand there was no doubting the fairness of the Indian democratic system itself, with its open franchise, etc. The Government's political mandate was interpreted as seeming to make changes but not actually doing so. The armed forces in many developing countries were used to defend the existing power structure against any threat of change.

None the less, it was incorrect and unrealistic to pose a choice between fundamental structural change and no change at all, for India and for a number of other countries. He agreed that people's organisation was essential for an effective literacy programme, adding that all institutions in India were required to organise literacy and adult education programmes, and did so. The real problems concerned the different pressures and allegiances at village level; this applied also to problems of coordination. As to the success of the NAEP so far, perhaps one should give the plant a chance to grow before looking at the roots. There had been two commissions of evaluation already since the 1979 Programme start. These pointed out failures in terms of functionality and of civic rights aspects, but suggested reasonably good results in terms of literacy work itself.

As to incentives and coercion, Bordia explained that the Indian Programme approach was to provide and persuade, but not to employ sanctions; it was felt to be wrong to force people to go to classes. There had been thought given to tangible economic rewards such as grants of additional fertiliser. The decision went against this on the ground that illiterate people should have equal right to such resources.

The session concluded with some discussion of criteria for success, and modes of evaluation. The Indian NAEP had a substantial research and evaluation built into it. None the less Bordia echoed earlier speakers who referred to the difficulties of measuring some of the more important gains. Rubenson, calling for more attention than had been given to the link between process, system and outcome in adult education, and Stock criticised the 'hard-nosed econometrician style' evaluation seen as characterising the World Bank approach. Rubenson cited a Swedish outreach illustration: the old lady taking an English language course in a small northern community who was hopeless in English at the end and therefore a 'failure' but learned in the process that she was being cheated by prices at the supermarket and now dared to complain. Stock also referred to 'meta-learning' quite outside the original programme and evaluation specifications within the U.K. literacy programme. Learners' own words and experience revealed gains in terms of discovering the possibility and potentiality of learning, resulting in new self-concepts and new behaviour. For Bordia the first function was to make people speak, and break the culture of silence with reading and writing coming later; this too was very hard to evaluate.

Chapter 8

The Training of Adult Educators

The Symposium concluded its study of systems with consideration of the lifeblood of any system of adult education - the adult educators themselves, and their professional preparation and training. Stock, introducing the lead paper, underlined the essential practicality of most training of adult educators, although this was based on an increasing body of knowledge and of theory. His selection of British and Western European examples reflected personal knowledge, not a judgement about the superiority of these approaches. In fact, within this particular tradition, the approach described is quite novel and systematic in its attempt to address the needs of the great army of part-time adult, usually nonformal, educators, and to help them to become better teachers irrespective of their subject specialism. Behind this paper and the subsequent discussion there lurked an inescapable tension between professionalism and a movement, also between adult education per se and the transmission of specialised knowledge and skills of all kinds to people who happen to be adults. The same two tensions - and possible syntheses - may be discerned through much of the Symposium, especially insofar as it was a dialogue between China and other parts of the world about both past and present approaches.

A. The Training of Adult Educators

Arthur Stock

Introduction

It is not possible here to examine all existing training systems and the total experience of training adult educators on a whole world scale. This paper concentrates on the current state of training and staff development in Western Europe with particular reference to the well-developed models and practice in the United Kingdom. This is not to imply that equal, alternative or better training schemes do not exist in other parts of the world; it is merely that this writer has had only small opportunity to examine such schemes in Africa, Latin America, Eastern Europe, North America and Asia.

Working Definitions

'Training'

This term is commonly deployed in U.K. and North America in a rather loose way. Strictly speaking the notion of **training** implies **designed instruction and learning experiences to ensure competent performance in a designated operational role.** However, the complex business of education - especially for adults - makes it difficult to pre-determine **all** the role requirements and necessary behaviours in every circumstance which an adult educator may encounter. Nowadays, for full-time adult educators, a preferred concept is 'staff development', which implies an expectation of continuing growth in personal and professional skills, knowledge, experience and capability. However, even in training courses for part-time or occasional teachers or volunteer helpers it is unusual for the design to concentrate exclusively on mechanistic conditioning to produce pre-determined behaviours. There tends always to be a recognition of the right of tutors (and to the great advantage of their work) to learn, to enquire, to speculate and to develop in positive ways. The resulting rather wide objectives, varied training experiences and holistic approach tend to contrast sharply with a great deal of operator training in industry and commerce where the objectives are frequently expressed in limited performance behavioural terms, and the instructions and learning systems employed (often quite successfully) are of an operant conditioning kind.

Adult Educators

This term, although perfectly acceptable as a generic label to attach to the many types of active workers engaged in the education of adults, needs further qualification when training systems are being designed. Very commonly administration and training authorities divide adult educators into three categories resulting from the degree and extent of their attachment both operationally and financially to the work: full-time paid (several sub-categories); part-time paid (mostly teacher, but some organisers); and part-time voluntary (ie., non-paid). Such a categorisation is not necessarily the best way to analyse the range of workers; indeed, as regards training it is not uncommon in several training schemes for part-time paid **and** voluntary (ie., unpaid) workers to be catered for at the same. More often the differentiation comes about because many voluntary workers are attached to voluntary, independent organisations with constitutional forms and structures different from statutory organisations which are the main employers.

Full-timers specifically in adult education in Western Europe are not very numerous as compared to the part-time and volunteer workers, but are nevertheless crucial to the successful operation of the service. In the U.K. there are approximately 2,500 full-time designated staff (plus a similar number of full-time industrial trainers) as compared to approximately 150,000 part-time paid staff and about 100,000 volunteers. This staffing relates to an adult population of nearly 40 million with an annual participation rate in adult education programmes of around 15 per cent.

But even with this relatively small select band of full-time staff the roles vary considerably: manager, adviser, organiser, community developer, **animateur**, 'subject' head of department (in larger colleges and centres), tutor-organiser, researcher, trainer, evaluator. Most full-time workers take on more than one of these roles, quite often three or four of them; and so the case for a core of generic training common to all becomes obvious. However, the specific demands upon (say) managers/administrators of large centres or colleges do vary significantly from those upon (say) advisers/trainers, and there are sometimes difficulties in reconciling all these demands in the design of training courses.

Structures and Systems of Training

There is a curious paradox in most of Western Europe: although very little legislative or regulatory requirement exists regarding the minimum qualifications for adult educators or their continuing professional development, nevertheless there are extensive systems of provision for both initial training and in-service further training. In the United Kingdom the systems could be, in part at least, regarded as a defined structure or framework at least for full-time and part-time teachers, although systematic structured training for the organisers and managers of education for adults is rather patchy.

Much of the structured training in English and Welsh parts of the

U.K. stems from the recommendations of the national Advisory Council for the Supply and Training of Teachers (ACSTT). During the years 1975-78, this body produced three reports which addressed the training of full-time vocational education teachers; the training of full-time and part-time teachers of adults; and the training for management of post-school educational services, respectively. The second report (known as ACSTT2) never received the endorsement of the central government ministry (the Department of Education and Science) as did ACSTT1, but has had a profund influence on the development of systematic training for part-time teachers in local education authorities and regional advisory councils - the latter being ten groupings of local authorities in England and Wales.

In essence the report recommended the establishment of a three-stage structure of provision for part-time teachers, with the first two stages involving a total of approximately 100 hours of course attendance in all and at least 30 hours of monitored teaching practice; the third, more advanced, stage required some 300 hours of course attendance plus teaching practice. Stage I is intended to be a "brief initiation into basic teaching skills preferably to precede a part-time teacher's first actual encounter with a group of students". Stage II is intended as a "...degree of training in pedagogical skills beyond that which can be given in the first stage and this should be provided by means of ... in-service modules involving at least 60 hours of course attendance ...". Stage III is designed to enable those part-time teachers who so wish to proceed to 'full qualification' equivalent to that of full-time college-based training (as per ACSTT1) "... by means of courses of some 300 hours and appropriate teaching practice".

Although not endorsed by central government as a requirement of part-time teacher employment or for the operation of education services for adults, this scheme has been taken up by most authorities; and the co-ordination and validation of specific modules or whole courses have proceeded in all regions of England and Wales. In Scotland and Northern Ireland there is a substantial amount of in-service training particularly at the introductory (more or less Stage 1) level. But as yet there is not the same degree of structuring of the training as in England.

A concept embedded in the ACSTT2 Report which has been seized upon by the planners of training courses is that of the **module,** which might be defined in the context of training schemes as a **'discrete element of instruction and learning experience for the purpose of achieving an identified pedagogical capability'.** The inter-linkage of such modules into 'courses' which in turn add up to a 'stage' of training requires much creativity and ingenuity. A great variety of 'knowledge', 'performance', 'sensitivity', 'experiential' modules has been designed and inter-related in the attempt to produce flexible but also holistic patterns of training experience. Such designs also have a better chance of meeting the life patterns and available time schedules of busy working people of the kind likely to be employed as part-time teachers. The modules, courses and stages can be promoted each with specific 'credit' ratings which can be accumulated, thus allowing a considerable degree of flexibility and of 'self-pacing' in the approach to work-effectiveness and, ultimately, qualifications.

'Initial' training for full-time adult education organising staff in U.K. is based on the assumption that all will either have been involved part-time in the provision of local education authority institutions, voluntary agencies, universities or polytechnics or have been employed in alternative relevant occupations such as broadcasting, industrial training or community work. Thus the courses provided at some thirteen British universities leading to diplomas or advanced degrees are essentially **post-experience** in character, and assume that the participants are mature adults with valuable perceptions and experience which they bring to their study. Subsequent in-service training of these full-time professional organisers depends on the policy of their employing organisations: some will encourage further academic training in adult education (usually on a part-time basis); others will encourage staff to take part in regional seminars, exchange visits or study conferences.

The initial training of U.K. full-time teachers of young people and adults, most of whom will work in district vocational colleges (termed colleges of further education or technical colleges in the U.K.), is either conducted as one-year full-time or four-term 'sandwich' courses in the seven specialist training colleges or departments designated for this purpose; or, for serving teachers, there is the recently introduced system of one day per week release from duties for specialist training continuing throughout one full academic year. Continuing in-service training of this category of staff is by regionally organised short courses and seminars.

Some Other West European Systems

Following investigation in 1979 by the Council of Europe of the very diverse provision made for training both full-time and part-time adult educators throughout the twenty-one countries in membership, it was decided that a major contribution might be made by the production of a range of multi-media materials which would involve video-cassettes and supporting multi-lingual print-on-paper units, and would be flexible enough to be used in many specific contexts and environments. Experts in Austria, the Federal Republic of Germany, The Netherlands and United Kingdom formed the original team; more recently they were joined by colleagues from Denmark. The materials are organised in 3 groups:

(1) learning about the **learner,** comprising two topics:
- the learner (units 1 and 2)
- learning and the learner (units 3 and 4);

(2) learning about the **teachers** - 1 topic:
- (units 5 and 6)

(3) learning about **learning** - 4 topics
- processes for the acquisition of knowledge (units 7 and 8)
- processes for the acquisition of skills (units 9 and 10)
- problem-solving learning (units 11 and 12)
- special issues in adult education (unit 13)

The whole programme was scheduled for completion in 1984. All 13 units would be recorded in all participating countries together with a training handbook and student workbook. The Open University (U.K.) is co-ordinating the project particularly at the editing stages.

An interesting specialist adult education programme has been instituted in **France** as part of the complete transformation of **agriculture policy** in that country. During the last 30 years the production of food in France has more than doubled, but the proportion of the whole population employed in agriculture has fallen during the same period from 32 per cent to less than 9 per cent. This has required a major vocational training effort among paid and self-employed agricultural workers. Over the last ten years the numbers trained per annum have increased from 5,000 to 130,000; now one quarter of all workers under 35 years of age have received intensive training. The work is carried out at the 122 Centres of Vocational Agricultural Training through France, and a crucial element in the success of the project has been the policy of training the trainers (**formation des formateurs**) established by the Higher Education Institute connected with the Ministry of Agriculture (L'Institut National de Promotion Superieure Agricole) based at Dijon. The training recognises the importance of fundamental education in science and technology, and the University of Grenoble has made an important co-operative contribution in this respect. The course extends over 900 hours: one third theory, one third in a training centre, one third private study. The course must be completed within 3 years, and at the conclusion the trainee-trainer must present two documents for examination: a critical evaluation of the courses taken, with full bibliographical references, and an 'action-research' report describing an agricultural training experiment with a full theoretical analysis, also proposing short-term and longer-term educational alternatives. The emphases are on flexibility, creativity and competence in a variety of field situations.

The German Adult Education Association (DVV) has long engaged in systematic study - curriculum and methodology of language learning. This was extended to other countries following the inception in 1969 of the International Certificate in Language Learning in which Austria, Switzerland, Denmark, Sweden and England have co-operated. These countries again joined the German Association in founding in 1973 the International Certificate Conference, at which a plan was made to develop an international training course for foreign language teachers in a European framework. Pilot projects were examined in subsequent years, and trial workshops held in England and Germany. The present form emerged in 1978/79 as a three-module structure (3 x 16 hours per module) usually spread over three linked weekend courses in a year.

Module 1 - is about adult learners' needs, the teacher's role and the factors influencing the process of communication.

Module 2 - looks at learning processes and teaching methods, and also covers the analysis and deployment of course materials. It includes micro-teaching practice.

Module 3 - concerns itself with the Certificate syllabus and the Certificate examinations and analyses these elements in the context of curriculum methods and materials.

However, these current modules are not regarded as fixed and immutable elements. The modular system allows for regular evaluation and replacement by improved elements or whole modules. It is also the intention of the Conference members to attach more modern materials (particularly video systems) to the scheme.

Volunteer training is often rather neglected in many countries, although volunteers form a large proportion of the committed personnel who organise, promote and (in several instances) teach. In The Netherlands there are two training initiatives of particular interest in this respect. The first is the **School for Volunteers for Work in Adult Education** which was founded in 1977 and has received grants from the Dutch Ministry of Culture. This was set up initially by one of the broadly based voluntary organisations in The Netherlands but has attracted support and interest from others. The main course programme (short-term residential) tries to meet the two major study-aims of participants: to obtain information quickly along with training in various relevant techniques; and to exchange problem-solving experiences with others in similar voluntary work. The course is resourced by books, films and videos taken directly from the daily activities of voluntary workers themselves, thus ensuring a concrete reality to the learning experience. Members of courses are encouraged to set up local training groups in their home situations after concentrated training on the residential courses.

The other interesting innovation in The Netherlands is the development of training **Study Circles for Volunteers.** This system has been introduced by a consortium of seven voluntary organisations. It is designed to meet the needs of the many voluntary workers who cannot leave their home districts to travel to residential courses of the School for Volunteers type. Moreover, many volunteer members of these organisations regard the courses of the School for Volunteers as being too difficult, too expensive and not sufficiently geared to individual needs. This Study Circle model is derived from extensive Scandinavian experience in which a learning/training group gathers for mutual improvement in a local centre (or even a member's house) and shapes its own training supported by **centrally produced** books, learning units, videos, audio tapes and assignments organised on a session-by-session basis. An evaluation is being carried out by the Dutch national adult education centres (NCVO and SVE) of four experimental community-based training study circles.

Some Special Features of Modern Training

Probably the most important and effective element in the recent training of actual **teachers** of adults has been **micro-teaching.** This term was coined at Stanford University , U.S.A., but similar procedures - 'sheltered' teaching exercises subject to sympathetic expert or peer-group review - were in operation in Europe in the early 1960s. The video-recording of limited duration sessions either with students or simulating a 'real' situation with other trainees can add powerful perceptual and feedback dimensions to training which are difficult to achieve to the same extent in other training strategies. For the first time trainee-teachers see themselves as others see them. Moreover, micro-teaching can be a cathartic experience for many trainee-teachers producing, after its successful conclusion, confidence which was not previously present. With careful sympathetic use by trainers it can form the climax of a sequence of training, especially for short-cycle work with part-time teachers.

A further interesting development in the last two decades is the development of **experiential** exercises (in addition to micro-teaching) for trainee teachers and organisers. These may be confidence-building exercises, problem-solving exercises, role-play and simulations which enable affective as well as cognitive learning to take place.

Another phenomenon, noted in the Council of Europe and Dutch examples above, is the linkage of centrally produced 'distance' training materials and units to local groups and institutions. This enables high quality inputs by experts and graphic audio-visual materials to be available in a wide diversity of local adult education situations. Also, if carefully designed, it allows for the essential local-specific elements to be inserted as well. The Open University in U.K. is currently engaged in producing such materials in a widely based national collaborative programme involving local trainers, university staff and invited experts, plus the renowned distance-education production capabilities of the Open University itself.

A final feature of modern training attempts to resolve what has been for many years a constant source of disagreement amongst trainers and trainees ie., 'general' pedagogical (or andragogical) training as opposed to subject-specific training. It is known that many subject teachers perceive their difficulties and inadequacies only in the context of their own subject. Their major requirement, as they see it, is to obtain expert help, advice and preferably simple guidelines to enable them to teach their own subject. They are unsympathetic to the notion that there is common ground material in the art of teaching adults which can be learned to advantage by all teachers of whatever subject. Equally, some 'generalists' have been unwilling to recognise that there are useful approaches and methodologies which are specific to certain subject areas. Recently, the **modular** structures of training systems have been able to cater in a reasonably balanced way for both the general and the specific, but this still requires an accumulation of module-credits of both kinds.

Conclusion

Modern training for adult educators has taken a great leap forward in recent years, but still needs to evolve further. Evaluation procedures are still not applied as rigorously as might be expected, nor used in re-design activities as would clearly be helpful. More recent 'systems' approaches may tend to correct this, but care must be taken to avoid the trend towards inflexibility and abstraction which can sometimes arise in over-dogmatic systems application.

All training procedures should exemplify the best field practice. Trainers should use methods and techniques themselves which they would expect trainees to apply in the classroom, workshop or community group.

Affective learning is just as important as cognitive for trainee adult educators. Tolerance, confidence, warmth, enthusiasm and sensitivity are important attributes which can be **learned**, if they are not spontaneously evident.

Much individual growth - in personality, judgement, interests and knowledge - should be looked for in trainees as well as purely performance skills.

Some of the best methodological and organisational curriculum **development** in adult education institutions and agencies has stemmed from challenging and skilful training programmes.

Notes for further reading

(1) The DATABASE selective bibliographical review system operated by the National Institute of Adult Continuing Education (19B De Montfort Street, Leicester, England) has approximately 250 article or book references available as a computer print out using a modified ERIC thesaurus of descriptors (cost 7 pounds).

(2) A 78 page monograph "The Training of Tutors" surveying the state of training up to 1982 - based on a careful review of research, documentation and scholarly writing from several countries - is available from NIACE, Leicester, England (cost 3 pounds).

(3) A comparative, selective, overview Newsletter of the "Training of Adult Educators" in Western Europe published by the European Bureau of Adult Education is available form NIACE (cost 2 pounds).

(4) An Advisory Council Report entitled "Teachers of Adults: Voluntary Specialist Training and Evaluating Training Courses" is available from NIACE (cost 1.75 pounds).

B. Discussion

Mulusa described the paper as an eloquent description of the training environment of adult educators in Europe in general, and Great Britain in particular. He noted the distinction between training of adult educators and 'operator' training as a model associated with industry and commerce, and the three-way classification between full-time, part-time paid and part-time voluntary workers, also the distinction between elements of the teaching environment: management structures, training procedures and methods, course content, accreditation and emerging trends in the training function.

Selman recalled that until recently adult education was by and large provided by private and voluntary agencies, while Jennings suggested that adult education emerged gradually out of the efforts of individuals and groups interested in the welfare of disadvantaged communities (see chapters 1.A, and 2.A, above). The pioneers were not trained adult educators. For nearly two hundred years there was no training of adult educators, yet the adult education movement had grown from strength to strength. A profession of adult educators had emerged, but the professionals joined it mainly as a result of taking an interest in social problems and wishing to do something about it.

Why did the training of adult educators become a necessity some three decades ago? Stock referred to the general goals of education and training: to acquire skills, knowledge, experience and capability. A number of content areas, course outlines and training strategies did suggest some of the motives which those initiating programmes might have had. But no direct reason is given as to why the core of predominantly nonformal education was formalised. Why did people who themselves came to adult education without training establish training schemes for newer generations of adult educators?

One obvious explanation is that they realised their own inadequacy, felt that adult education needed a larger body of workers, and could no longer rely upon individuals who dropped in casually and often took a long while to internalise the purpose of adult education. It was however equally possible that adult educators were acting in part in their own interests (a) to create an exclusive class of professionals (b) to create more secure employment for themselves (c) to find alternative or additional work for themselves at a time when adult education was beginning to lose momentum in Europe in the post-war years. If these were major reasons then adult education itself was only served by default. A knowledge of the original purposes in establishing training programmes for adult educators would help us to determine what the programme had achieved, what changes have occurred to the original objectives, what innovations are emerging, and so on.

Has adult education benefitted from training? Why do we still encounter problems of low enrolment in adult education, high drop-out, growing illiteracy, etc? What has training done to remedy these problems? Are today's trained adult educators equal to or better than their untrained predecessors in terms of ideological commitment and academic excellence? Or is the university diploma or degree, for example, their main qualification? What does training give to them beyond unintelligent use of common concepts which occur in the standard adult education texts by Roby Kidd and Malcolm Knowles? Any adult educator diploma-trained in Kenya would normally say that a child learns faster than an adult. When asked how old his child and adult are he gets confused. Mulusa had got into trouble by asking whether an illiterate child of six would learn all skills faster than a young adult of sixteen.

In short Mulusa did not find in Stock's paper satisfactory answers to his own questions: what the original purpose of training was; what developments had taken place in training; and how this had benefitted the adult education movement. For his own part, he earned a living by training adult educators, having been trained as a secondary school teacher and taught in secondary school for two years before joining adult education. Like other pioneers, he trained others for ten years before himself being formally trained as an adult education trainer. In his University, only one person had three years' training in adult education; others had had a year of training and others again none at all, not even in other sectors of education. Since adult education is not accorded high priority in this country, those trained tend to be below university level, who would not qualify for diploma courses in other departments of the University. Mulusa described the courses offered, all of them in-service and drawing people from practically all sectors of development. He concluded that the training might not be very effective because some of the educators are not themselves trained, trainees' academic background tends to be weak, and there was no precise supporting philosophical framework backed up by eloquent metaphors such as China's 'walking on two legs'.

Horn, whose tabled description of the training approach and kinds of courses arranged by the German Adult Education Association, D.V.V., is not included here, pointed out the importance of being frank about shortcomings in the interests of mutual exchange and learning - a feature which distinguished many of the proceedings and notably the Chinese contributions - and commended Mulusa both for his openness and for his work in Kenya.

Kamla Bhasin, an experienced trainer of Third World adult educators in a highly participative mode, stepped back from the practical details of good training practice to ask some larger questions of adult educator training, and of adult education itself, from a Third World perspective. She began by asking the question 'adult education for what?'

> I refuse to accept **that** adult education which helps people cope with and adjust to socio-economic, political, military changes uncritically. I cannot accept adult education which completely ignores the real issues our societies and mankind are facing. I reject adult education which not only justifies but supports systems which are producing hunger, inequalities, alienation, dehumanisation, nuclear bombs.

Bhasin borrowed the Chinese metaphor of walking on two legs to refer to the need for clear cultural and ideological values as well as economic developments and production. Her impression of most papers from the West was nurturance of a one-legged monster: economic and material development the only preoccupation. There was need for and value in providing technical knowledge but this alone was not enough. She felt that most industrialised country contributions had not mentioned, much less challenged, the diseases their societies suffered and which were spreading to other societies. There was needed a sense of urgency, not apparently uncritical and complacent acceptance of the status quo. Could it be that adult educators in industrialised societies averted their eyes from international exploitation, neo-colonialism and militarism because this enabled them to enjoy a comfy and affluent 'good life'? Those who did not feel a sense of urgency were themselves also in a sense victims of an alienating and dehumanising system which made them, too, feel impotent and helpless.

It was no use to talk about refining adult and continuing education provision and training to produce better workers for a sick society: "the throw-away culture, the consumerist ethos and individualistic mentality in the West". Bhasin referred to the disproportionate consumption of the world's resources by the United States and other industrialised countries, and the drain which this represented on the Third World. How did adult education in these countries relate to these issues, and to those groups in the West who sought to mobilise public opinion about them? Was compartmentalisation between self and work dehumanising this as other professions? Bhasin wanted to see the slogans of adult education taken seriously, for example (from the opening sessions) 'Adult education an awakening force'. Similarly, appreciation of China's achievements should lead to reflection on the values and structures of each one's own society.

> Unless we address ourselves to the real issues seriously our adult

education will continue to be one-legged. It will continue blindly to train people to become pawns of an inhuman system. I expect adult education to be an awakening force in every society, capitalist, socialist, communist. It should make every person feel that it is her business to ask questions, to have a say in the direction her society takes. It should make them vigilant to challenge undemocratic, unfair practices and to accept nothing uncritically.

The main task, then, with reference to the training of adult educators, should be to provide them with a set of values and an understanding of socio-economic and political issues in addition to providing the technical skills: to provide them with two legs to walk on so that they can in turn do the same with their students.

Hall, in the final panel comment, observed that much in Stock's commentary would apply equally in North America. A growing concern there was the over-emphasis on psychology, specifically the psychology of the adult learner, which had resulted sometimes in the individual being treated as the only focus for adult education: not only as learner but also as the central cause of any lack of learning. In this North American training was neither red nor expert.

While the Chinese could learn from a number of the efforts at systematisation of training as illustrated in Europe, including the improved use of television and printed materials, in terms of content, this was an area where the West perhaps had more to learn from the Chinese. Papers by Guan Shih Xiong, Wang Wenlin and Gao Benyi all made contributions to the question of content of training. Guan talked of cultural knowledge, sociology and modern technology, as content for training; Wang drew attention to the relationship of research to training, suggesting that the research process should itself be part of adult education training. Gao outlined a set of content areas for training which could provide for broad understanding, and which could be taken up by many institutions outside China:

Marxist theory concerning adult education;
knowledge related to the planning, economics and management of education;
the history of education;
knowledge of new technologies.

Other lessons had been learned from the pre-Symposium visits:

the importance and means of linking training to productive work in the workplace;

the use of older workers as teachers to teach the younger;
a continuous spirit and drive towards excellence;
the necessity of maintaining a balance between the teaching of the two civilisations - the political and cultural as well as the technical.

In subsequent discussion Bordia suggested broadening Bhasin's perspective, using her own insights and concerns. One industrialist in India itself created more pollution than a thousand defecating peasants. The disease of militarism and greed could be found in India, Pakistan and China, also in socialist Europe as well as in the West. It was an **international** problem of greed and exploitation. Certainly it was crucial to ask who was being trained in adult education to what end, and to see it in broad socio-economic context.

Jennings referred to the long-standing interest of the Workers' Educational Association in these issues, for instance in the preparation for very rapid decolonisation. The WEA had always sought to provide training for unpaid teachers. There was in short a long history of rather feeble attempts to provide training.

Gajardo, sharing in part Bhasin's Third World perspective on training, asked what importance was attached to the education of local civic and similar leaders. Most Latin Americans could not look to the universities for systematic training - often these were closed - but had to rely on themselves. Some of the great revolutionary leaders were untrained adult educators. Several North American speakers supported the case for balance between ideology and technology, suggesting that modern training programmes produced trainers 'with no fire in their belly', and who could not perceive the ideology in which they were immersed. Dore suggested that in Africa the higher the level of professional preparation and standing the less efficient was the educator. Those from the countryside were good in their own locality. University training tended to produce polite but inefficient and ineffectual small bureaucrats.

Hunter, taking up Hall's concern about over-emphasis on psychology, suggested that sociology was under-represented as a perspective. In line with Bhasin's concerns, she considered that adult education should encourage and assist citizens to think about and understand the many major threats to society. For Maydl, what came out of the debate was the fact that while all indeed lived in one world, we were at different phases of development, in different cultural settings, and so on. Intelligent debate required great attention to these differences. Selman, dissociating himself from 'training' in favour of educating adult educators, in effect echoed Maydl's point in rejecting any one unified model or type of training experience for adult educators, within, let alone between, societies: training should take many forms in each society.

In concluding responses from the panel, Hall asserted that the fire was still in the belly of some North American adult educators (such as graduate students selecting the political economy of adult education as a subject), but could be generated especially from adult educators' social roles in larger social movements. Stock (recalling that he had been asked for a technical paper and expressing agreement with the values expressed in the debate) agreed with Mulusa that professionalisation and elitism were a real threat: one could get so remote from the roots of the work and the needs of people that training could become useless. He saw adult education in the West as almost always radical, subversive, questioning, seeking change. It was a matter for adult educator training what the possibilities and most effective modes might be. Adult education had a crucial role to play in popular organisations and movements such as the peace movement. The affective element, the context and milieu in particular, were very important. While role-playing and simulation could be effective, training should never be too far removed from its milieu - a point which echoed Dore's. It was not however impossible to continue one's own education and professional development through advanced study while keeping genuinely in touch with the environment and key social issues.

Summing up, and recommending study groups to take the discussion further on various points of detail concerning both ideology and methodology, the Chinese session chairman commended those who had contributed for speaking their minds openly, expressing views without reserve, and thereby benefitting the cause of adult education as well as modelling good behaviour. Mao had said that the educator must be educated first; it was a crucial issue for the success of adult education. The groups, in the event, largely echoed and amplified the main points from the plenary session. However, one group also added to Stock's agreed basic approach the importance of further improving oneself during the process of practice as an adult educator: by taking part in relevant seminars and similar opportunities; by visiting factories and other workplaces; and by taking part in some research work, writing and contributing to the development of theory from a practical base so that this enlarged knowledge could in turn support better practical teaching.

Postscript

'Theories, Applications, Systems' was an ambitious and successful international symposium. Yao Zhongda's judgement, expressed at the concluding session, was that it had "added a new chapter to the history of adult education of the Chinese". The proceedings have in consequence been published in full in Chinese. The symposium structure - theories, applications, systems - emerged logically from the planning negotiations but may appear arbitrary in terms of where discussion of research, for example, appears in this volume. This does not detract from the quality of the papers. What is lost, rather, is the anchorage of symposium discussion in the four days of shared experience as participants in four mixed groups visited 28 different educational sites, in agricultural and industrial enterprises as well as in institutions designated as educational. The Chinese, like the Latin American popular educators also represented at Shanghai, commonly speak of anchoring theory in the concrete reality, or in actual practice. This symposium commenced with four days anchored in a common experience of learning together about the actual practice of the education of adults in Shanghai. The proceedings cannot adequately reflect this symposium sequence - practice to theory to applications and systems.

Nor can it fully convey the richness of exchange which occurred in the many hours of mixed-group dialogue, where communication of complex concepts and purposes was gradually achieved across different languages and from the base of widely differing experience and assumption. It was this patient unfolding of understanding through increasingly open dialogue which led Wang Wenlin to exclaim that "we are unifying the contradictions", and Yao at the end to praise the sincerity and candidness of expressed opinion. This may have been more comment-worthy to Chinese only recently emerging from the fear and intellectual oppression into which the Cultural Revolution deteriorated. Especially for participants from the West, themselves of widely differing ideological persuasions and forced to be on their best behaviour in front of strangers, the experience doubtless stirred in many an unusual level of critical self-awareness: one heard one's own words more clearly - and perhaps they sounded less clear - in a context of unshared assumptions and different socio-historical circumstance. Hopefully some at least of this thought-provoking disorientation and maybe reformulation will be stirred in readers of this volume: such is the main value of comparative study.

What lessons did the symposium teach? First, without being facile, that it is possible at least in some part to 'unify the contradictions'. Creative tension and dialectic may replace sterile dichotomies. Among those explored at Shanghai may be listed:

an adult education movement versus a profession;
the liberal versus the instrumental (or vocational);
the individual versus society;
centralisation versus decentralisation, and planning versus participation;
reform versus, or phasing into, structural transformation, into revolution.

The Chinese experience spanning pre- and post- 1949, with both phases represented by architects of adult education either side of Liberation at the symposium, provided a means of connecting purposes and experiences from different regions of the world which tend to be seen as unconnected opposites. On the other hand it was confusing for radical adult educators from the West and the Third World to see the Chinese achieving the purposes for which they too were striving, through a State system of provision. On the other hand, the historical perspectives with which the formal symposium opened (Selman, Yao, Jennings and Cadena) provided links between the early radicalism of the 'liberal tradition' in its context and the popular education of Latin America today. At the same time, present priorities in China provided unexpected connections with the practices of modern Western societies against which critical adult educators in these countries protest. To make such connections between contradictions across time and place is not to embrace historical determinism; Chinese no less than other speakers conveyed during the symposium the strength of an adult education movement as a creative and human force in many differing circumstances.

Greater understanding led also to greater respect and mutual acceptance of differences. Straight transfer of models and practice in whatever direction was unanimously rejected. As Dame Nita Barrow concluded in her final summing up, shared insights were equally valuable to all parties, but each had to take from the symposium what was relevant while retaining their own special strengths: all had to forge their own answers.

Many who read this set of papers and discussion summaries will live and practise adult education in societies variously characterised as late-industrial, post-industrial, or collapsed industrial: satirically as over-developed or optimistically as emerging high technology societies. It has been recognised, rather recently, but now quite generally, that these societies can learn from the Third World, if only for the sake of their own underprivileged, the 'Fourth World' within the North. Exchange and gain of experience can be not only North-South and South-South (itself still a rather novel idea to the more arrogant North) but also South-North. The other quarter of the world, modern China, is only now entering the picture. China calls itself a developing country, which in some obvious senses it is. It also manifests the resurfacing of a very old and sophisticated civilisation. Balancing or integrating the instrumental (for modernisation) and the cultural (in the western sense) was a half-submerged theme in the Chinese dialogue at Shanghai. Already in this symposium, and no doubt with increasing rapidity in the future as many in the nation rapidly acquire facility in English, Japanese and other foreign languages, China will come to give more to (and learn from) both the South and the North. For the Chinese the main needs in adult education are felt to be more and better research, contributing to and linked with better teaching methodology as well as more modern and sophisticated curricula, equipment and materials.

For Western societies the list is rather different. A list of possible relevant learnings from China, as indicated in the Shanghai symposium, might read somewhat as follows. First, that politics is central (a lesson no doubt learned at one level in the harder times since the late seventies but still perhaps grasped only in a superficial sense). Secondly, that the individualistic tradition of the West, fine and noble though it is, can also be an obstacle to human development; the collectivity too needs better understanding and attention. Thirdly, the struggle for priority and resources between the liberal and instrumental (or vocational) is by no means new, nor exclusively the preserve of the British tradition. Paradoxically, the Chinese are seeking balance and integration from the side of rigorous instrumentality, whereas British adult educators are fighting to retain the tatters of 'liberal tradition' against what is perceived as an onslaught of governmental barbarism. Allied to this, notably in contemporary Britain, is a battle between local initiative and individualism, through local authorities and educational institutions, and the central purposes of the State - paradox again, since that State Administration favours 'free enterprise' more than has any for many years. Sir Keith Joseph has puzzled audiences by accusing himself, as Secretary of State for Education, of being slightly socialist "in seeking to protect the job market by the use of manpower planning". The Manpower Services Commission (MSC) and other instrumentalities of the State in Britain are however indeed means for quite massive intervention in the educational activities of institutions nominally the responsibility of local authorities. While the Chinese State prescribes in great detail the requirements and standards for formal adult education, that political system is striving towards a free market system of motivation which curiously echoes prescriptions of the monetarist West. At the least, reflection on the Chinese tensions and contradictions helps to illuminate similar contradictions nearer home.

Another, less confusing, area of relevant learning is the sheer scale of, and the government commitment to, the formal adult system in China. It is indeed a case of 'walking on two legs'. Moreover, there is no doubt about the size and strength of the second, adult education, 'leg'. The nature of the Chinese State and its system of administration means that quite precise statistics of scale and cost of (formal) adult education can be provided; contrast the extreme difficulty in most Western societies of approaching even an intelligent guess at how much education of adults occurs or how much, through its various channels and in its various forms, it costs the taxpayer. This State-directed provision (often through enterprises, unions etc. rather than directly by the State) is also unashamedly, and proudly, formalised and systematised. ('Formalisation', and 'formal-non-formal' were sources of great confusion in the symposium; one group resolved to lay these matters aside only during its final meeting.) Not for Chinese adult educators the ambivalence of their western counterparts who wish to foster equity and second chance, yet baulk at examination and accreditation as the road to equality of attainment for the (labour) market place.

Then there is the success with which the Chinese have integrated learning and working (learning and earning, to borrow the title but not the lesser substance of a recent Australian report on higher education). 'Continuing education' in USA, Britain and elsewhere is charged with 'brokerage' between education and industry. In the main this means looking for opportunities for mutual benefit between the two kinds of system, each contained within its own culture, concepts and criteria for measuring success. Chinese (formal) adult education has gone far towards what is now increasingly called for, but seldom attained, in the West (excepting perhaps in the area of military R & D): the interpenetration of higher education and industry. Teachers are drawn from the workplace and are responsible for a large proportion of instruction in adult education, especially adult higher education, while full-time adult educators seek to play the role of guide and counsellor to this enterprise-based teaching force. Workers study at all levels through a great variety of imaginative forms of release from work, full-time, part-time and spare-time (supported by a substantial levy on enterprises for adult education). In the final stages students undertake research and development projects on real life problems of their actual workplaces, in consultation with their work groups as well as teaching staff. Many of the results of these projects are applied back in the workplace and result in improved quality or reduced cost or waste. Faced with the problem of the 'double generation' (young adults coming through the system plus the generation who missed out through the disruption of the 'Ten Years' Turmoil') China has responded to the need for adult continuing education on a scale barely yet conceived in many countries.

If the lesson of the Shanghai symposium for the Third World is to have confidence in finding your own way, and taking what you choose from 'the North', the lesson for the North is more complex. Post-industrial societies are discovering new illiteracies and new inequalities. 'North and South' is acquiring a new and bitter meaning within Britain itself. A modest shift has been attempted through government reallocation of some resources to higher education, to boost science and technology and to equip the nation for a high technology future. Yet this shift, even were it successful, is modest in its objectives and, like the interventions of the MSC and the Department of Education and Science, it has aroused great hostility. Meanwhile the liberal tradition becomes attenuated and feels more beleaguered, despite some fine attempts to respond to the new inequalities. The need to shift educational resources and effort, not just marginally into pre-service science and technology but system-wide into continuing 'culture', in the broad sense which includes technical training and civic education as well as 'education for living', is acutely clear; not only to adult educators but, to judge by their words, to many in politics and administration. The papers in this volume suggest many ways forward. They do not however show just how to convert understanding into will, and will into action and provision. Perhaps it requires a more traumatic and unwelcome change, something analagous to the destructive Cultural Revolution, if not the experience of liberation in 1949, to bring practice into line with understanding in the post-industrial West. Is institutional change on the required scale, addressing the new inequalities as well as new economic needs, possible without real trauma?

Appendix

List of Participants

Mr Sabah Al-Nassri
Vice-President,
University of Technology,
Tel Mohammed,
Baghdad, Iraq,

Mr Musare Al Rawi,
Director, ARLO,
113 Abu Nawas Street,
Baghdad, Iraq

Dame Nita Barrow,
President, ICAE,
37 Donhead Close,
Barbados

Ms Kamla Bhasin,
FFHC/Action for Development,
FAO,
PO Box 3088,
New Delhi 110003 India

Mr Anil Bordia,
Additional Secretary,
Ministry of Labour,
C-11/61, Bapa Nagar,
New Delhi 110 003
India

Mr Felix Cadena,
Mexican CESTEEM,
C/- Prolongacion
Peten 830, Dept 102,
Delegacion Benito
Juarez 03310 Mexico

Ms Chanida Chanyapate,
Dept of Nonformal
Education,
Ministry of Education,
Bangkok 10300 Thailand

Mr Nat Colletta,
The World Bank,
1818H Street, N.W.,
Washington DC 20433
U.S.A.

Ms Lea Cousineau,
President,
Institut Canadien
d'Education des Adultes,
506 Est Ste Catherine,
Suite 800, Montreal
Quebec H2L 2C7 Canada

Dr Phyllis Cunningham,
Graduate Studies in
Adult/Continuing Education,
Northern Illinois University,
De Kalb Illinois
60115 U.S.A.

M. Dirus Dore,
Director-General,
Service National
Alphabetisation,
Ministere de l'education
Conakry, Guinea (Africa)

Dr Glen Farrell,
Director, University Extension,
University of Victoria,
PO Box 1700,
Victoria BC V8W 2Y2
Canada

Ms Marcela Gajardo,
Inter American Institute
for Cooperation on
Agriculture,
R do Passeio 61-13
Andar Sala 1303
20021 Rio de Janeiro
RJ Brazil

Dr Budd Hall,
Secretary-General,
International Council
for Adult Education,
29 Prince Arthur Avenue,
Toronto, Ontario
M5R lB2 Canada

Mr Jakob Horn,
Deutscher Volkshoschul
Verband (DVV)
Rheinallee 1,
5300 Bonn 2 FR Germany

Dr Carman Hunter,
196 Carroll Street,
Brooklyn N.Y. 11231,
U.S.A.

Ms Michele Jean,
College de Bois du
Boulogne,
ICEA,
506 est Ste Catherine,
Suite 800, Montreal
Quebec H2L 2C7 Canada.

Prof. Bernard Jennings,
Head,
Dept of Adult Education
University of Hull,
Hull, HU6 7RX
United Kingdom

Prof Ana Krajnc,
President,
Yugoslav Federation for
Adult Education,
Filozofska Fakulteta,
University of Ljubjlana
Askerceva 12 6100
Ljubljana Yugoslavia

Mr P. Maydl,
European Centre for
Leisure & Education,
Czechoslovak Academy
of Sciences,
Jilska 1, Prague 1
Czechoslovakia

Mr John D. McNie,
Chairman, Management
Advisory Board,
ICAE,
29 Prince Arthur Avenue
Toronto, Ontario M5R lB
Canada

Mr A. P. Montenegro,
Officer-in-charge,
FFHC/Action for Devolopment,
FAO,
Via delle Terme di
Caracalla,
00100 Rome Italy

Prof K. Moro'oka,
Faculty of Education,
Kyushu University 03,
Hakozaki, Higashi-ku,
Fukuoka 812
Japan

Mr Tom Mulusa,
African Adult Education
Association,
Institute of Adult Studies,
University of Nairobi,
Nairobi, Kenya

Mr Cesare Poloni,
Chief, Workers Education
Branch, Bureau for
Workers Activities,
International Labour
Office,
CH-1121 Geneva 22,
Switzerland

Prof Kjell Rubenson,
Adult Education Division,
Dept of Admin., Adult
& Higher Education,
University of British Columbia,
Vancouver BC V6T 1L2,
Canada

Mr Guy Saez,
Peuple et Culture,
30 Rue de Rivoli,
75001 Paris,
France

Mr Hans Schütze,
C/- Centre pour la
Recherche & l'Innovation
dans l'Enseignment,
OECD,
2 Rue Andre-Pascal,
75775 Paris Cedex 16
France

Professor Gordon Selman,
Adult Education Divn.,
Dept of Admin, Adult & Higher Education,
University of British Columbia,
Vancouver BC V6T 1L2
Canada

Mr Arthur Stock,
Director,
National Institute Of Adult & Continuing Education,
17B de Montfort St.,
Leicester LE1 7GE
United Kingdom

Nikolai Sichev,
USSR National Commission for Unesco,
Moscow, USSR

Dr W.M.K. Wijetunga,
Executive Member,
ICAE,
30/63A Longden Place,
Colombo 7, Sri Lanka

Chinese Participants

Zhang Buoping,
President,
Adult Education Association of China,
Ministry of Education,
Beijing.

Zhao Wenqing,
Deputy Director,
Division of Worker Peasant Education,
Dept of Education,
Jilin Province

Yao Zhongda,
Secretary-General,
Adult Education Assoc.
Ministry of Education,
Beijing

Wang Wenlin,
Standing Committee,
Adult Education Ass.
Ministry of Education,
Beijing

Guan Shih Xiong,
Deputy Director,
Worker Peasant Education Commission,
Beijing

Xu Xieju,
Teacher,
Harbin University,
Harbin

Zhou Jianshu
Director,
Correspondence College,
People's University,
Beijing

Yang Shangde,
Registrar,
Harbin Workers Spare-time University,
Harbin

Li Jianwei,
Vice-President,
Postal & Telecomunicat-
ions College,
Beijing

Wang Yongxian,
President,
Shanghai Adult Education
Research Society,
Shanghai

Zhao Dingfu,
President,
Shanghai Workers Educat-
ion Research Society,
Shanghai

Min Shufeng,
Director,
Shanghai Workers Higher
Education Res. Unit,
Shanghai

Chen Hao,
Director,
Division of Sparetime
Education,
Tongji University,
Shandong Province

Gao Benyi,
Director,
Division of Sparetime
Education,
East China Normal
University

Lian Qimin,
Lecturer,
Hebei Workers Sparetime
University,
Heibei

Fang Xingyuan,
Deputy Director,
Shanxi Dept of Education,
Shanxi

Liang Zhepei,
Deputy Director,
Division of Worker
Peasant Education,
Dept of Education,
Shanxi

Gao Xieyong,
Deputy Director,
Worker Peasant Divn.,
Dept of Education,
Fujian

Cai Tiemin,
Associate Professor,
Xiamen University,
Xiamen

Li Ruiyuan,
Associate Professor,
Vice President,
Guangzhou Sparetime
Guangzhou

Ning Xin,
Deputy Director,
Worker Peasant Division,
Department of Education,
Hunan Province

Huang Hong,
Director,
Correspondence Study for Cadres,
Hubei College of Finance,
and Economics, Hubei

Xu Yuntai,
Deputy Director,
Workers Institute of
Technology,
Ansham Steel Works

Biladi Abudulengyimu,
Worker Peasant Division,
Xinjiang Uygur Autonomous
Region
Dept of Education

ICAE Secretariat

Professor Chris Duke,
Conference Convenor,
Dept of Continuing &
Adult Education,
University of Warwick,
Coventry CV4 7AL
United Kingdom

Mr Charles Wong,
Dept of Extramural Studies,
Chinese University of Hong
Kong,
67 Chatham Road, South,
13F Kowloon,
Hong Kong

Local Secretariat

Li Li (Mdm.),
Division of Worker-
Peasant Education,
Dept of Education,
Shanghai

Tong Li,
Dept of Adult Education,
Ministry of Education,
Beijing

Index